Praise for
HOW CIVILIZATIONS DIE

⚜⚜⚜

"In *How Civilizations Die*, David Goldman muses on population trends and religion with a breathtaking depth, originality, and panache. Some of his startling but documented predictions: Europe is in its death throes. Muslim demographic collapse will undercut Islamic triumphalism. The United States and Israel will emerge triumphant. And that's just the start."

—DANIEL PIPES,
President of the Middle East Forum and Taube Distinguished Visiting Fellow at the Hoover Institution of Stanford University

⚜⚜⚜

"Ask anyone in the intelligence business to name the world's most brilliant intelligence service and we'll all give the same answer: Oswald Spengler. David P. Goldman's 'Spengler' columns provide more insight than the CIA, MI6, and the Mossad combined."

—HERBERT E. MEYER,
Special Assistant to the Director of Central Intelligence and Vice Chairman of the CIA's National Intelligence Council in the Reagan Administration

⚜⚜⚜

"*How Civilizations Die* is a clever book: sharply constructed, nicely written, and filled with the mischievous spirit that makes a book fun to read. And yet, most of all, David Goldman has produced a *frightening* book. This is a horror story, more disturbing than anything from *Frankenstein* to *The Shining*—because it's set in the real world. Our world and its terrifying future."

—JOSEPH BOTTUM,
Contributing Editor, *The Weekly Standard*

More praise for

HOW CIVILIZATIONS DIE

"Oswald Spengler's *Decline of the West* was required reading when I was a college student and David Goldman's contemporary argument should be required reading today."

—HERB LONDON,
President Emeritus of the Hudson Institute

"David Goldman has explored the political implications of demography with rare insight. *How Civilizations Die (and Why Islam Is Dying Too)* is a mind-expanding peek into the likely political future of our planet."

—MARY ANN GLENDON,
Learned Hand Professor of Law, Harvard University

"Spengler at his best is dazzling, a philosophical high-wire act, swinging gracefully from platform to platform."

—MICHAEL LEDEEN,
Freedom Scholar at the Foundation for the Defense of Democracies and former Special Adviser to the Secretary of State and consultant to the Departments of Defense and State and the National Security Council

HOW
CIVILIZATIONS
DIE

HOW
CIVILIZATIONS
DIE

(AND WHY ISLAM
IS DYING TOO)

DAVID P. GOLDMAN

Since 1947
REGNERY
PUBLISHING, INC.
An Eagle Publishing Company • Washington, DC

Library of Congress Cataloging-in-Publication Data

Goldman, David P.
 How civilizations die (and why Islam is dying too) / by David P. Goldman.
   p. cm.
 Includes bibliographical references.
 ISBN 978-1-59698-273-4
 1. Civilization--History. 2. Regression (Civilization) 3. Civilization--Philosophy. 4. Islamic civilization. 5. Civilization, Arab. 6. Islam and culture. 7. Religion and civilization. 8. United States--Civilization. I. Title.
 CB151.G64 2011
 909'.09767--dc23
                    2011030144

Published in the United States by
Regnery Publishing, Inc.
One Massachusetts Avenue, NW
Washington, DC 20001
www.regnery.com

Manufactured in the United States of America
10 9 8 7 6 5 4 3 2 1

Books are available in quantity for promotional or premium use. Write to Director of Special Sales, Regnery Publishing, Inc., One Massachusetts Avenue NW, Washington, DC 20001, for information on discounts and terms or call (202) 216-0600.

Distributed to the trade by:
Perseus Distribution
387 Park Avenue South
New York, NY 10016

To my teachers, for my children

Contents

⟁⟁⟁

THE FIFTH HORSEMAN OF THE APOCALYPSE

Population decline is the elephant in the world's living room. As a matter of arithmetic, we know that the social life of most developed countries will break down within two generations. Two out of three Italians and three of four Japanese will be elderly dependents by 2050.[1] If present fertility rates hold, the number of Germans will fall by 98 percent over the next two centuries. No pension and health care system can support such an inverted population pyramid. Nor is the problem limited to the industrial nations. Fertility is falling at even faster rates—indeed, at rates never before registered anywhere—in the Muslim world. The world's population will fall by as much as a fifth between the middle and the end of the twenty-first century, by far the worst decline in human history.

The world faces a danger more terrible than the worst Green imaginings. The European environmentalist who wants to shrink the world's population to reduce carbon emissions will spend her declining years in misery, for there will not be enough Europeans alive a generation from now to pay for her pension and medical care.[2] For the first time in history, the birth rate of the whole developed world is well below replacement, and a significant part of it has passed the demographic point of no return.

But Islamic society is even more fragile. As Muslim fertility shrinks at a rate demographers have never seen before, it is converging on Europe's catastrophically low fertility as if in time-lapse photography. Iranian women in their twenties who grew up with five or six siblings will bear only one or two children during their lifetimes. Turkey and Algeria are just behind Iran on the way down, and most of the other Muslim countries are catching up quickly. By the middle of this century, the belt of Muslim countries from Morocco to Iran will become as gray as depopulating Europe. The Islamic world will have the same proportion of dependent elderly as the industrial countries—but one-tenth the productivity. A time bomb that cannot be defused is ticking in the Muslim world.

Imminent population collapse makes radical Islam more dangerous, not less so. For in their despair, radical Muslims who can already taste the ruin of their culture believe that they have nothing to lose.

Political science is at a loss in the face of demographic decline and its consequences. The wasting away of nations is an insoluble conundrum for modern political theory, which is based on the principle of nations' rational self-interest. At the threshold of extinction, the political scientists' clever models break down. We "do not negotiate with terrorists." But a bank robber holding hostages is a terrorist of sorts, and the police negotiate with such miscreants as a matter of course. And what if the bank robber knows he will die of an incurable disease in a matter of weeks? That changes the negotiation. The simple truth—call it Spengler's Universal Law #1—is *A man or a nation at the brink of death does not have a "rational self-interest."*

Conventional geopolitical theory, which is dominated by material factors such as territory, natural resources, and command of technology, does not address how peoples will behave under existential threat. Geopolitical models fail to resemble the real world in which we live, where the crucial issue is the willingness or unwillingness of a people inhabiting a given territory to bring a new generation into the world.

Population decline, the decisive issue of the twenty-first century, will cause violent upheavals in the world order. Countries facing fertility dearth, such as Iran, are responding with aggression. Nations confronting their own mortality may choose to go down in a blaze of glory. Conflicts may be prolonged beyond the point at which there is any rational hope of achieving strategic aims—until all who wish to fight to the death have taken the opportunity to do so.

Analysis of national interests cannot explain why some nations go to war without hope of winning, or why other nations will not fight even to defend their vital interests. It cannot explain the historical fact that peoples fight harder, accepting a higher level of sacrifice in blood and treasure, when all hope of victory is past. Conventional geopolitical analysis cannot explain the causes of population collapse either, any more than its consequences— for example, under what circumstances strategic reverses (notably the two World Wars of the past century) may crush the aspirations of the losers and result in apathy and demographic death.

Why do individuals, groups, and nations act irrationally, often at the risk of self-destruction? Part of the problem lies in our definition of rationality. Under normal circumstances we think it irrational for a middle-aged man to cash in his insurance policy and spend money as fast as possible. But if the person in question has a terminal illness and no heirs, we think it quite reasonable to spend it all quickly, like Otto Kringelein in *Grand Hotel* or his updated equivalent, Queen Latifah's character in *The Last Holiday*. And if we know that we shall presently die of rabies, what is to prevent us from biting everyone we dislike?

Countries sometimes suffer the equivalent of terminal illness. What seems suicidal to Americans may appear rational to an existentially challenged people confronting its imminent mortality.

Self-immolation of endangered peoples is sadly common. Stone-age cultures often disintegrate upon contact with the outside world. Their culture breaks down, and suicides skyrocket. An Australian researcher writes about "suicide contagion or cluster deaths—the phenomenon of indige-nous people, particularly men from the same community taking their own lives at an alarming rate."[3] Canada's Aboriginal Health Foundation reports, "The overall suicide rate among First Nation communities is about twice that of the total Canadian population; the rate among Inuit is still higher—6 to 11 times higher than the general population."[4] Suicide is epidemic among Amazon tribes. The *London Telegraph* reported on November 19, 2000,

> The largest tribe of Amazonian Indians, the 27,000-strong Gua-rani, are being devastated by a wave of suicides among their children, triggered by their coming into contact with the mod-ern world.
>
> Once unheard of among Amazonian Indians, suicide is ravaging the Guarani, who live in the southwest of Brazil, an area that now has one of the highest suicide rates in the world. More than 280 Guarani have taken their own lives in the past 10 years, including 26 children under the age of 14 who have poisoned or hanged themselves....
>
> Alcoholism has become widespread, as has the desire to own radios, television sets and denim jeans, bringing an awareness of their poverty. Community structures and family unity have broken down and sacred rituals come to a halt.[5]

Of the more than six thousand languages now spoken on the planet, two become extinct each week, and by most estimates half will fall silent by the end of the century.[6] A United Nations report claims that nine-tenths of the languages now spoken will become extinct in the next hundred years.[7] Most endangered languages have a very small number of speakers. Several are disappearing tribal languages spoken in the Amazon rainforest, the Andes Mountains, or the Siberian taiga. Perhaps a thousand distinct languages are spoken in Papua New Guinea, many by tribes of only a few hundred mem-bers. Eighteen languages have only one surviving speaker. It is painful to imagine how the world must look to these individuals. They are orphaned in eternity, wiped clean of memory, their existence reduced to the exigency of the moment.

But are these dying remnants of primitive societies really so different from the rest of us? Mortality stalks most of the peoples of the world—not this year or next, but within the horizon of human reckoning. A good deal of the world seems to have lost the taste for life. Fertility has fallen so far in parts of the industrial world that languages such as Ukrainian and Estonian will be endangered within a century, and German, Japanese, and Italian within two. The repudiation of life among advanced countries living in prosperity and peace has no historical precedent, except perhaps in the anomie of Greece in its post-Alexandrian decline and Rome during the first centuries of the Common Era. But Greece fell to Rome, and Rome to the barbarians. In the past, nations that foresaw their own demise fell to the Four Horsemen of the Apocalypse: War, Plague, Famine, and Death. Riding point for the old quartet in today's more civilized world is a Fifth Horseman: Loss of Faith. Today's cultures are dying of apathy, not by the swords of their enemies.

The Arab suicide bomber is the spiritual cousin of the despondent aboriginal of the Amazon rain forest. And European apathy is the opposite side of the coin of Islamic extremism. Both apathetic Europeans and radical Muslims have lost their connection to the past and their confidence in the future. There is not a great deal of daylight between European resignation to cultural extinction at the hundred-year horizon and the Islamist boast, "You love life, and we love death." Which brings us to Spengler's Universal Law #2: *When the nations of the world see their demise not as a distant prospect over the horizon, but as a foreseeable outcome, they perish of despair.* Like the terminally ill patient cashing in his insurance money, a culture that anticipates its own extinction has a different standard of rationality than does conventional political science.

Game theorists have tried to make political strategy into a quantitative discipline. Players with a long-term interest think differently than players with a short-term interest. A swindler who has no expectation of encountering his victim again will take what he can and run; a merchant who wants repeat customers will act honestly as a matter of self-interest. By the same token, the game theorist contends, nations learn that it is in their interest to act as responsible members of the world community, for the long-run advantages of good behavior outweigh the passing benefits of predation.

But what if there isn't any long run—not, at least, for some of the "players" in the "game"? The trouble with applying game theory to the problem of existential war is that the players may not expect to be there for the nth iteration of the game. Entire peoples sometimes find themselves faced with probable extinction, so that no peaceful solution appears to be a solution for them. Situations of this sort have arisen frequently in history, but never as frequently as today, when so many of the world's cultures are not expected to survive the next two centuries. A people facing cultural extinction may well choose war, if war offers even a slim chance of survival. That is just how radical Islamists view the predicament of traditional Muslim society in the face of modernity. The Islamists fear that if they fail, their religion and culture will disappear into the maelstrom of the modern world. Many of them would rather die fighting.

Paradoxically, it is possible for wars of annihilation to stem from rational choice, for the range of choices always must be bounded by the supposition that the chooser will continue to exist. Existential criteria trump the ordinary calculus of success and failure. If one or more of the parties knows that peace implies the end of its existence, it has no motive to return to peace. That is how the radical Islamists of Hamas view the future of Muslim society. A wealthy and successful Jewish state next to a poor and dysfunctional Palestinian state may imply the end of the moral authority of Islam, and some Palestinians would rather fight to the death than embrace such an outcome. Rather than consign their children to the Western milieu of personal freedom and sexual license, radical Muslims will fight to the death.

But why are Muslims—and Europeans, and Japanese—living under a societal death sentence? Why are populations collapsing in the modern world? Demographers have identified several different factors associated with population decline: urbanization, education and literacy, the modernization of traditional societies. Children in traditional society had an economic value, as agricultural labor and as providers for elderly parents; urbanization and pension systems turned children into a cost rather than a source of income. And female literacy is a powerful predictor of population decline among the world's countries. Mainly poor and illiterate women in Mali and Niger bear eight children in a lifetime, while literate and affluent women in the industrial world bear one or two.

But what determines whether it is one child or two? Children also have a spiritual value. That is why the degree of religious faith explains a great deal of the variation in population growth rates among the countries of the world. The industrial world's lowest fertility rates are encountered among the nations of Eastern Europe where atheism was the official ideology for generations. The highest fertility rates in the developed world are found in countries with a high degree of religious faith, namely the United States and Israel. And demographers have identified religion as a crucial factor in the differences among populations within countries. When faith goes, fertility vanishes, too. The death-spiral of birth rates in most of the industrial world has forced demographers to think in terms of faith. Dozens of new studies document the link between religious belief and fertility.

But why do some religions seem to provide better protection against the sterilizing effects of modernity than others? The fastest demographic decline ever registered in recorded history is taking place today in Muslim countries; demographic winter is descending fastest in the fifth of the world where religion most appears to dominate. And even more puzzling: Why does one religion (Christianity) seem to inoculate a people against demographic decline in one place (America) but not in another (Europe)? In many parts of the world, what once looked like an indestructible rock of faith has melted in the hot light of modernity. In others, modernity has only added compost for the growth of faith. Apparently some kinds of faith will survive in the modern world, and others will fail.

Strategic analysts and politicians are poorly equipped to understand these new and disturbing circumstances, with their overarching implications for political strategy and economics. To make sense of the world today we must do better than secular political science, which pigeon-holes faith as one more belief-structure among the other belief-structures in its collection of specimens.

Our political science is uniquely ill-equipped to make sense of a global crisis whose ultimate cause is spiritual. But this was not always so. From the advent of Christianity to the seventeenth-century Enlightenment, the West saw politics through the lens of faith. St. Augustine's fifth-century treatise *The City of God* looked through the state to the underlying civil society, and understood that civil society as a congregation—a body bound together by common loves, as opposed to Cicero's state founded only on common interests. (In the concluding chapter, we will consider Augustine's view as a lodestar for an American foreign policy that realistically addresses the threats created by the imminent demographic collapse of nations.)

We might call Augustine's view "theopolitics." A millennium later, Niccolo Machiavelli and Thomas Hobbes changed the subject, to the individual's desire for power, wealth, and personal survival. Hobbes, the seventeenth-century grandfather of modern political science, introduced a radically truncated anthropology, centered on the individual's struggle for survival. The state, he argued, was a compact among individuals whose survival prospects were poor in a "state of nature"; thus they ceded their individual rights to a sovereign in return for protection. A century later Montesquieu added differences in climate, terrain, and resources to the mix. The modern view of atomized man motivated only by the pursuit of material advantage is loosely known as "geopolitics."

What prompted this revolution in political thinking that has left modern political theory without the tools to understand the causes and implications of the current demographic collapse? Undoubtedly, the terrible religious wars of the sixteenth and seventeenth centuries poisoned the idea of faith-based politics. Europe fought dynastic and political wars under the false flag of religion until the Thirty Years' War of 1618–1648 destroyed almost half the population of Central Europe. The Peace of Westphalia that ended this fearful war forever buried the political model that Christendom had advanced since Augustine: a universal Christian empire that would keep the peace and limit the arbitrary power of kings.

But things are not as simple as they seem in the standard account of the violence that soured the West on theopolitics. For—as we shall see—the nation-states that opposed universal empire were founded on a contending kind of faith, a fanatical form of national self-worship whose internal logic was not played out until world war and genocide in the twentieth century, and the collapse of faith and fertility in the twenty-first. But when Thomas Hobbes published his great book *Leviathan* three years after the end of the Thirty Years' War, it seemed credible that "the papacy is no other than the ghost of the deceased Roman Empire, sitting crowned upon the grave thereof."

One powerful attraction of the Hobbesian revolution in political thinking was the power it promised to intellectuals. If politics reduces the individual to his material concerns, then it is possible to manipulate the individual through the alternation of his material circumstances. A clever elite could fix all the problems of the world. Immanuel Kant boasted in 1793 that he could write a constitution for a race of devils, "if only they be rational." Europe ignored him and proceeded to destroy itself in the Napoleonic Wars and the two World Wars of the past century. Today, as in Kant's time, the great frustration in world affairs is the refusal of some players to act rationally. Something was gained, but much more was lost, in the seventeenth-century Hobbesian revolution in political thought. To view human beings as creatures concerned solely with power, wealth, and security is an impoverished anthropology. The missing tools—the ones Machiavelli and Hobbes removed from the toolbox—are exactly the ones we need to understand and cope with the dangers inherent in the wholesale collapse of cultures that faces us today.

Secularism in all its forms fails to address the most fundamental human need. Sociologist Eric Kaufmann, who himself bewails the fecundity of the religious and the infertility of the secular, puts it this way: "The weakest link in the secular account of human nature is that it fails to account for people's powerful desire to seek immortality for themselves and their loved ones." Traditional society had to confront infant mortality as well as death by hunger, disease, and war. That shouldn't be too troubling, however: "We may not be able to duck death completely, but it becomes so infrequent that we can easily forget about it."[8]

Has death really become infrequent? Call it Spengler's Universal Law #3: *Contrary to what you may have heard from the sociologists, the human mortality rate is still 100 percent.*

We can refuse for only so long to face the fact that we will die. Religion offers the individual the means to transcend mortality, to survive the fragility of a mortal existence. *Homo religiosus* confronts death in order to triumph over it. But the world's major religions are distinguished by the different ways in which they confront mortality. We cannot make sense of the role of religion in demographic, economic, and political developments—and of the different roles of different religions in different places and times—without understanding the existential experience of the religious individual. It is challenging to recount this experience to a secular analyst; it is somewhat like describing being in love to someone who never has been in love. One doesn't have to be religious to understand religion, but it helps.

Without understanding humankind's confrontation of his own morality in religion, political science is confined to analysis on the basis of the survival instinct—which suddenly seems to be failing whole peoples—and rational self-interest—at a time when nations and peoples are not behaving in a conspicuously rational manner.

At the conclusion of a previous eruption of irrationality, a young German soldier at a remote post in Macedonia jotted down his thoughts on army postcards in the final months of the First World War. A small, bespectacled man with a thin mustache, he had been groomed to be one of the mandarins of the German academy, a philosopher whose function was to reinforce the country's confidence in its culture. Just before the war began he had returned to Judaism, after a near conversion to Christianity. As the casualty lists rose in inverse proportion to the hope of victory, the consolations of philosophy seemed hollow. Philosophers, he wrote, were like small children who clapped their hands over their ears and shouted, "I can't hear you!" before the fear of death. "From death—from the fear of death—comes all of our knowledge of the All," the soldier began. It was not the individual's fear of death that fascinated the young soldier, but the way entire nations respond to the fear of their collective death. He wrote,

> Just as every individual must reckon with his eventual death, the peoples of the world foresee their eventual extinction, be it however distant in time. Indeed, the love of the peoples for their own nationhood is sweet and pregnant with the presentiment of death. Love is only surpassing sweet when it is directed towards a mortal object, and the secret of this ultimate sweetness only is defined by the bitterness of death. Thus the peoples of the world foresee a time when their land with its rivers and mountains still lies under heaven as it does today, but other people dwell there; when their language is entombed in books, and their laws and customs have lost their living power.[9]

The soldier was Franz Rosenzweig, and the postcards would become his great book, *The Star of Redemption*. Awareness of death defines the human condition, so that human beings cannot bear their own mortality without the hope of immortality. And our sense of immortality is social. The culture of a community is what unites the dead with those yet to be born.

The death of a culture is an uncanny event, for it erases not only the future but also the past, that is, the hopes and fears, the sweat and sacrifice of countless generations whose lives no longer can be remembered, for no living being will sing their songs or tell their stories.

The first surviving work of written literature, the *Epic of Gilgamesh* written perhaps 3,700 years ago, recounts the Sumerian king's quest for immortality. After a journey beset by hardship and peril, Gilgamesh is told: "The life that you are seeking you will never find. When the gods created man they allotted to him death, but life they retained in their own keeping."

In the pre-Christian world, Rosenzweig points out, the peoples of the world anticipated their eventual extinction. Every nation's love of itself is "pregnant with the presentiment of death," for each tribe knows that its time on earth is limited. Some fight to the death. Others cease to breed. Some do both.

Christianity first taught the nations of the world the Jewish promise of eternal life. To talk of "man's search for meaning" trivializes the problem. What humankind requires is meaning that transcends death. This need explains a great deal of human behavior that otherwise might seem irrational. One does not have to be religious to grasp this fundamental fact of the human condition, but religion helps, because faith makes explicit the human need to transcend mortality. Secular rationalists have difficulty identifying with the motives of existentially challenged peoples—not so much because they lack faith, but because they entertain faith in rationality itself, and believe with the enthusiasm of the convert in the ability of reason to explain all of human experience.

But not only the religious need the hope of immortality. The most atheistic Communist hopes that his memory will live on in the heart of a grateful proletariat. Even if we do not believe that our soul will have a place in heaven or that we shall be resurrected in the flesh, we nonetheless believe that something of ourselves will remain, in the form of progeny, memories, or consequences of actions, and that this something will persist as long as people who are like us continue to inhabit the earth. Humanity perseveres in the consolation that some immortal part of us transcends our death.

Sadly, our hope for immortality in the form of remembrance is a fragile and often vain one. Immortality of this sort depends upon the survival of people who are like us—that is, upon the continuity of our culture. If you truly believe in a supernatural afterlife, to be sure, nothing can really disappoint you. But there is no consolation in being the last Mohican.

And that's because of Spengler's Universal Law #4: *The history of the world is the history of humankind's search for immortality.* When nations go willingly into that good night, what should we conclude about human nature?

Human beings may not be the only animals who are sentient of death. (Elephants evidently grieve for their dead, and dogs mourn their masters.) But we are the only animals whose sense of continuity depends on culture as much as it does upon genes. Unlike men and women, healthy animals universally show an instinct for self-preservation and the propagation of their species. We do not observe cats deciding not to have kittens the better to pursue their careers as mousers.

I do not mean to suggest that human beings of different cultures belong to different species. On the contrary, the child of a Kalahari Bushman will thrive if raised in the family of a Glaswegian ship's engineer. (As Jared Diamond, the author of *Collapse: How Societies Choose to Fail or Succeed*, observes, it is easier to be stupid in a modern welfare state than in a hunter-gatherer tribe in New Guinea.)

But culture performs a role among human beings similar to the role species plays for animals. An adult Bushman would never fully adapt to industrial society, any more than a Glaswegian ship's engineer would last a fortnight in the Kalahari. Insofar as an animal can be said to experience an impulse toward the future beyond his own life, that impulse is fulfilled by the propagation of the species. But individual human existence looks forward to the continuation of the culture that nurtures, sustains, and transmits our contribution to future generations. Culture is the stuff out of which we weave the hope of immortality—not merely through genetic transmission but through inter-generational communication.

In the absence of religious faith, if our culture dies, our hope of transcending mere physical existence dies with it. Individuals trapped in a dying culture live in a twilight world. They embrace death through infertility, concupiscence, and war. A dog will crawl into a hole to die. The members of sick cultures do not do anything quite so dramatic, but they cease to have children, dull their senses with alcohol and drugs, become despondent, and too frequently do away with themselves. Or they may make war on the perceived source of their humiliation.

The truth is—to invoke Spengler's Universal Law #5—*Humankind cannot bear mortality without the hope of immortality.* When men and women lose the sacred, they lose the desire to live. Despairing of immortality, we stand astonished before the one fact we know with certainty—that some day we must die. This is as true of modern *homo sapiens sapiens* as it was of our remotest ancestors. Even Neanderthal burial sites have been unearthed with grave gifts. "Man does not live by bread alone," Moses said on the east bank of the Jordan River. The affluent peoples of the world have all the bread they need, but have lost the appetite for life.

Americans are ill-equipped to empathize with the existential fears of other nations. America is the great exception to the demographic collapse sweeping the modern world. As an immigrant nation we regenerate ourselves. We bear no baggage from a tragic past. The glue that holds us together is a common concept of justice and opportunity. The United States is what John Courtney Murray called "a propositional nation." In our benevolence and optimism we assume that all peoples are like us, forgetting that we are or descend from people who chose to abandon the tragic fate of their own nations at the further shore and selected themselves into the American nation. But we have learned that our capacity to influence events in the rest of the world, even in the absence of a competing superpower, is limited, and that the dissipation of our resources can be deadly for us.

Our strategic thinking suffers from a failure to take into account the existential problems of other nations. We think in the narrow categories of geopolitics, but we need to study theopolitics—the powerful impact of religious beliefs and aspirations on world events. Even we exceptional Americans must come to grips with the collapse of faith and fertility, especially in the rapidly and dangerously declining Muslim nations, in order to prevail in a world in which tragic outcomes are more common than happy endings.

PART ONE

THE DECLINE OF THE EAST

CHAPTER 1

THE CLOSING OF
THE MUSLIM WOMB

If demographic winter is encroaching slowly on the West, a snap frost has
overtaken the Muslim world. Europe has had two hundred years to make
the transition from the high fertility rates of rural life to the low fertility
rates of the industrial world. Iran, Turkey, Tunisia, and Algeria are attempting it in twenty. The graying of the Muslim world in lapsed time, as it were,
can have only tragic consequences.

The Muslim world is on the brink of the fastest population decline in
recorded history. Academic demographers are stunned. "In most of the
Islamic world it's amazing, the decline in fertility that has happened," Hania
Zlotnik, head of the United Nations' population research branch, told a
2009 conference.[1]

Think of a train wreck: the front car hits an obstacle, and the rear cars
collapse accordion-style with the momentum. Driving the demographics
of Iran, Turkey, Algeria, Tunisia, and other Muslim countries is a "locomotive"

1

made up of people in their teens and twenties. They were born into families of six or seven children. But this "locomotive" has hit a demographic wall: these young people are having only one or two children. Today's "bulge" generation of young Muslims, whose political humiliation and frustration over economic stagnation stoked the Arab rebellions of 2011, will be followed by a generation dramatically smaller than their own.

Today there are more Iranians in their mid-twenties than in any other age bracket. But they are not reproducing. An educated twenty-five-year-old Iranian woman today probably grew up in a family of six or seven children, but will bear only one child. The consequences will be catastrophic. Today there are nine Iranians of working age for every elderly dependent. By 2050, when the bulge in Iran's population will be at retirement age, there will be more Iranians in their mid-sixties than in any other age bracket—seven elderly dependents for every ten working Iranians. The country produces just $4,400 per capita, about a tenth of America's GDP, and most of that comes directly or indirectly from oil and natural gas reserves—which are running out.

It's already too late to fend off the population decline. That Iranian twenty-five-year-old's mother married in her teens and had several children by her mid-twenties. Her daughter has postponed family formation, or foregone it altogether, and spent her most fertile years on education and work, if she can find it—a quarter of young Iranians are unemployed by the official count, and the true number is probably worse.

Aging populations present a danger even to rich countries with well-funded public pension systems. For poor countries with a primitive social safety net or none at all, a graying society will be a disaster.

The Muslim world will re-enact in lapsed time the demographic winter of the industrial world, with a deadly difference: the industrial nations are wealthy enough to cushion the impact, but the worst-affected Muslim nations are not. With GDP per person of $30,000 in 2009, Europe is wealthy enough to support its elderly—with sacrifice, skimping, and a certain amount of social dislocation. Egypt and Indonesia have less than a tenth of

Europe's per capita GDP. Algeria, like Iran, earns $4,400 per capita, while Pakistan shows barely $1,000 per capita—half of Pakistanis live on $1 a day or less. Even Turkey, the one Muslim country with a semblance of a modern economy, generates only $8,000 per capita, about a quarter of Europe's GDP.

By the end of the century, under the assumption of constant fertility, the economically active population (aged 15 to 59 years) of Western Europe will fall by two-fifths, and of Eastern Europe and East Asia by about two-thirds. The working-age population of the United States will grow by about a quarter. The least fertile European countries will see their total populations drop by 40 to 60 percent in the course of the present century.

This is the great underreported story of our time. Population collapse across almost the entire industrial world is threatening to disrupt the world's economy and endangering political stability. Eastern Europe and especially Russia are already facing a demographic death spiral. As the working-age population shrinks in most of the industrialized world, elderly dependents will make up most of Europe and East Asia's population. (But only two-fifths of America's.) Economies and tax revenues across Europe and East Asia will implode while pension and health care costs skyrocket. Pundits who preach America's inevitable decline should be sentenced to a year's hard labor at the United Nations database. For all the concern about the future cost of pensions and health care as America's population ages, America will still have the people to shoulder the burden. In the rest of the world, there simply will not be enough workers to support the elderly. Demographic winter means fiscal ruin and social upheaval.

But even more remarkable than the demographic decline of the industrial nations in Europe and the Far East is the speed at which Muslim nations are catching up to and in some cases overtaking the rest of the world in fertility collapse. World fertility has fallen by about two children per woman in the past half century—from about 4.5 children per woman to about 2.5. Fertility in the Muslim world has fallen two or three times faster than the world average. The drastic drop-off in fertility has hit Arab, Persian, Turkish, Malay, and South Asian Muslims. Iran's fertility has fallen by almost six children per woman, Turkey's has fallen by five children per woman, Pakistan's by more than three children per woman, and Egypt's and Indonesia's by four.

Muslim Countries' Fertility Falls Much Faster Than the World Average

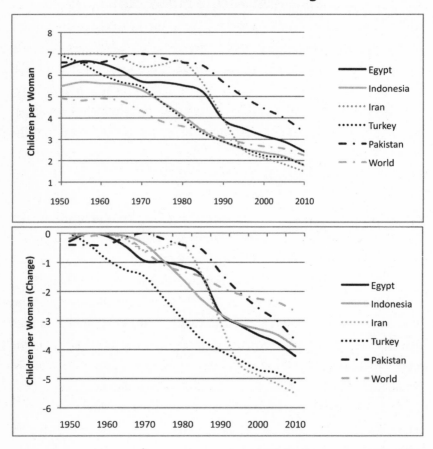

Source: United Nations World Population Division

Most Muslim countries have no public pension or health systems. The aged rely on their children to care for them. Muslims now in their sixties and seventies have on average several working-age children. In Iran, Turkey, and Algeria, most old people will have one or two children at mid-century. Europe is already struggling to cope with an aging population and increased demands for pensions and health care. During the next forty years, the average age of the European population will increase only from forty to forty-six years. In most Muslim countries, the average age today ranges from late teens to late twenties—but by 2050, it may rise to forty years or more. Many of the largest Muslim countries may well catch up with Europe's geriatric crisis in a generation and a half. By 2070, Iran will be grayer than Europe.

By the year 2070, several Muslim countries will have a higher proportion of elderly dependents than Western Europe. And the relative economic burden will be much, much heavier in the fast-aging Muslim countries.

Percentage of Population over 65 Years, Europe vs. Selected Muslim Countries

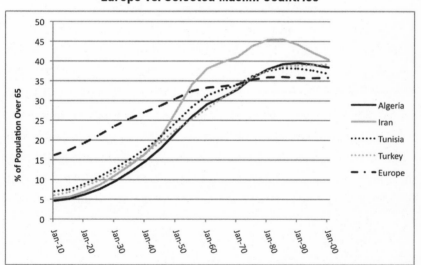

Source: United Nations World Population Division (Low Variant Scenario)

Most of the variation in birth rates among Muslim countries is explained by a single factor: literacy. Literacy is the threshold that separates traditional society from modernity. The moment Muslims learn to read, family size falls below replacement. Literacy explains about 60 percent of the fertility differential across the Muslim world.

Across the entire Muslim world, university-educated Muslim women bear children at the same rate as their infecund European counterparts. As soon as Muslim women break the constraints of traditional society, they have one child and sometimes two, but rarely three or four—and almost never the six or seven children that their mothers bore. This correlation holds whether we compare fertility among different Muslim countries or compare the fertility of women with differing educational levels within the same country, as we will see in the detailed data for Iran and Turkey.

Other factors impinge, to be sure: Bangladesh has promoted contraception more than some of its neighbors. In consequence its fertility rate of just under three children per woman is a bit lower than its 38 percent literacy would predict. "The contrast between Pakistan and poorer Bangladesh is stark," writes sociologist Eric Kaufmann. "Pakistan's religious authorities resisted family planning far longer than their counterparts in Bangladesh, who are much less influenced by…fundamentalist ideology."[2] Whether Muslim governments support or oppose contraception, though, makes only a small difference. Pakistan has the same literacy rate as Bangladesh, and Pakistani women have only one child more on average than Bangladeshi women; Pakistan's fertility rate of about four is just what the literacy rate there predicts. The only Muslim countries where women still give birth to seven or eight children are the poorest and least literate: Mali, Niger, Somalia, and Afghanistan.

Another factor is religious practice, itself inversely correlated with literacy. The more frequently Muslims attend mosque, the more likely they are to have big families, according to the World Values Survey—although data are available for only a small number of countries, and from years during which rapid change was under way. A third of the 88 percent-literate Turks never attend the mosque, according to the WVS polls, along with a quarter of 82 percent-literate Iranians (some recent news reports put mosque attendance in Iran even far lower)—and in both countries fertility is below replacement. By contrast, only a fifth of Egyptians never visit a mosque, and their fertility is correspondingly higher, at around 3 children per woman. And in illiterate Mali only 3 percent of respondents say they never to go a mosque—and the fertility rate jumps to 5.5 children per woman.

The Muslim world is trapped between two extremes. Some countries—notably Pakistan, Bangladesh, and Egypt—have populations nearly half of which cannot read. Those populations retain the habits of the tribal world, including high fertility rates. But these countries can barely feed the illiterate half of their people, let alone employ them; and the persistence of extreme poverty and the threat of hunger keep them poised at the precipice of social instability. At the other extreme, countries that have achieved a high degree of literacy—Iran, Turkey, Tunisia, and Algeria—are facing an even more devastating degree of social failure, in the form of deficient family formation and a dearth of children.

Modernity has attacked Muslim society in its most vulnerable organ—indeed, in the organ that was supposed to ensure Islamic triumph over the decadent West: the womb. But fragility does not make vulnerable Muslim countries less dangerous. On the contrary: whereas Europe tends toward pacifism because it knows it has nothing to gain from aggression, Iran tends toward belligerence because it knows it has nothing to lose.

Demographics and Desperation

Muslim leaders show more panic about their own demographic decline than the most despondent Western pessimist. The presidents of Iran and Turkey, Mahmoud Ahmadinejad and Tayyip Erdogan, both warn that their nations may be extinguished in a single generation. For the most part, the English-language media has ignored their warnings, but they permeate the Turkish- and Persian-language press and blogs. The sense of impending doom that pervades much of the Muslim world makes these countries dangerous and unstable. The real risk to world security is not the gradual triumph of Islam by demographic accretion, but an era of instability, social breakdown, and aggression impelled by despair.

"They want to eradicate the Turkish nation," Turkey's Prime Minister Tayyip Erdogan averred in 2008. "That's exactly what they want to do!" The "they" to whom Erdogan referred in his speech to a women's audience in the provincial town of Usak means whoever is persuading Turkish women to stop bearing children. Turkey is in a demographic trap. Its birth rate has fallen, and its population is aging almost as fast as Iran's. Speaking as a "worried brother" to his "dear sisters," Erdogan implored his audience, "In order that our people may remain young, you should have at least three children." No one listened. "Erdogan asked women to have three children, and demand for contraceptives went up," sniffed a prominent Turkish academic. Behind the fertility data, Erdogan sees nothing less than a conspiracy to destroy Turkey. "If we continue the existing trend, 2038 will mark disaster for us," he warned in May 2010.

Erdogan is right: the future of the Turkish nation is at risk. The demographic problem is not without remedies, but Erdogan's Islamism may not have access to them. Turkish fertility today is already below replacement and converging on European levels. It shows the same pattern we have seen in Iran and across the Muslim world: educated and literate Turkish women are having one and sometimes two children, while illiterate women in Anatolia's eastern back country are having four. For Turkey, that constitutes an existential threat. The most fecund group in Turkey is the Kurds, the restive fifth of the country who have been fighting for independence for decades. By the middle of this century, two-fifths of the total Turkish population and the majority of military-age men likely will be Kurdish.

Iran's Ahmadinejad, meanwhile, warns that national extinction will be the result of his country's collapsing birth rate. On September 10, 2010, the Iranian president declared during a meeting with officials in Alborz province, "'Two children' is a formula for the extinction of a nation, not the survival of a nation…. The most recent data showing that there are only 18 children for every 10 Iranian couples should raise an alarm among the present generation…. This is what is wrong with the West. Negative population growth will cause the extinction of our identity and culture. The fact that we have accepted this places us on the wrong path. To want to consume more rather than having children is an act of genocide."[3] The Persian-language website Javan Online quoted President Ahmadinejad and also cited sociologist Majid Abhari, warning of a "tidal wave of elderly" due to "decreased fertility" coming in the next few decades, leading to "workforce reduction and higher social insurance and medical costs due to an over-whelmingly elderly population."

The Iranian Train Wreck:
Projected Population by Age Bracket, 2010 vs. 2050

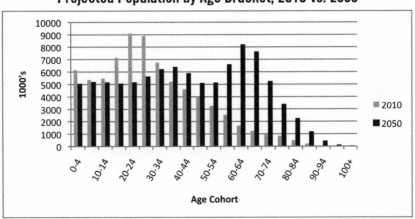

Source: United Nations Population Division (Constant Fertility)

The factors reducing fertility, Javan pointed out, include "increased education for women, increasing employment of women, improved health care and family planning, higher marriage age, more frequent divorce, changing view of family in the global culture, the changing family structure, and urbanization." The consequences of low fertility will include "a reduced labor force, an elderly population, a reduction of the country's international strength, a gradual deterioration of culture and community identity, migration of qualified personnel due to lack of opportunity, and psychological problems for only children."

In November 2010 President Ahmadinejad demanded that Iranian girls marry at the age of sixteen and produce more children. As he told the government newspaper *Jam-e Jam*, "We should take the age of marriage for boys to 20 and for girls to about 16 and 17."[4] For years, Ahmadinejad has denounced Iran's falling birth rate as a Western conspiracy to hobble his country. In 2006 he declared that Iran's population should nearly double: "I am against saying that two children are enough. Our country has a lot of capacity. It has the capacity for many children to grow in it. It even has the capacity for 120 million people. Westerners have got problems. Because their population growth is negative, they are worried and fear that if our population increases, we will triumph over them."

But Iranian women are doing the opposite of what Ahmadinejad asked. Back in 2006, when he first discovered the supposed Western plot to depopulate his country, Iranian women were having two children on average. By 2010 their fertility had dropped to only 1.7 children. Among the Persians who make up just over half of Iran's people—the rest are Turkish-speaking Azeris, Kurds, Arabs, and Baluchis—fertility is even lower. And in Iran's urban centers, there are even fewer births. In Tehran, the nation's capital, fertility is just 1.5 children per woman.

Demographers have never seen anything like it. In a 2008 study entitled "Education and the World's Most Rapid Fertility Decline in Iran," a team of European and Iranian demographers at the International Institute for Applied Systems Analysis observed,

> A first analysis of the Iran 2006 census results shows a sensationally low fertility level of 1.9 for the whole country and only 1.5 for the Tehran area (which has about 8 million people).... A decline in the TFR [total fertility rate] of more than 5.0 in

roughly two decades is a world record in fertility decline. This is even more surprising to many observers when one considers that it happened in one of the most Islamic societies. It forces the analyst to reconsider many of the usual stereotypes about religious fertility differentials.[5]

Education explains a great deal of Iran's fertility collapse, the team concluded. As we have seen, literacy explains most of the variation in fertility rates among the different Muslim countries. Within every Muslim country where data are available, the same pattern applies: education accounts for most of the variation in fertility within the population of each country.

The Iranian mother of seven children in the 1960s or 1970s had a primary school education, if any. By the mid-1980s, illiterate Iranian women had nearly five children. Women with a primary school education had an average of three and a half. Those with a high school diploma had slightly over two. But university-educated Iranian women had a fertility rate of just 1.3, about the same as the lowest levels registered in Western Europe. As more Iranian women went through the school system, the researchers conclude, fewer had children. The fertility rate for each education level also declined steadily, and the overall fertility rate imploded.

The few remaining illiterate women in Iran—mainly in the restive eastern province of Baluchistan—still have seven children, and the minority of Iranian women with only a primary school education still have four children. But, no thanks to the Islamist regime, Iran's women are the best educated in the Muslim world. Iran's secular government under the late Shah put enormous efforts into education during the 1970s and 1980s, with the goal of eliminating adult illiteracy by 1985. A "Literacy Corps" allowed young men with a high school diploma to teach reading to illiterate children as an alternative to military service, and two hundred thousand volunteered.[6] Ayatollah Khomeini's Islamic Revolution slowed but could not stop the literacy movement set in motion by the deposed Shah.

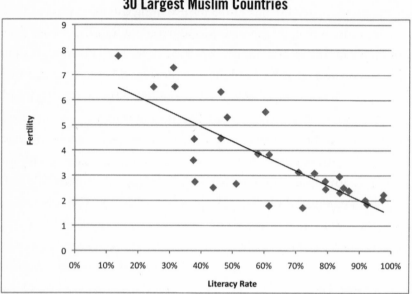

Total Fertility Rate vs. Literacy,
30 Largest Muslim Countries

Source: CIA World Factbook

Educated Iranians in their childbearing years are far less religious than their parents. As Iranians leave traditional society for secondary and university education, religious practice attenuates. Data are sparse, but as noted, the international survey data show less mosque attendance in Iran than in any Muslim country except Turkey. The nation that established the first Islamist state in the wake of the first Islamist revolution and that is ruled by a council of clerics and patrolled by religious police is becoming irreligious. After the fall of Communism in 1990, the world learned that outside of the ruling elite, there weren't many Communists in Russia. Outside of the governing theocracy, there don't seem to be many Muslims in Iran—not Muslims, that is, who turn up at mosques for prayers on Friday, Islam's holy day. Only 2 percent of Iran's adults attend Friday services, Zohreh Soleimani reported in a 2008 BBC broadcast.[7] Millions of Iranians demonstrated against vote fraud after the 2009 presidential elections, giving the world a glimpse of the extent of disaffection with the theocratic regime. Quietly and gradually, though, Iran's young people have been protesting for years, and in a far more decisive way: they refuse to bring children into the world.

Iran, moreover, appears to have set a precedent for other parts of the Muslim world; Turkey and Algeria, in particular, are not far behind. Muslim birthrates on average still exceed those in moribund Western Europe by a large margin, but with a rate of decline far and away the fastest in the world, Muslim fertility could easily fall below European fertility in the near future. Iran has already dropped to the lower part of the Western European range. A generation hence some of the world's poorer societies will be saddled with an elderly-dependency ratio like Europe's, as today's shriveled generation succeeds the very large generation of Muslims now in their working years.

This is why Mahmoud Ahmadinejad vocalizes a desperate sense of urgency: Iran was the first country to throw out a Western-oriented, secular government and replace it with an Islamist theocracy. On its own terms, Iran's Islamist experiment has failed. The treatment is killing the patient. That makes Iran dangerous. Iran is a mortally wounded beast, but a beast still at the peak of its destructive power.

Declining populations do not necessarily portend a peaceful outcome. On the contrary, in the short term they may well motivate aggressive behavior, provoked by a belief that the opportunity to fight may never return.

Hitler was decidedly pessimistic about the future of the Aryan race. He opined in *Mein Kampf,* "Aryan races create cultures which originally bear all the inner characteristics of their nature; however, the conquerors transgress against the principle of blood purity. They begin to mix with the subjugated inhabitants and thus end their own existence; for the fall of man in paradise has always been followed by his expulsion."[8] Hitler believed that the Aryan race in his own time stood at the edge of extinction because of interbreeding and the poisoning of blood through syphilis; he thought it might be saved only by early and extreme action that, in any case, would only postpone the inevitable Gotterdämmerung.

In the Islamists' own view, the encounter of Islam with the globalized world has had catastrophic effects on a religion so deeply rooted in the habits of traditional society that it cannot survive in the harsh light of modernity. The closing of the Muslim womb is a symptom of a shock to the spiritual condition of the Islamic world, a loss of faith more sudden and more devastating than the past century's trend towards secularism in the West.

The vast majority of educated young Muslims are alienated from the traditional Islamic culture of previous generations and rebel quietly against the Islamists' attempt to reimpose it on them by force. They have voted with their wombs. Like Europe, the Muslim world is engaged in the slow-motion suicide of failing to create the next generation. But the flip side of suicide by infertility is jihad. Islamists have responded to the disappearance of what former Iraqi minister of Finance, Defense, and Trade Ali A. Allawi calls "Muslims' basic identity and autonomy"[9] by mounting holy war on the West.

The Muslim world is committing suicide. But we could die in the implosion.

CHAPTER 2

⁂

FAITH, FERTILITY, AND THE WORLD'S FUTURE

Islam's demographic freeze is unique in world history for its speed. Otherwise, it follows a pattern documented exhaustively by demographers. As societies secularize, they become infertile. *Shall the Religious Inherit the Earth?* is the title of Eric Kaufmann's 2010 account of the secular birth dearth.[1] "Liberalism's demographic contradiction—individualism leading to the choice not to reproduce—may well be the agent that destroys it," Kaufmann complains. In 2004, journalist Phillip Longman, a fellow at the liberal New America Foundation, had already observed in his book *The Empty Cradle* that people of faith have children while secular liberals do not:

> Not since the fall of the Roman Empire has the world ever experienced anything on the scale of today's global loss of fertility. As sociologist Rodney Stark demonstrates in his well-respected

book on the rise of Christianity, at that time Christians had marginally higher birthrates than pagans and practiced less infanticide.... The resulting demographic advantage, Stark argues, slowly transformed a marginal Jesus movement into the dominant cultural force of the Western world, as Christian communities gradually outbred and out-lived their pagan counterparts. Demographic conditions today suggest that a culture transformation of similar proportions may be in store if secularists increasingly avoid the growing economic cost of raising children, while fundamentalists of all stripes do not.[2]

Demographic winter arises from a crisis of faith, in the West as well as the Islamic world. In many respects the demographic tailspin of Muslim countries repeats a well-studied pattern in the West: as traditional society gives way to modernity, faith and fertility vanish together. We have seen that a crisis of faith afflicts Muslim nations as much as it does the West. The façade of religious authority seems unbroken in most of the Muslim world. Behind the façade, though, the deterioration of traditional society hollows out religious faith.

It appears that Islam cannot survive outside the cocoon of traditional society. But to understand the wrenching changes in the Muslim world, we require a more general understanding of how civilizations decline. Oswald Spengler, whose *Decline of the West* remains the standard for pessimism, claimed that human civilizations followed a biological cycle of growth and decay. But there is no reason to believe this to be true; some very ancient civilizations—China and India, for example—are in resurgence.

The truth is that humankind cannot survive without faith, specifically faith that our lives have meaning beyond the mere span of our years. Civilizations that lose their faith also lose their desire to continue and fail to reproduce themselves. This premise is supported by extensive statistical evidence, most of it gathered by demographers during the last ten years— years that have produced a wealth of data about demographic decline.

But if we accept that secularism versus faith is the answer to the puzzle of the demographic death spiral—and many secular sociologists now accept it—that conclusion only leads to another question: Why do some faiths survive while others perish? Why is Islam collapsing in a generation, when it took European Christianity centuries to succumb to modern secularism? And, even more mysterious, why do some manifestations of the same faith manage to survive modernity in some places, but not in others? Why, for example, is the United States the only large industrial country in which a majority of people confess religious faith, as well as the only large industrial country with a fertility rate above breakeven? Why has Christianity flourished in the United States while it died out in Europe? That is the more important and more difficult question.

Why the "Overpopulation" Scare Was an Aberration

In retrospect, the West will look at the overpopulation scare of the late twentieth century as passing whimsy. Not overpopulation but rather depopulation has been the danger through almost all of recorded history. As early as the fourth century B.C.E., with Aristotle's diagnosis of the decline of Sparta, the wise men of the West noticed that societies might fail of their willingness to bear and raise children. Humankind was the first endangered species.

The great population surge of the second half of the twentieth century briefly erased the enduring fear of depopulation. But it is important to understand that that bulge in world population was a one-off event in human history, not the harbinger of environmental doom. As traditional society dissolved into the modern globalized world, death rates plunged immediately, while birth rates fell only gradually. Antibiotics encountered traditional habits of family formation, and the outcome was the—necessarily temporary—fastest rate of population increase the world had ever seen.

During the thousand years between Charlemagne and Frederick the Great, the world's population rose on average by 2.5 percent every half-century. With the agricultural revolution of the late eighteenth century, the world's population rose by 20 percent in fifty years, for the first time in history. During the second half of the twentieth century, the world's population grew by 140 percent. But that growth rate was always unsustainable—a blip in the statistics, the short lag between the point at which modern prosperity and medicine began to prolong lives and the point at which that improvement in life expectancy inevitably affected the birthrate. And it is about to fade in the rearview mirror. Population growth peaked in 2000 and will turn sharply negative during the last quarter of the twenty-first century.

World Population Growth
Every Half-Century

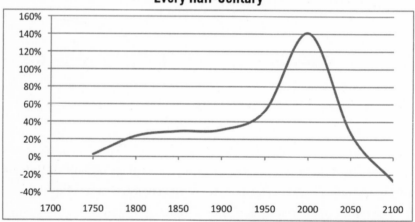

Source: United Nations (Data Point for 2100 from Low Variant Projection)

In 1994 the scientific academies of fifty-eight nations including the United States called for "zero population growth within the lifetime of our children," warning, "The world is undergoing an unprecedented population expansion. Within the span of a single lifetime, world population has more than doubled to 5.5 billion and even the most optimistic scenarios of lower birth rates lead to a peak of 7.8 billion people in the middle of the next century."

That may have been the dumbest idea that ever occurred to a group of smart people. It's true that the world's population will probably peak somewhere above 8 billion around the middle of this century. But it is likely to fall by nearly 2 billion between 2050 and 2100 under the United Nations' "low variant" projection. World population starts to decline in the second half of this century even in the UN's "medium variant" projection. And the actual population data have surprised the demographers on the downside during the last twenty years; there is good reason to believe that the low variant is more realistic. The world is facing a demographic collapse unlike anything in human experience.

What the zero population growth movement misunderstood is that the dissolution of traditional society drove down birth rates as well as death rates in a tortoise-and-hare race. First infant mortality fell to nearly zero in the developed world and to very low levels in all but the poorest countries. Then, although fertility fell slower, it fell much farther. The fear expressed as far back as the Hellenistic world—that human beings in the absence of constraint might fail to bring a new generation into the world—turned out to be right after all.

Faith and the Fertility Shift

Why do people raise children? Human beings are the only animals whose continuity depends on culture as much as it does on DNA. We cannot make a future for ourselves without our past. All cultures exist to ward off the presentiment of death. Breaking continuity with the past implies that our lives have no meaning past our own physical existence.

Sigmund Freud, wondering at Europe's propensity for self-destruction, invented an inborn death-drive to explain this widely observed phenomenon. I understand it rather as a symptom of a culture's mortal illness. If we do not see ourselves as continuing the lives of those who preceded us, nor preparing the lives of those who will follow us, then we are defined by our physical existence and nothing more. In that case we will seek to maximize our pleasure. Entire peoples may live only for pleasure, numbing themselves to the prospect of their own obliteration. How else should we explain fertility rates in Europe and Japan, now at barely half of replacement?

Why have so many branches of the human family lost the will to live? They have lost the cultural resources that enabled them to cope with their own mortality. From awareness that we will die arises culture—the capacity to order our behavior consciously rather than by instinct. Culture is the stuff we weave out of the perception of immortality, the bridge between generations. Every echo of our earthly footsteps will die out unless those who follow us inherit more than our genes. To speak of a "search for meaning" is pointless unless that "meaning" endures beyond our lifetime. With sad frequency, ethnic groups will die rather than abandon their culture. And their culture is failing many peoples in the modern world.

You don't have to be religious to understand why religion must provide the foundation of human culture. The just-deceased dean of secular sociologists, Harvard Professor Daniel Bell, explained back in 1976 that humankind is not content with mere animal existence:

> Human culture is a creation of men, the construction of a world to maintain continuity, to maintain the "un-animal" life. Animals seeing others die do not imagine it of themselves; people alone know their fate, and create rituals not just to ward off mortality but to maintain a "consciousness of kind" which is a mediation of fate. In this sense, religion is the awareness of a moment of transcendence, the passage out of the past, from which one has to come (and to which one is bound), to a new conception of the self as moral agent, freely accepting the past (rather than just being shaped by it).[3]

Bell's sociological account of religion, to be sure, views it as merely a human creation, a device to perpetuate the things that define us in a unique way—our customs, language, and so forth. Secular sociologists like Eric Kaufmann and his mentor Bell understand why religion is important. But they have no way to explain why some religions thrive and others fail—why the devout Catholicism of 1960s Quebec was headed towards extinction while the evangelical Protestantism of Middle America was poised for explosive growth at home and throughout the Global South.

What Determines Fertility?

Demographers speak of the "great fertility transition" between the old rural society and modern industrial society. In pre-modern society, most people had no choice but to raise children. Children were an economic asset to farming families who comprised nine-tenths of the American population at the time of the Revolution. They were also a retirement investment; before public pension systems, children cared for aged parents.

Married couples today ask themselves questions that did not occur to their great-great-grandparents. Do we want children? Can we afford an extra bedroom for another child, or another college tuition? Would we rather spend the money on a boat or a vacation in Tahiti? In the industrial world today, a prospective child has to compete against material pleasures, and the child is losing the competition.

And so we get Spengler's Universal Law #6 (courtesy of Warren Buffett): *You don't know who's naked until the tide goes out.* To make sure that a family would have enough children to run the farm and care for the elderly infirm, women bore children through most of their reproductive lives. A hundred years ago, roughly one in seven American newborns died before their first birthday. Only one in 150 American infants born today dies before its first year (the rate for Caucasians is one in 200). Only a few pockets of the industrial world's population continue to raise six or more children, and they do so out of religious motivation—for example, the Amish and ultra-Orthodox Jews.

The term "faith" has different meanings in traditional society and in the modern world; if people are incapable of questioning the regimen of their lives, it is difficult to distinguish between faith and habit, or faith in a universal Creator God as opposed to faith in one's own ethnicity. (This distinction is crucial, as we shall see later when we examine the sudden collapse of faith as well as fertility among peoples in transition out of traditional society.)

At some point in the twentieth century, the economists tell us, children ceased to be an economic asset and became a cost. We know the "price" of children both as an asset to unskilled farmers and as a liability to modern urban families, because economists have made careers out of calculating it.

- How many children do you need in order to be sure that at least one son will be there to care for you at age sixty-five? (Married daughters would care for their husbands' parents.) If you lived in England at the turn of the twentieth century, where life expectancy had just reached the fifty-year mark, the answer is five children to be 95 percent sure that one son would be alive when you reached age sixty-five.
- What is the optimal number of children to raise to help run a subsistence farm? The answer is five or more; in a large enough family the older children can help raise the younger children.
- If life expectancy at birth is twenty-five years—about the level that prevailed until the beginnings of the Industrial Revolution in the eighteenth century—how many children must the average woman bear in order to keep the population stable? Again, the answer is five.
- In 1950, seven out of ten people in the world lived in farming communities, and women on average bore five children.

In the United States of 1800, nine-tenths of Americans lived on farms, and the average woman bore seven children during her lifetime. By 1900, when only half of Americans lived on farms, fertility had fallen to four children per woman, and in 2000 to only two children. The same thing is happening around the world. By 2007, the majority of the world's people lived in towns or cities for the first time in history, and global fertility had fallen to 2.5 children per woman. And by 2050, seven out of ten people will live in urban areas.

Children were a valued source of labor for traditional farming families. At first, the Industrial Revolution increased the economic value of children by opening new opportunities for child labor. Sociologist Viviana Zelizer combed through court cases in the late nineteenth and early twentieth centuries where damages were awarded in the case of negligent death of children. Juries calculated damages by estimating the child's prospective earnings, net of the parents' expenses. "Overall, the principles of legal valuation of children in nineteenth-century death actions were remarkably similar to those of adults. The measure of damages in the case of a husband-father was the lost value of his probable earnings; for a wife, the anticipated worth of her household services; for a child, the probable value of his or her services during minority less the costs of support." These estimates fell into a predictable range; "for both boys and girls," Zelizer reports, "most awards ranged from $2,000 to $5,000."[4]

But in economic terms, we speak of children today not as a source of labor or retirement care, but as a cost. Very few people in the industrial world still live on farms, and even fewer use child labor. Children still contribute to family businesses, especially in first-generation immigrant families, but this phenomenon is significant in only a tiny minority of families. Very few people expect their children to support them in retirement. Instead, they expect other people's children to support them, through public or private pension plans.

The average cost of raising an American child to age seventeen is $222,360, according to a 2010 survey by the U.S. Department of Agriculture. That's more than four years of after-tax income for the median American family, not counting university. Put it another way: a single child will cost nearly 30 percent of the median family's spending power over the first seventeen years. Young families go into debt to raise children and pay the debts off when the children are grown. It's not hard to finance a large family if you start having babies in your early twenties, take out a big mortgage to buy a family home, get the kids out of the house by your mid-forties, and spend the last twenty years of your working life saving for retirement. But that presumes that you plan your life around a prospective family, marrying young and having children right away. If you spend your first ten years out of college playing the field, you're not likely to raise a big family.

There is something perverse in the economists' reckoning, to be sure. Human beings are, in fact, incomparably more valuable today in purely economic terms than they were in the old rural life. In 1850, output per person in the United States was about $4,000 in constant 2009 dollars. Today it is more than eleven times higher, at $46,000. Every American child born today, that is, will produce eleven times more goods and services than his great-great-great-grandfather born in 1850. Raising a child today, in other words, is an investment that pays ten times as much as it did in the middle of the nineteenth century. But by whom, and for whose benefit, is this investment made? When children labored on the family farm (or turned in their wages to their parents) and cared for aged parents, they contributed directly to their own family. When today's children go into the job market, they pay taxes and contribute to society. Childless singles who spend their money on entertainment receive the same pension and medical benefits as people who raise big families.

Without other peoples' children, to be sure, the childless singles would starve in old age, because there would be no one to pay the taxes that fund their benefits. But nothing in the social safety net discourages free riding on other people's child-rearing. If everyone decided whether or not to raise children on purely economic grounds, everyone would opt to keep child-raising costs to a minimum—in other words, to have no children at all—and let others pick up the tab. Society would disintegrate in a generation. That perverse outcome is an example of a "Nash Equilibrium" (after Nobel Prize winner John Nash whose biography became the film *A Beautiful Mind*). In terms of economic theory, concluded a 1997 study by the Population Council, "there is no explanation for why Americans still want children."[5] The authors concluded, "While the economic value of children to their families has disappeared, their value as a social resource has persisted. Having children is an important way in which people create social capital for themselves." But this hardly explains why Americans should want "social capital" while Spaniards and Germans do not.

In traditional society, people did what was expected of them. Our ancestors did not ask whether they preferred children to a larger condo and a Caribbean vacation. Whether they raised children out of love or obligation, we shall never know, for they never asked this sort of question. We do not know of a single case of fertility failure in a traditional society, that is, a society in which most people worked the land for subsistence. But traditional society is fragile. In the ancient world, as we shall see, infertility arrived with the Spartan warrior-state in which citizens practiced arms while slaves farmed, and with the Athenian imperial state where colonies subsidized an urban population. The modern fertility shift follows the migration from farm to city.

Except for tiny pockets like the Amish, traditional society is dead in the industrial world and fast dying in the developing world. Affluence, security, and longevity have combined to give the people of the wealthier countries freedom to make their own lives as they see fit in a way that no peoples enjoyed before them. Most of them use that freedom to play the field, find their inner selves, or enjoy the new frontiers of entertainment. The world is gone in which young people did what was expected of them: choose a spouse, marry in a house of worship, and get on with the business of child-rearing right away. Fewer people in the industrial world marry today, and those who do marry later and have fewer children at later ages. American women marry on average at age twenty-six today. And more than half of American women today are unmarried, compared to just over a third in 1950.

Fertility rates in nearly all the wealthier countries have plunged far below replacement. The poorer countries are not far behind. The United Nations' median forecast for global fertility foresees a world fertility rate at just above two children per woman by the middle of this century, or a fraction less than replacement, compared to a global fertility rate of five children per woman in the middle of the twentieth century. There is a world of difference between a fertility rate just above two, however, and a rate just below replacement—it is the difference between having your nose half an inch above the waterline and half an inch below.

In reality, population decline may drown us faster and deeper. In the United Nations' low variant forecast, global fertility will drop to barely above 1.5 children per woman by 2050. The outcome is likely to fall somewhere between the median and low variants. For the past twenty years, the rate of fertility decline has been much faster than the forecasters anticipated. A decline in productive population accompanied by a rise in dependent retirees creates an economic tailspin, as the shareholders of U.S. auto companies and the taxpayers of California and Illinois well know—and the residents of two dozen other American states are about to find out. Three-quarters of all Japanese and half of all Europeans will be elderly dependents by the middle of this century if the present low fertility rate continues.[6]

CHAPTER 3

WHAT THE ARAB REVOLUTIONS MEAN

An extensive literature warns that Europe will turn into "Eurabia" as Muslims replace the declining population of the Old World. Bernard Lewis, the dean of Western experts on the Muslim world, predicted in 2006 that "Muslim minorities will turn into majorities in a series of European countries" before the end of the present century.[1] The depopulation of Europe's Christians and the resettlement of Europe by Muslim immigrants has inspired recent books by Bat Ye'or, Tony Blankley, and Mark Steyn, among others.[2] The "Four Horsemen of the Eupocalypse," Steyn quips, are "Death—the demise of European races too self-absorbed to breed; Famine—the end of the lavishly-funded statist good times; War—the decline into bloody civil unrest that these economic and demographic factors will bring; and Conquest—the recolonization of Europe by Islam."

A YouTube video on Muslim demographics released in 2009 attracted over 10 million viewers with the claim that France would be an Islamic republic by 2048, that Muslims would form a majority in the Netherlands within fifteen years, and that Germany will be a Muslim state by 2050.[3] Libya's eccentric leader Muammar al-Gaddafi boasted in 2006, "We have 50 million Muslims in Europe. There are signs that Allah will grant Islam victory in Europe—without swords, without guns, without conquests. The 50 million Muslims of Europe will turn it into a Muslim continent within a few decades."[4]

It did not occur to Gaddafi five years ago that Europe's most urgent problem in 2011 would be an inundation of Libyan refugees fleeing civil war. Barely into the fourth month since the beginning of the Arab revolutions, Europe's well of compassion appeared to have run dry. According to United Nations officials, eight hundred refugees drowned in the attempt to reach Europe in small boats during the first months of this year.

The despair of Islam's Lost Generation has forced a very different crisis from the one proponents of the "Eurabia" thesis expected. Europe may face a more urgent threat during the next several years: the spillover of Islam's social crisis in the wake of the upheaval that engulfed the Arab world in 2011. We may not have the opportunity to observe at leisure how demographic trends in the Muslim world play out. The childless twenty-somethings of Islam's Generation X do not have to wait another forty or fifty years until they face starvation upon retirement. They are hungry now.

Europe's biggest worry in 2011 is not colonization by Muslim immigrants but inundation by Muslim refugees fleeing the chaos in Arab North Africa. Twenty-five thousand refugees from Libya's civil war have landed on the tiny Italian island of Lampedusa, close to the Libyan coast, and thousands more have drowned in the attempt to reach Italy, some reportedly in sight of NATO ships that failed to rescue them. Reported *Time* magazine,

> The Arab uprisings have created a surge of migrants fleeing toward Europe's southern rim, triggering a political rumpus. In late April, Italian Prime Minister Silvio Berlusconi and French President Nicolas Sarkozy jointly called for border controls to

be reimposed, to cope with what they described as "exceptional difficulties." And on May 4, the European Commission declared that the governments involved in the Schengen zone—which allows passport-free travel between 22 participating E.U. countries, plus Norway, Iceland and Switzerland—could soon be able to set temporary border checks.[5]

On April 17, France stopped train traffic from Italy to repel an influx of North African refugees after Italy gave temporary residence visas to five thousand Tunisians, allowing them to travel outside Italy and become a burden on other European countries. "Arab Refugees Destroy European Union" was the terse headline in the April 19 edition of *Pravda*.

So far Europe has felt only the first wave of spillover from the disintegration of Libya and Tunisia, with a combined population of 16 million. At improvised refugee camps in Italy and Greece, thousands of hungry migrants are living in crowding and filth. If Egypt plunges into chaos—and the first symptoms of social disorder already are manifest there—refugees from among its 82 million people could overwhelm Europe's capacity to handle the flood of desperate migrants. What some hailed as an "Arab Spring" after the January 2011 uprising in Tunisia and the toppling of Egypt's president Hosni Mubarak a month later is descending into an Arab Nightmare—civil war in Libya, brutal repression in Syria, and a collapse of social order in Egypt marked by violence against the country's Coptic Christian minority and rampant criminality.

Egypt is running out of food, and, more gradually, running out of money with which to buy it. The most populous country in the Arab world shows all the symptoms of national bankruptcy—the kind that produced hyperinflation in several Latin American countries during the 1970s and 1980s—with a deadly difference: Egypt imports half its wheat, and the collapse of its external credit means starvation. The country's foreign exchange reserves fell by $13 billion, or roughly a third, during the first three months of 2011. The country lost $6 billion of official and $7 billion of unofficial reserves, and had only $24.5 billion on hand at the end of April. Capital flight probably explains most of the rapid decline. Egypt's currency has declined by only about 6 percent since January, despite substantial capital flight, because of market intervention by the central bank, but the rapid drawdown of reserves is unsustainable. At this rate Egypt will be broke before the end of 2011. Egypt imported $55 billion worth of goods in 2009, but exported only $29 billion of goods. With the jump in food and energy prices, the same volume of imports would cost considerably more now. Egypt closed the 2009 trade gap with about $15 billion in tourist revenues, and about $8 billion of remittances from Egyptian workers abroad. But tourism today is running at a fraction of last year's levels, and remittances are down by around half because of expulsion of Egyptian workers from Libya. Even without capital flight, Egypt is short perhaps $25 billion a year.

The industrial nations and international aid organizations have pledged emergency help, but the Egyptian economy is bleeding out. The International Monetary Fund, the United Nations agency dedicated to financial stability, has thrown out stupefying numbers. "In the current baseline scenario," according to the IMF on May 27, 2011, "the external financing needs of the region's oil importers is projected to exceed $160 billion during 2011-13." That's almost three years' worth of Egypt's total annual imports as of 2010. As of 2010, the combined current account deficit (that is, external financing needs) of Egypt, Syria, Yemen, Morocco, and Tunisia was only $15 billion a year.

What the IMF says, in effect, is that the oil-poor Arab economies—especially Egypt—are not only broke, but dysfunctional, incapable of earning more than a small fraction of their import bill. And the private markets will not help countries at risk of takeover by extremists. "In the next 18 months," the IMF added, "a greater part of these financing needs will need to be met from the international community because of more cautious market sentiments during the uncertain transition."[6]

It will look like the Latin American banana republics, but without the bananas. That is not meant in jest: few people actually starved to death in the Latin inflations. Egypt, which imports half its wheat and a great deal of the rest of its food, will actually starve. Revolutions don't kill only their children. They kill a great many other people as well. The 1921 famine after the Russian civil war killed an estimated five million people, and casualties on the same scale are quite possible in Egypt. Half of Egyptians live on $2 a day, and that $2 is about to collapse along with the national currency. The result will be a catastrophe of, well, biblical proportions.

Desperation among Arab refugees is not the only threat to Europe. Libya's security forces used to prevent migrants from sub-Saharan Africa from leaving its shore in small boats headed for Europe. With the collapse of public order, Libyan police are taking bribes from West Africans to arrange boat passage. These are some of the world's poorest people, willing to take desperate risks. By some estimates a tenth of prospective migrants drown in the attempt to reach Europe.[7]

Tunisia's Lost Generation

It is no accident that the Arab revolts began in Tunisia, where expectations were the highest, and disappointment commensurately the greatest. Tunisia was supposed to be the poster child for Arab economic success. An October 27, 2010, evaluation on the website of the World Bank gushed with enthusiasm about the country's economic performance:

> Through a range of development policy loan programs with IBRD, Tunisia has boosted its global competitiveness and seen exports double over a little more than 10 years. The best illustration of Tunisia's improved competitiveness is its total factor productivity growth, which often drives investment. Total factor productivity rebounded from a negative rate in the 1980s to 1.24% in the 1990s and 1.4% in 2000-2006. While productivity growth in 2000-2006 remained below South Korea's and Malaysia's, it represented one of the best performances in the Middle East and North Africa region. Furthermore, exports of goods doubled in value between 1996 and 2007, while annual foreign direct investment flows increased steadily, averaging 2.2% of

GDP in 1996-00, 2.6% in 2002-05 and 5% in 2006-2008. Tunisia ranked as Africa's most competitive country in Davos' 2009 Global Competitiveness Report. All this translated into a 5% growth since the mid-1990s despite recurrent internal (e.g., droughts) and external shocks.[8]

It seemed like Tunisia was doing all the right things. The country spends 7.3 percent of GDP on education, a higher proportion than the U.S., Finland, or Israel. Of course, its GDP is far lower, so absolute education expenditures are lower as well. Nonetheless, Tunisia's education effort exceeds that of any other Muslim country, including 2 percent of GDP for university education. About 30 percent of secondary school graduates go onto university although 60 percent of them fail exams.

The trouble is that their diplomas are largely worthless. Like most developing countries, Tunisia teems with diploma mills that issue worthless degrees to half-trained graduates. Even in India and China, the majority of engineering graduates do not meet international standards—although the elite universities in those countries do produce a huge number of first-rate engineers. No Arab country produces graduates who can compete with their East Asian counterparts; the only Muslim country whose graduates meet world standards is Turkey.

University graduates throughout the Arab world have miserable prospects. "The average unemployment rate for the age group 15-24 years in the Group of Arab Countries reaches to 30%, compared with an average rate of world 14.4%," according to the Arab Labor Organization. "Problem [*sic*] of high unemployment rates among the educated graduates from universities and colleges, which reaches to 26.8% in Morocco and 19.3% in Algeria, 17.7 % in Jordan. It was noted that 94% of the unemployed in the Arab Republic of Egypt are in the age group 15-29 years, reflecting a lack of consistency of education plans to the needs of the Labor market."[9]

Tunisia had attracted a modest amount of foreign investment, most importantly in tech-support call centers for French-language customers of hardware and software companies. Outsourcing added perhaps two thousand jobs in 2010, or one for every 180 university students. Although Tunisian engineers will work for a fifth of the cost of their European counterparts, there aren't enough good engineers and not enough jobs even for the good ones. And the most qualified university graduates seek greener pastures overseas. Today's bulge of young Tunisian university graduates is a day late and a dollar short for the global world economy. If a new government were to cast off the constraints of bureaucracy and bribery that weigh so heavily on the Tunisian economy, it is conceivable that this country of just 10 million people might achieve a somewhat higher growth rate than Ben Ali's 5 percent per annum, and absorb a few more of its army of university graduates.

The average young Tunisian woman—like her Iranian or Turkish counterpart—grew up in a family of seven children, but will bear only one or two herself. Her mother was born into traditional society, and could barely read and write; the daughter may have attended university, and has neither the inclination nor the income to raise a large family.

Tunisia: Fertility vs. Elderly Dependent Rate
(Fertility Rate is a blend of UN "medium" and "low" variants.)

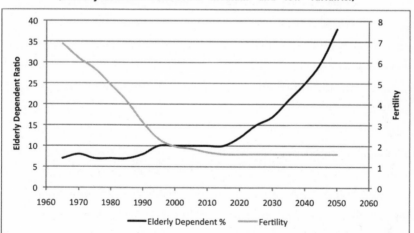

Source: United Nations World Population Prospects

By 2000, Tunisia's fertility rate had already fallen below replacement, and it is likely to fall much further (the UN "low variant" scenario puts it at only an astonishing 1.35 children per woman by 2015). One out of ten Tunisians is an elderly dependent today; as the present generation ages, the ratio will rise to about the same level as in Western Europe, or two out of five. Even for wealthy Western Europe, caring for this army of pensioners will strain resources to the limit; a poor country simply has no way to manage. The trouble is that Muslim countries that invest heavily in education, of which Tunisia is the best example, never achieve a critical mass of graduates capable of competing with their East Asian peers in world markets. Excepting a thin stratum of Turkish university graduates, the products of Muslim universities are mostly unemployable.

Wherever Muslim countries have invested heavily in secondary and university education, they have wrenched their young people out of the constraints of traditional society without, however, providing them with the skills to succeed in modernity. An entire generation of young Muslims has lost its traditional roots without finding new roots in the modern world. The main consequence of more education appears to be a plunge in fertility rates within a single generation, from the very large families associated with traditional society to the depopulation levels observed in Western Europe. Suspended between the traditional world and modernity, impoverished and humiliated, the mass of educated young Muslims have little to hope for and every reason to be enraged. In maleducated, underemployed, and depopulating Tunisia, the world can see the impending future of Arab societies.

Famine Stalks Egypt

Egypt is Iran without oil, and Turkey without an educated elite. One might add that it is Gaza without foreign aid. Whether Egypt will remain a militarized state, or become a democratic state, or an Islamist state, cannot be guessed as this book goes to press. It seems most likely that Egypt will be a failed state.

Pundits and political scientists talk of a choice of political models as if they were at a Ford dealership rather than the scene of a national catastrophe. *New York Times* columnist Roger Cohen's February 7, 2011, offering was titled "Tehran 1979 or Berlin 1989?" That is, the Iranian or the German model? Israeli Prime Minister Benjamin Netanyahu warns that Iran wants "a new Gaza in Egypt." Swiss Muslim Tariq Ramadan opined on Egypt's political future in the *Huffington Post* on February 8 under the title, "Democratic Turkey is the Template for Egypt's Muslim Brotherhood." (Ramadan is the grandson of Muslim Brotherhood founder Hassan al-Banna, whom he praises without mention of al-Banna's allegiance to the Nazis during the 1930s and 1940s.) But Spengler's Universal Law #7 warns, *Political models are like automobile models: you can't have them unless you can pay for them.* It is whimsical to compare Egypt to Iran, which has enough oil to pay for a lot of blunders—let alone to Germany. And unlike Turkish educational institutions, Egyptian universities do not meet world standards.

As Mohamed ElBaradei, the Egyptian Nobel Peace Prize winner, said after the January uprising, his country "is on the list of failed states,"[10] and the Arab world is "a collection of failed states who add nothing to humanity or science" because "people were taught not to think or to act, and were consistently given an inferior education."[11] Even that glum assessment, though, does not capture the intractability of Egypt's backwardness. According to a World Health Organization study, 97 percent of Egypt's married women have suffered genital mutilation, and 70 percent stated their intention to arrange the similar mutilation of their daughters, even though the Egyptian government outlawed the practice in 2007.[12] It is not simply that more than 40 percent of Egyptians are functionally illiterate, or that half the population lives on $2 a day or less. Most of the country is immured in a traditional society so rigid and remote from the modern world that modern political structures are as alien to it as quantum physics.

Even Islamists have to eat. Egypt is the world's largest wheat importer, beholden to foreign providers for nearly half its total food consumption. Food comprises almost half the country's consumer price index, and much more than half of spending for the poorer half of the country. This will get worse, not better.

Not the destitute, to be sure, but the educated, aspiring, and frustrated young confronted the riot police and army on the streets of Egyptian cities in the first months of 2011. The uprisings in Egypt and Tunisia were not food riots; only in Jordan have demonstrators made food the main issue. But the regime's weakness reflects the dysfunctional character of the country.

Countries can languish in backwardness only so long before some event makes their position untenable. The greatest risk to the impoverished citizens of oil-poor Arab countries is competition from East Asia for scarce resources. In effect, Chinese and Indian demand has priced food staples out of the Arab budget. As prosperous East Asians consume more protein, global demand for grain increases sharply (seven pounds of grain produce one pound of beef). East Asians are rich enough, moreover, to pay a much higher price for food whenever prices spike because of temporary supply disruptions. Egyptians, Jordanians, Tunisians, and Yemenis are not. Episodes of privation and even hunger will become more common. The miserable economic performance of all the Arab states has left a large number of Arabs so far behind that they cannot buffer their budget against food price fluctuations.

Not only Egypt, but all the oil-importing Arab countries are vulnerable to hunger. A 2009 World Bank report on Arab food security warned, "Arab countries are very vulnerable to fluctuations in international commodity markets because they are heavily dependent on imported food. Arab countries are the largest importers of cereal in the world. Most import at least 50 percent of the food calories they consume."[13] The price of wheat, the staple food in the Arab world, has doubled in the past several years. Soaring food prices were one of the triggers for the political upheaval in the Arab world in 2011.

Price of Wheat (U.S. Dollars per Bushel)

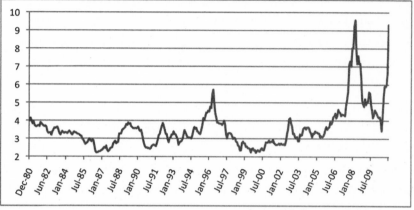

Source: U.S. Department of Agriculture

Low agricultural productivity is not only an artifact of incompetence, but a deliberate policy decision. Like most Arab countries, Egypt for decades discouraged increases in agricultural productivity because higher productivity means fewer peasants on the land, and more crowding into major cities. With 17 million people, most of them extremely poor, Cairo is already an unmanageable city.

How dangerous it is to dislodge inefficient smallholding farmers is evident from the destabilization of Syria. The Syrian government's liberalization of the agricultural sector, compelled under international trade agreements, resulted in the displacement of tens of thousands of small farmers, according to a March 2011 study by Paul Rivlin of Tel Aviv University. Rivlin explains,

> Syrian agriculture is suffering from the country's move to a so-called "social market economy" and the introduction of a new subsidy regime in compliance with international trade

agreements, including the Association Agreement with the European Union (which Syria has still not ratified). The previous agricultural policy was highly interventionist, ensuring (at great cost) the country's food security and providing the population with cheap access to food items. It is now being replaced with a more liberal one that has harsh consequences for farmers and peasants, who account for about 20% of the country's GDP and its workforce.[14]

Syria's farm sector, Rivlin adds, was further weakened by four years of drought: "Small-scale farmers have been the worst affected; many have not been able to grow enough food or earn enough money to feed their families. As a result, tens of thousands have left the northeast and now inhabit informal settlements or camps close to Damascus.... In early 2008, fuel subsidies were abolished and, as a result, the price of diesel fuel tripled overnight. Consequently, during the year the price of basic foodstuffs rose sharply and was further exasperated [sic] by the drought." Against that background, Syrian food prices jumped by 30 percent in late February, Syrian bloggers reported, after the regime's attempt to hold prices down provoked hoarding. The rise in global food prices hit Syrian society like a tsunami, exposing the regime's incapacity to modernize a backward, corrupt, and fractured country.

As Syria appeared to be descending into civil war in May of 2010, the UN Food and Agriculture Organization warned that the prospect of widespread starvation loomed: "Continuing unrest in Syria will not only affect economic growth but could disrupt food distribution channels leading to severe localized shortages in main markets.... Syria hosts one of the largest urban refugee populations in the world, including nearly one million Iraqis who have become more vulnerable because of rising food and fuel prices."[15]

Food and fuel provisions are shrinking in Syria and Egypt, but in Yemen, the most backward Arab state, the capital city of Sanaa is running short of drinking water. "Amid the ancient tower houses of Sanaa's Old City, men, women and children rushed to a water tanker when it arrived outside a mosque," the Newscore agency reported in June 2011. "Tensions rose as residents jostled to fill cans and plastic containers. The cost of a water tanker delivery, usually 1,300 Yemeni rials ($6.07), has soared to 7,000 amid the escalating conflict. 'They spend their money on bullets, but I can't even afford water for my family,' shouted one desperate resident as he waited for his can to fill from a communal water tanker. As with many cities and towns across the country, most of the capital's population relies on water being brought in. With fuel in short supply and roads increasingly dangerous, the delivery system is on the brink of collapse."[16] Yemen's GDP is just $1,200 per capita, half of Syria's, the country's infrastructure is primitive, and incipient civil war threatens life-endangering privation.

Arab dictatorships kept a large proportion of their people in rural backwardness as a matter of social control, a failed policy that set in motion the present crisis. Egypt's wheat yields are only eighteen bushels per acre, compared to thirty to sixty for non-irrigated wheat in the United States, and up to a hundred bushels for irrigated land. The trouble isn't long-term food price inflation: wheat has long been one of the world's bargains. The International Monetary Fund's global consumer price index quadrupled between 1980 and 2010 while the price of wheat, even after the price spike of 2010, only doubled in price. What hurts the poorest countries isn't the long-term price trend, though, but the volatility. People have drowned in rivers with an average depth of two feet.

It turns out that China, not the United States or Israel, presents the greatest existential threat to the Arab world, and through no fault of its own: rising incomes have gentrified the East Asian diet, and, more importantly, insulated East Asian budgets from food price fluctuations. Economists call this "price elasticity." Americans, for example, will buy the same amount of milk even if the price doubles, but they will stop buying fast food if hamburger prices double. East Asians now are wealthy enough to buy all the grain they want. If wheat output falls, for example, because of drought in Russia and Argentina, prices rise until demand falls. The difference today is that East Asian demand for grain will not fall, because the Chinese are so much richer than they used to be. Someone has to consume less, and it will be the people at the bottom of the economic ladder, in this case the poorer Arabs.

The volatility of the wheat price (the rolling standard deviation of percentage changes in the price over twelve months) has trended up from about 5 percent during the 1980s and 1990s to about 15 percent today. There is now only a roughly two-thirds likelihood that the monthly change in the wheat price will be less than 15 percent.

Wheat Price Volatility

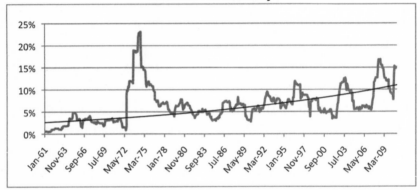

Source: USDA, Author's Calculations

With newly rich East Asians buying more grain at any price, the occasional poor harvest will push the wheat price through the ceiling, as it did during the past twelve months. To make life intolerable for the Arab poor, the price of wheat does not have to remain high indefinitely; it only has to trade out of their reach once every few years. And that is precisely what has happened. After thirty years of stability, the price of wheat has had two spikes into the $9 per bushel range at which very poor people begin to go hungry. The problem isn't production. Wheat production has risen steadily, very steadily in fact. Wheat supply dropped by only 2.4 percent between 2009 and 2010—and the wheat price doubled. That's because affluent East Asians don't care what they pay for grain. Prices depend on what the last (or "marginal") purchaser is willing to pay for an item (what was the price of the last ticket on the last train out of Paris when the Germans marched in on June 14, 1940?). Don't blame global warming or unstable weather patterns: wheat supply has been fairly reliable. The problem lies in demand.

The deposed President of Egypt, Hosni Mubarak, was an American ally, at least in appearance.[17] In place of allies, America now has Facebook friends. The image of tech-savvy young people deposing a dictatorship captured the imagination of a credulous Western media. A month after the Egyptian uprisings began, a search in Google News turned up more than five thousand news reports including the search terms "Facebook," "Egypt," and "revolution." The search terms "Egypt," "revolution," and "genital mutilation" turn up just seven stories in Google News. But female genital mutilation is in fact still much more common in Egypt than Facebook use; the Egyptians who "circumcise" their daughters have many more votes than the Egyptians who hang out at internet cafés.

For two reasons, the Facebook revolutionaries of Tahrir Square have scant hope of ruling Egypt. The first is that there are very few of them; as of the most recent data (for 2007), Egypt had only 437,000 broadband Internet connections for a population of nearly 80 million, or a penetration rate of five per one hundred residents, about the same as Iran and Pakistan. South Korea had thirty-four broadband connections per hundred people; Israel has twenty-five.[18] Roula Khalaf, writing in the *Financial Times*, pointed out, "The euphoric youth say they ran Tahrir Square so perfectly that they can also manage Egypt—except that their country is a land of 80 million people, 40 per cent of whom live in poverty. By official accounts, 44 per cent of the labor force is illiterate or semi-illiterate."[19]

And Egyptian young people with university degrees do not have sufficient skills to get a job with a multinational company, let alone run a country. Egypt churns out seven hundred thousand university graduates a year qualified to stamp each other's papers and not much else, and employs perhaps two hundred thousand of them, mostly in government bureaucracy.[20]

Officially, Egypt's unemployment rate is slightly above 9 percent, the same as America's. But independent studies say that a quarter of men and three-fifths of women are jobless. As Egypt's new Finance Minister Samir Radwan said of the young people who put him in power, "I'm generalizing, but a large number of the Egyptian labor force is unemployable. The products of the education system are unemployable."[21] "Many people have degrees but they do not have the skill set," Masood Ahmed, director of the Middle East and Asia department of the International Monetary Fund, said in February 2011. "The scarce resource is talent," agreed Omar Alghanim, a prominent Gulf businessman. The employment pool available in the region "is not at all what's needed in the global economy."[22] There are countless capable Egyptians, to be sure, but most of them study, and many of them work, outside the country. Google employee Whalid Ghonim, the poster child for Egypt's revolution, did not have a job in Egypt, but in Dubai.

Two years' output of the country's diploma mills will fill Tahrir Square with young people who have nothing else to do. They know the Internet, to be sure; the Internet café is the ubiquitous peephole on the great world available to anyone in the global South with a couple of dinars or pesos to spend. One finds Andean Indians in colored blankets and round hats at computer screens in Quito, and kaftaned Senegalese online in Dakar. Whether they are voyeurs or participants in the modern world is the question. The benign view of the Egyptian uprisings presumes that a relatively tiny caste of semi-educated urban residents can steer a backward and destitute country in the direction of representative democracy.

Eurabia or Eu-grave-ia?

Critics of the "Eurabia" thesis point out that Muslim birth rates have fallen sharply in Europe, just as they have at home. Evidence is fragmentary—many European nations refuse to collect or publish information on Muslim birth rates—but the available data point to a fertility bust among some Muslim immigrants to Europe comparable to the fertility bust in their own countries. Conditions vary. The drop in the birthrate seems especially true of Turkish immigrants, but not at all true of Pakistanis.

The most-cited study of Muslim fertility rates in Europe finds, "Based on official data on religion, national origin, and other indicators of ethnic origin, Muslim fertility in 13 European countries is higher than that for other women, but in most countries with trend data the differences are diminishing over time."[23] In Germany, for example, Turkish women had on average two more children apiece than German women in 1970. But by 1996, the gap had narrowed to a one-child advantage for the Turks. Muslim women in Austria bore an average of 3.1 children each in 1981, almost double the 1.7 fertility rate for Catholic Austrians. Twenty years later, in 2001, the Catholic fertility rate was down to 1.3, but Muslim fertility had fallen to 2.3. In Holland, Turkish immigrant women were at a fertility rate of 3.2 children in 1990, double the Dutch fertility rate of 1.6. But by 2008, Turkish women in Holland were having only 1.9 children apiece. And in Denmark, the fertility of native-born women reached 1.9 in 2009, against 1.6 for immigrant women. (The figure for Danish women, though, includes second-generation immigrants.)

The pattern also appears to apply to African Muslim immigrants to France, which takes in more immigrants from Muslim Senegal than from any other country in sub-Saharan Africa. Although Senegal's total fertility rate of 5.2 (four children in cities and six children in the countryside) is one of the world's highest, Senegalese immigrants average only 2.12 children, slightly higher than the French average, a recent study finds.[24] A French researcher claims that "excess fertility of immigrants compared with women born in France" is only half a child per female on average, taking into account the drop in fertility after immigrants settle in France.[25]

That is small comfort for the United Kingdom, where Muslims from the Indian subcontinent form the dominant group of immigrants. Pakistan with its 50 percent literacy rate still has a fertility rate of more than three children per woman. And Pakistani fertility survives emigration to Britain. According to the Population Research Bureau, Britain's population will rise to 77 million in 2050 from 63 million today. More than half of new births will come from immigrant mothers, and it is not known how many of the remaining births will come from second-generation immigrants.[26] It appears that Muslim immigrant fertility will make Britain the most populous European country by 2050.

It may be that the threat of a "Londonistan" in the United Kingdom is insufficiently appreciated while the prospect of a Turkish takeover in West Germany and the Senegalization of France are exaggerated. Whether Muslim immigrants to Europe comprise a much larger share of population or not during the next generation or two, the evidence is that the Muslim world is only a generation or two behind the Europeans in the slide towards depopulation. Instead of a Muslim takeover of Europe by immigration and high fertility rates, the simultaneous demographic decline of Europe and the adjacent Muslim countries may bring about mass starvation, political instability, and an unmanageable refugee crisis—and common ruin—before the end of the present century.

CHAPTER 4

✠✠✠

SEX, DRUGS, AND ISLAM

The underside of Islam's demographic freeze is an appalling breakdown of traditional mores. Political Islam returned to the world stage with Ruhollah Khomeini's 1979 revolution in Iran. And Iran soon became the aggressive patron of Muslim radicals outside its borders, including Hamas in the Palestinian territories and Hezbollah in Lebanon. After the June 2009 presidential elections, mass demonstrations against vote fraud in major Iranian cities brought to the surface long-simmering resentment against the Islamic regime, especially among young educated city dwellers. Despite the extent of the protests, opposition wilted before a regime that continues to control money and gunmen. But disaffection among young Iranians takes other and more alarming forms.

Under the façade of radical Islam, Iran suffers from an eruption of social pathologies such as drug addiction and prostitution on a scale much worse than anything observed in the West. It appears that Islamic theocracy promotes rather than represses social decay. A spiritual malaise has over-come Iran despite the best efforts of the totalitarian Islamists. Popular morale has deteriorated much faster than in the "decadent" West against which the Khomeini revolution was directed.

Spengler's Universal Law #8: *Wars are won by destroying the enemy's will to fight. A nation is never really beaten until it sells its women.* The French sold their women to the German occupiers in 1940, and the Germans and Japanese sold their women to the Americans after World War II. Hundreds of thousands of female Ukrainian "tourists" entered Germany after the then-Foreign Minister Joschka Fischer loosened visa standards in 1999. That helps explain why Ukraine has the world's fastest rate of population decline.

And prostitution has become a career of choice among educated Iranian women. On February 3, 2009, the Austrian daily *Der Standard* published the results of two investigations conducted by the Tehran police but suppressed by the Iranian media.[1] "More than 90% of Tehran's prostitutes have passed the university entrance exam, according to the results of one study, and more than 30% of them are registered at a university or studying," according to the Austrian daily. "The study was assigned to the Tehran Police Department and the Ministry of Health, and when the results were tabulated in early January no local newspaper dared to so much as mention them":

> Eighty percent of the Tehran sex workers maintained that they pursue this career voluntarily and temporarily. The educated ones are waiting for better jobs. Those with university qualifications intend to study later, and the ones who already are registered at university mention the high tuition as their motive for prostitution…they are content with their occupation and do not consider it a sin according to Islamic law…. This study isn't the only unwanted gift that the regime received on the thirtieth anniversary of the Islamic Revolution. A second investigation about the condition of young people presents more problems

for the authorities. It was assigned to the Education Ministry. A portion of the results were published, but others were suppressed. It was made public that less than a third of young people in Tehran between 15 and 29 years of age say they are satisfied with their situation. 62.5 percent complain about unemployment, the social order and lack of money. They have no perspective for the future. Only 31.6 percent find the social norms of the regime acceptable; 35.8 percent want to emigrate.

It is hard to obtain reliable data on prostitution inside Iran, but anecdotal evidence suggests that it has increased since Mahmoud Ahmadinejad was re-elected in 2009. Anti-regime sociologists claim that at least three hundred thousand women are selling themselves in Tehran alone. On April 25, 2009, the ADNKronos website reported:

> Prostitution is on the rise in Iran.... Sociologist Amanollah Gharaii Moghaddam told ADNKronos International (AKI) that he believes Iran's deteriorating economy and the high unemployment rate among youths to be the main causes of this worrying phenomenon. In Iran, 28% of young people between the ages of 15 and 29 are unemployed.... The age of prostitutes is increasingly younger, and girls as young as 12 are selling their bodies on Iran's streets. Overall, the number of prostitutes is also on the rise and there are an estimated 300,000 of them in Tehran alone.... Nevertheless, Gharaii Moghaddam says "the number isn't so high when compared [with] the 4 million unemployed only in Tehran and the 5 million drug addicts today in Iran."

By "prostitute," the Iranian authorities mean a woman who exchanges sexual services directly for money. No data are available on the extent of "temporary marriages," which are permitted in Shi'ite Islam. According to a document translated and published by *Eurasia Review,* the Imam Reza shrine offers temporary marriage licenses for pilgrims priced according to duration; five hours costs the equivalent of $50, twenty-four hours costs $75, and so forth.[2] There is also an extensive international trade in poor Iranian women; they are trafficked to the Gulf States and to Europe and Japan.

Prostitution as a response to poverty and abuse is one thing, but the results of the new Iranian Health Ministry study reflect something quite different. The educated women of Tehran are choosing prostitution in pursuit of upward mobility—as a way of sharing in the oil-based potlatch that made Tehran the world's hottest real estate market during 2006 and 2007.

The popular image of the Iranian sex trade is one of tearful teenagers abused and cast out by impoverished parents. Such victims abound, but a high proportion of Tehran's prostitutes are educated women seeking affluence. Only in the former Soviet Union after the collapse of Communism in 1990 did educated women choose prostitution on a comparable scale, but they did so under very different circumstances. Russians went hungry during the early 1990s as the Soviet economy dissolved and the currency collapsed. Today's Iranians suffer from shortages, but the data suggest that Tehran's prostitutes are not so much pushed into the trade by poverty as pulled into it by the dream of wealth. That is consistent with Spengler's Universal Law #9: *A country isn't beaten until it sells its women, but it's damned when its women sell themselves.*

The second fail-safe indicator of social decay is drug addiction. The *Der Standard* piece reported that "the most unpleasant news for the government are the statistics about drug use among Iranian youth. Those were kept secret. 30 percent of schoolchildren have tried drugs at least once, and 10 percent of schoolchildren are addicted." And according to a 2008 report from the U.S. Council on Foreign Relations, "Iran serves as the major transport hub for opiates produced by [Afghanistan], and the UN Office of Drugs and Crime reports that Iran has as many as 1.7 million opiate addicts." The United Nations report is close to Iran's official numbers, which report 1.2 million addicts and eight hundred thousand occasional users.

Last year the BBC cites non-governmental organizations who estimate that the actual number of users of hard drugs (including opiates, methamphetamine, and hallucinogens) is as high as 5 million.[3] In other words, 12 percent of Iran's non-elderly adult population of 35 million uses drugs. That is an astonishing number, unseen since the peak of Chinese addiction during the nineteenth century. The closest American equivalent, from the 2003 National Survey on Drug Use and Health, found that 119,000 Americans reported using heroin within the prior month, or less than one-tenth of 1 percent of the nonelderly adult population. Despite fearsome restrictions—a third conviction for alcohol possession merits the death penalty—alcoholism is also extensive, if hard to measure. The government estimates that 14 million liters of spirits are smuggled in to the country annually, and Iranians distill illegal spirits as well. Cheap opium from neighboring Afghanistan, though, makes the narcotic the Iranian drug of choice.

Iran's economy is a sick entity kept going through infusions of oil money. Iran's central bank reports inflation at 14 percent for the year through May 2011, but the research center of the Iranian parliament claims that the actual inflation rate was over 50 percent in 2010.[4] How do households survive? The average Iranian urban household spends a total of $316 a month. A high proportion of Iranian families are priced out of the rental market, which suffered increases of over 100 percent during 2007 and 2008. Foodstuffs, fuel, and other essentials have registered double- or triple-digit price increases during the last two years. Germany's *Suddeutsche Zeitung* reported from Tehran on June 17, 2008, "Price increases follow one another in batches. After the prices of rice and detergent suddenly jumped by a multiple, tea prices have their turn. In just a few days different types of tea have become 300% to 700% more expensive."

Official Iranian data report that the average household earns too little to purchase the minimum consumption level of basic goods. In fiscal year 2005–2006, according to the country's central bank, the average Iranian household of four people earned the local-currency equivalent of about $6,100, or just over $1,500 per person—and that number includes the rental equivalent of owner-occupied houses and other imputed income. Those are the last numbers available, and they reflect the position of Iranian city-dwellers before economic sanctions began to bite. Iranian families were barely keeping their heads above water before Western governments imposed sanctions in response to Tehran's efforts to acquire nuclear weapons. In December 2010 the government eliminated fuel subsidies, quadrupling the price of gasoline and doubling the price of bread, while giving Iranians a $37 per month cash subsidy. In 2006 the central bank reported that one in six Iranian urban households had no member with a job; the national unemployment rate probably exceeds 20 percent.

Oil Runs Out as the Iranian Bulge Generation Retires

Just as Iran's bulge generation approaches retirement, Iran's output of oil and gas is likely to shrink drastically. Iran's GDP is just $7,000 per capita, mostly derived from oil and gas, and Iran's oil production may fall to below domestic consumption requirements before 2020 because of the gradual exhaustion of reserves and neglect of needed investment.[5] Estimates of Iran's available reserves and explanations of the causes of its supply problems vary, but it seems likely that a combination of geology and incompetence will shrink state oil revenues—and the country's capacity to subsidize consumption—precisely when Iran will need them the most. "Iran's natural gas exports will be minimal due to rising domestic demand even with future expansion and production from the massive South Pars project," according to the U.S. Department of Energy.[6] Iran's aging oil fields will lose an estimated 8 percent of output per year, according to the DOE, although secondary recovery measures can slow the rate of decline. In 2010, the International Energy Agency predicted that by 2015, Iran's oil production would fall by 18 percent, to 3.30 million barrels a day, compared to a 1970s peak of 6 million barrels per day.[7]

Even if secondary production methods reduce the decline from 8 percent a year to only 2 percent a year, oil output will fall by more than half by

2050, when an avalanche of retirees will make impossible demands on the Iranian economy. We have never seen anything like this before; we have difficulty imagining the degree of misery that will befall Iran. Assuming a 2 percent per annum decline in oil output—a relatively benign scenario— Iran will encounter precisely the sort of national disaster of which Ahmadinejad warns. The years of the institutionalized Islamic Revolution have been, relatively speaking, economically fat years, subsidized by oil and natural gas production. And yet in those fat years, the educated urban population is slipping into drug addiction, prostitution, and despair. What will Iran's lean years look like?

Iran's Elderly Dependent Ratio vs. Oil Production
(Assuming 2 percent/Year Production Decline)

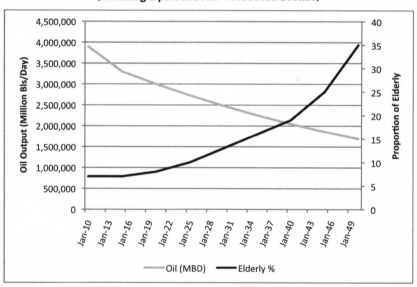

Source: UN Population Prospects

CHAPTER 5

⚜⚜⚜

"THEY WANT TO DESTROY THE TURKISH NATION!"

Turkish President Tayyip Erdogan, we have seen, predicts national destruction by the year 2038. That's when the cost of supporting the bulge-generation of Turkish retirees will bankrupt the national Treasury, and when Kurdish speakers will threaten to outnumber Turks in Anatolia.

These considerations put the much-vaunted "Turkish" model in a different light. Rarely has a fatally flawed political system received so much praise. "The 'Turkish model' emerges as nations face transformation," ran a March 3 headline by the Chinese state news agency Xinhua. "Turkey could be an example for its political, socio-cultural and economic progress achieved in recent years," Atilla Sandikli, president of the Istanbul-based Wise Men Center for Strategic Research (BILGESAM), told Xinhua on the occasion of a visit to Egypt that week by Turkish President Abdullah Gul.[1]

Turkish analysts, though, hear such statements with incredulity. The online *Hürriyet Daily News* in March 2011 tried to catalogue the innumerable mentions of the "Turkish model" for "entertainment value," and cited the following:

> A headline from the Jerusalem Post: "A Turkish model for Egypt?" Or the essay in America's National Journal: "What is the Turkish model?" The Daily Star in Cairo phrased the question differently in its headline: "Is there a Turkish model?" The Wilson Center in Washington DC apparently thinks there is. On that think-tank's website you can find the tome: "Egypt and the Middle East: The Turkish Model." At the Brookings Institution, a think-tank a few blocks away, there appeared less certainty: "An Uneven Fit? The Turkish Model and the Arab World" is that outfit's contribution. With typical German conciseness, a think-tank there offered us simply, "The Turkish Model."[2]

Turkey was supposed to be the poster child for Muslim democracy. But it is rapidly turning into an Islamist tyranny. In 2002, Turkey's Justice and Development Party, or AKP, formed the country's first Islamist government in nearly eighty years. Then Deputy Defense Secretary Paul Wolfowitz singled Turkey out as an exemplar of moderate Islam in a September 2002 address.[3] The Bush administration gave the AKP party leader Tayyip Erdogan star treatment during a 2003 Washington visit, including a presidential press conference and high-profile meetings at the Pentagon, even though Erdogan was still barred from the prime minister's office for Islamist pronouncements he had made a decade earlier.

When Erdogan was re-elected prime minister in 2007, though, Turkey transmogrified from the West's (and Israel's) most reliable ally in the region to a spoiler intent on carving out its own regional role. According to Rachel Sharon-Krespin, a researcher for the Middle East Media Research Institute,

As Turkey's ruling Justice and Development Party (Adalet ve Kalkinma Partisi, AKP) begins its seventh year in leadership, Turkey is no longer the secular and democratic country that it was when the party took over. The AKP has conquered the bureaucracy and changed Turkey's fundamental identity. Prior to the AKP's rise, Ankara oriented itself toward the United States and Europe. Today, despite the rhetoric of European Union accession, Prime Minister Erdogan has turned Turkey away from Europe and toward Russia and Iran and re-oriented Turkish policy in the Middle East away from sympathy toward Israel and much more toward friendship with Hamas, Hezbollah, and Syria.[4]

Turkey's sudden transition from Eastern linchpin of NATO to ally of extremist regimes was motivated by a deep sense of national despair. Turkey is locked in a demographic trap: to compete in the world economy, it must educate and employ its women. The more years of education a Turkish woman receives, however, the fewer children she is likely to bear. According to demographer Sutay Yavuz, improvements in female education have suppressed fertility. "The proportion of women aged 15 to 49 that have completed at least the second level of primary school increased from 15 percent in 1993 to 24 percent in 2003," he wrote in a recent study. As in Iran and the rest of the Muslim world, the consequence is a sharp decline in the birth rate: "Fertility differentials among women with different educational backgrounds are striking; the mean number of children ever born (a measure of completed fertility) among women aged 40 to 49 without formal education is 5, while the same figure is only 2 for women at the same ages who have completed high school or higher level education."[5]

That's half the problem. During the period 1995–1998, overall Turkish fertility was 2.29 children per woman, while Kurdish fertility was 4.27 children per woman.[6] The Kurds comprise 18 percent of the Turkish population by the narrowest definition (Kurdish rather than Turkish as a mother tongue), which means that the Turkish fertility rate excluding the Kurds during the late 1990s was only 1.5, as low as Europe's. For native Turkish-speakers in Turkey, fertility has been in a death-spiral for the past fifteen years. Erdogan is right: if the trend continues until 2038, the Turkish economy will collapse under the strain of caring for its dependent elderly, while the country's young people will be concentrated among minorities demanding independence from the hard hand of the Turkish state. According to a recent study in *Population Policy Review*, "Fertility levels of Turks and Kurds are significantly different. At current fertility rates, Turkish-speaking women will give birth to an average of 1.88 children during their reproductive years. The corresponding figure is 4.07 children for Kurdish women. Kurdish women will have almost 2 children more than Turkish women."[7] The study adds, "Results show that despite intensive internal migration movements in the last 50 years, strong demographic differentials exist between Turkish and Kurdish-speaking populations, and that the convergence of the two groups does not appear to be a process under way. Turks and Kurds do indeed appear to be actors of different demographic regimes, at different stages of demographic and health transition processes." The Kurds of Turkey's undeveloped east, in short, continue to bear four children while Turkish citizens whose cradle tongue is Turkish have one or two.

The Holy Roman Empire was neither holy, nor Roman, nor an empire, in Voltaire's quip. One might say that Muslim democracy in Turkey is neither Muslim, nor democracy, nor Turkish. Excluding the country's Kurdish minority, Turkish fertility has fallen to Western European levels, a test for secularization. Within two generations, Turks once again may be a minority in Anatolia, as they were after they first conquered Asia Minor in the thirteenth century. For eight years, Turkey has had an energetic Islamist government, which is trying—but failing—to reverse these trends. Turkey's fragile democracy is in doubt, with thousands of regime opponents, including prominent academics and journalists, in jail or under investigation.

There is a bizarre edge to Tayyip Erdogan. He is given to lurid, sometimes bloodthirsty outbursts. During a February 2008 visit to Germany, Turkey's most important European trading partner, Erdogan scandalized his hosts when he told an audience of twenty thousand Turks that assimilation into German culture was "a crime against humanity." Germany, after all, knows a thing or two about crimes against humanity. German opinion was outraged, and Turkey's chances for membership in the European Community—a pillar of Turkish diplomacy for a generation—fell to negligible. Erdogan ignored the uproar, and told the Turkish Parliament upon his return to Ankara, "I repeat…assimilation is a crime against humanity…. We can think differently from (Chancellor Angela) Merkel about this, but that is my opinion." The German attitude towards its Turkish minority has swung from multicultural outreach to pessimism about their future in German society. In October 2010, German Chancellor Angela Merkel told a gathering of her political party that Germany's attempt to create a multicultural society has "utterly failed." As press reports paraphrased her remarks, "Allowing people of different cultural backgrounds to live side by side without integrating has not worked in a country that is home to some four million Muslims."[8]

Optimists say that the glass is only half poisoned: Erdogan, in a widely held view, is an old-fashioned populist playing to the prejudices of a backward constituency. "Just turn on American television and listen to the hate speech coming from the evangelical Christians!" one Turkish politician told me. Whatever one thinks of Pat Robertson, though, no one elected him president of the United States. The prime minister's outbursts and paranoid style appear at odds with what critics concede to be pragmatic economic management. Turkey has the only strong economy in the Muslim world. A small-town boy made good, a devout Muslim in a country long ruled by secular governments, an autodidact with a deep suspicion of his country's elites, Erdogan displays all the eccentricities of a political outsider. Some of his tantrums can be interpreted as characteristically Asian haggling. The

Chinese government feared that Turkey was quietly encouraging unrest among the Uyghurs when riots erupted in 2009, and Erdogan's "genocide" remark did nothing to alleviate Beijing's concern. After the dust settled, though, China and Turkey agreed that Chinese imams will train in Turkey, rather than in Saudi Arabia or Iran as in the past.[9] It is possible that Ankara used the Uyghurs as a bargaining chip with Beijing.

But there is something troubling about the prime minister's personal edge. His rage reflects a deep crisis of Turkish identity—an unresolvable tension between Europe and Asia, secularism and Islam, the educated elite of the western cities and the intractable backwardness of the Anatolian hinterland. And it is energized by the realization that Turkey's catastrophic fertility decline marks its failure to find its way from traditional society to modernity.

From an economic standpoint, Turkey might break down. From a political standpoint, it might break up. The hysteria that Erdogan displays towards domestic and foreign opponents draws on a deep reserve of existential angst about problems that are anything but imaginary.

From the prime minister's office to the man in the street in Istanbul, a deep sense of malaise impels Turks to lash out against real and perceived enemies at home and abroad. The AKP government has arrested or charged about forty-three hundred individuals with complicity in an amorphous coup plot called Ergenekon, including hundreds of senior military officers, journalists, and academics. AKP critics denounce the Ergenekon case as a pretext for an Islamist coup against Turkey's secular constitution. "Ergenekon has become a larger project in which the investigation is being used as a tool to sweep across civic society and cleanse Turkey of all secular opponents. As such, the country's democracy, its rule of law and its freedom of expression are at stake," a former Justice Minister told the *New York Times*.[10] In February 2011, Francis Ricciardone, America's ambassador to Turkey, told a press conference, "On the one hand there exists a stated policy of support for a free press. On the other hand, journalists are put under detention. We are trying to make sense of this."[11]

Erdogan's Islamist government is still running on the reserves that Turkey built up over three generations of secular rule. A poor country without natural resources, Turkey's only economic advantage is a highly qualified managerial and technical caste. As in Europe, secularism has failed as a source of national identity. Erdogan wants to revive Islam as the source of Turkish identity. Rather than batter the Kurds into accepting "Turkishness," as his secular predecessors did, at frightful human cost, Erdogan argues that Kurds are brother Muslims. But the Kurdish problem simmers away beneath the surface. Kurdish parties continue to demand the right to use their language in media and in private educational institutions, now forbidden by Turkish law.

After the Ottoman Empire's catastrophic defeat in the First World War, Kemal Atatürk, the founder of modern Turkey, established an explicitly secular state and banned the outward symbols of Islamic practice—the flat-topped red felt fez worn by men and the headscarf. Atatürk built a new national university system on the German model, and offered refuge to a generation of academics fleeing Nazi Germany and the Second World War. The Turkish army guaranteed the strictly secular character of the state, and the military seized power—most recently in 1980—when civilian politicians crossed the line. Turkey looked to the West, formed the southeastern flank of NATO during the Cold War, and trained a highly qualified cadre of managers and engineers.

Turkey has never been a country so much as a stopping-place for migrations. The Turkish coast was Greek from the middle of the third millennium B.C.E. to the early 1920s, when the million and a half remaining Greeks were expelled. No Turk lived in Anatolia until the end of the eleventh century, when the Seljuk Turks began conquering territory from the Byzantine Empire. The Westernization of Turkey rested on more than Atatürk's personal vision; it was physically a Western phenomenon, the result of an enormous migration into Turkey from the West. By the end of the First World War, refugees or children of refugees from the collapsed European outposts of the Ottoman Empire—along with Crimean Muslims driven out of Russia—comprised more than a quarter of the 21 million people living within the frontiers of what is now modern Turkey, in the Anatolian rump of the once vast Ottoman territories. The liberation of the Balkans from Ottoman rule and Russian expulsions drove between 5 and 7 million people into Anatolia during the century before the First World War.[12] After the war, another half million Muslims were expelled from Greece in the population exchange that settled the Greek-Turkish war. Turkey in turn massacred or expelled 3 to 4 million Armenian and Greek Christians during and after the First World War. Atatürk's constituency resided on the country's coast, swollen with Turkish refugees from Western lands, rather than in the backward Anatolian plain.

But now the migration has reversed: the shrinking birth rate of the European Turkish population requires a population shift from backward Anatolia to the relatively modern western half of Turkey. The great tension in Turkish politics derives from a great uncertainty: Will modern Turkey assimilate the Anatolians, or will the eastern migrants, as so many times in the past, swamp the west? Turkey's Westernized elite is suffering from the same malaise and demographic collapse as the European nations whence it derived, and to whom it looked for an example. The return of Islamism to secular Turkey reflects not just a failure of secular parties' leadership or the military, but also a sociological failure of the Westernized population.

Atatürk's secularism defined "Turkishness" as a national identity, emulating the European nationalism of the nineteenth century. The old Ottoman identity had had nothing to do with nationality in the Western sense. It was religious and ethnic. A fifth of the population of Anatolia before World War I was Christian, mainly Armenian and Greek; virtually all were expelled or murdered. The Turks killed more than a million and a half Armenians, employing Kurdish militia to do most of the actual dirty work (that is why what is now "Turkish Kurdistan" was until 1916 "Western Armenia"). The modern Turkish state was born in a bloodbath and founded on massive population shifts. The Kurdish minority that now makes up a fifth to a quarter of the population, depending on definition, got the southeast as a consolation prize but still longs for its own language, culture, and eventual national state.

By the turn of the millennium, Kemalist secularism was a grotesque relic of 1930s European nationalism. To the extent that there was some hope of keeping Turkey in the Western camp, though, the Bush administration's nation-building blunders in Iraq and credulous admiration of "moderate Islam" in Ankara destroyed it. Iraqi leader Saddam Hussein was a monster, but for the Turks a useful monster. The 1988 Anfal campaign against the Kurds in northern Iraq killed up to 180,000 of them, and the crackdown on the Kurds after the 1991 First Gulf War killed as many as a hundred thousand. The Turks, in contrast, killed perhaps only twenty to forty thousand Kurds during the 1980s and 1990s.

Turkey in 2003 rejected America's plan to open a northern front against Saddam out of fear that the war would ruin Turkey's ability to control its restive border. The destruction of the Iraqi state, moreover, created a de facto independent Kurdish entity on Turkey's border, the last thing Ankara wanted. If America had simply installed a new strongman and left, Turkey would have been relieved. But America's commitment to "nation-building" and "democracy" in Iraq, to Ankara's way of thinking, meant that Iraq inevitably would break up; the Kurdish entity in the north would become a breakaway state; and Iran would come to dominate an Iraq with a Shi'ite majority. Despite Turkey's friendship of convenience with Iran, the two countries are natural rivals.

The Iraq war undermined the position of the Kemalist military, which had bloodied its hands for decades in counter-insurgency operations against the Kurds. Erdogan's Islamists argued that the weak glue of secular Turkish identity could no longer hold Turkey together and proposed instead to win the Kurds over through Islamic solidarity. The Kurds are quite traditional Muslims; unlike the Turkish Sunnis, the provincial Kurds of southeastern Turkey and northern Iraq often practice female circumcision. After 2003, the George W. Bush administration saw no reason to back the Turkish generals who had let it down in Iraq, and instead threw its backing to the

Islamists, on the theory that Erdogan represented a sort of "moderate Islam" that would provide an example to other prospective democratic Muslim regimes.

Some American analysts, for example the American Enterprise Institute's Michael Rubin, warn that Turkey may be headed toward an Iranian-style Islamic revolution, and point to the huge influence of the Islamic spiritual leader Fethullah Gülen in Erdogan's Turkey.[13] Gülen exiled himself to the United States in 1998 to avoid prosecution for allegedly plotting an Islamic state; from America he presides over a vast organization in Turkey and a network of religious organizations and schools throughout the Muslim world, but heavily concentrated among the Turkic states of central Asia. Sharon-Krespin writes,

> Gülen now helps set the political agenda in Turkey using his followers in the AKP as well as the movement's vast media empire, financial institutions and banks, business organizations, an international network of thousands of schools, universities, student residences (ışıkevis), and many associations and foundations. He is a financial heavyweight, controlling an unregulated and opaque budget estimated at $25 billion. It is not clear whether the Fethullahist cemaat (community) supports the AKP or is the ruling force behind AKP. Either way, however, the effect is the same.[14]

Sharon-Crespin quotes Adil Serdar Saçan, the ex-chief of the organized crimes unit at the Istanbul Directorate of Security, who claims that 80 percent of supervisory-level officers in Turkish security services are Gülen supporters. Saçan since has been charged as an "Ergenekon" coup conspirator, in what Sharon-Crespin considers a heavy-handed attempt to neutralize opposition to the Gülen takeover of the security services.

Gülen strives to project an image of moderation and modernity; he has met with religious leaders of other faiths, including Pope John Paul II.

Whether he is dissimulating, as the Ayatollah Khomeini did to Western reporters before his triumphal return to Iran with the implicit backing of the Carter administration, and as his critics claim, is impossible to prove. What is evident, though, from his published writings is that he is utterly mad, at least by Western standards. When he speaks about the virtues of science, Gülen means something entirely different from what Westerners do. This "imam from rural Anatolia," as his website describes him, inhabits a magical world of *jinns* and sorcery. Science is just a powerful form of magic of which Turks should avail themselves to enhance their power, as he writes in his 2005 book, *The Essentials of the Islamic Faith*:

> Jinn are conscious beings charged with divine obligations. Recent discoveries in biology make it clear that God created beings particular to each realm. They were created before Adam and Eve, and were responsible for cultivating and improving the world. Although God superseded them with us, he did not exempt them from religious obligations.
>
> As nothing is difficult for God almighty, he has provided human beings, angels and jinns with the strength appropriate for their functions and duties. As he uses angels to supervise the movements of celestial bodies, he allows humans to rule the Earth, dominate matter, build civilizations and produce technology.
>
> Power and strength are not limited to the physical world, nor are they proportional to bodily size.... Our eyes can travel long distances in an instant. Our imagination can transcend time and space all at once...winds can uproot trees and demolish large buildings. A young, thin plant shoot can split rocks and reach the sunlight. The power of energy, whose existence is known through its effect, is apparent to everybody. All of this shows that something's power is not proportional to its physical size; rather the immaterial world dominates the physical world,

and immaterial entities are far more powerful than material ones.[15]

Gülen goes on to warn about sorcery and the danger of spells; he allows that it is meritorious to break spells (evil witches are everywhere, casting them), although a good Muslim should not make a profession of this, for then he might be mistaken for a sorcerer himself. "Although our Prophet met with *jinn*, preached Islam to them, and took their allegiance, he never explained how to contact them or how to cast or break a spell," Gülen writes. "However, he taught how *jinn* approach us and seek to control us, and how to protect ourselves against their evil."[16] The notion that "wind" and "energy" are "immaterial" forces betrays the magical thinking of an Anatolian peasant; the miracles of technology are the secret actions of *jinn*, just as the planetary movements are the actions of angels. When Gülen talks about the union of religion and science, he means very specifically that the magical view of *jinn* in the Koran aids the believer in enlisting these "immaterial" forces to enhance the power of Islam. Science for Gülen means simply the management of *jinn*. Gülen, in short, is a shaman, a relic of pre-history fixed in the cultural amber of central Anatolia.

That is the spiritual world of the "Anatolian Tigers," who have one foot in world markets and another in the magical miasma of the ancient world. To the extent Western media have reported on Turkish Islam, though, they have ignored the beliefs of the hugely influential Gülen, and focused instead on putative reformists at the University of Ankara's theology department. A flurry of reports in 2008 proclaimed that Turkey would initiate nothing less than a Muslim reformation. In a widely quoted report, the BBC's religion correspondent Robert Pigott wrote in February 2008,

> Commentators say the very theology of Islam is being reinterpreted in order to effect a radical renewal of the religion. Its supporters say the spirit of logic and reason inherent in Islam at its

foundation 1,400 years ago are being rediscovered. Some believe it could represent the beginning of a reformation in the religion.

Turkish officials have been reticent about the revision of the Hadith until now, aware of the controversy it is likely to cause among traditionalist Muslims, but they have spoken to the BBC about the project, and their ambitious aims for it. The forensic examination of the Hadiths has taken place in Ankara University's School of Theology.[17]

Copycat reports followed in other Western outlets, which hailed the Ankara effort as the harbinger of the long-awaited Muslim reformation. Nothing of the sort was happening. Felix Koerner, a German Jesuit who taught for a while at Ankara and collaborated with the Turkish theologians, dismissed the result as an exercise with "tin-openers and baked beans." He wrote, "The [Ankara University] revisionists' vision is still restricted to one type of question: ethics. If they ask only, 'How can we make the Koran ethically acceptable today?', they are selling the Koran under price.... Hermeneutics has then a merely mechanical function: we know what there is in the Koran, ethics; and we know what must come out, modern ethics. The only question left is, how do we get it out? Hermeneutics has become a tin-opener."[18]

Nothing much about "Islamic reformation" in Turkey has been heard of late. There is nothing "moderate" about Prime Minister Erdogan's devout Islamic faith. It is rooted in the *jinn*-haunted spirit world of the Anatolian plain. His emotional eruptions against Israel, China, and the Kurdish rebels play well to his Anatolian constituency, but they also offer a glimpse into Erdogan's deep-seated beliefs. Like Rubin and Sharon-Crespin, many secular Turks are convinced that Erdogan is simply biding his time, using the organs of state security to hobble his enemies, and waiting for the right moment to launch an Iranian-style revolution. Erdogan is trying to introduce Islamic norms piecemeal—for example, by raising the country's legal drinking age to twenty-four, which some view as a step towards prohibition of alcohol.

Still, there is a convincing argument that Erdogan could not transform Turkey into an Iranian-style Islamic republic even if he wanted to. Bilgi University professor Asaf Savas Akat, a Turkish television commentator and long-time official of Turkey's largest secular political party, explained why in a February interview at his Istanbul office. "People are misreading Erdogan," Professor Akat told me. "He knows how to take risks and make decisions. He's also a good manager; he knows how to choose the right policies and the right people. And he knows how to walk away from bad decisions. He's not analytical, but instinctive; he's more like a football player who has to make decisions in a split second."

"Some worry," Azat points out, "that he will be not another Khomeini, but an Ahmadinejad. Will he go in that direction? I don't know. He has the God-given gift of winning popularity, of knowing how to give people the one-minute story they can understand. To make sense of Erdogan, you have to remember that he was a nobody. He didn't go to good schools. He came from the lower middle class, and still has the outlook of the lower middle class. But he personally broke down the Islamic movement and reshaped it. The Islamic movement was anti-free enterprise, anti-Western, and anti-globalization. He made it pro-free-enterprise, pro-Western, and pro-globalization. He is a real leader. He doesn't follow the public agenda; he sets the public agenda. Unlike some earlier prime ministers, for example [Süleyman] Demirel, he doesn't maneuver within the limits of what seems possible. He creates new possibilities."

As Professor Azat reminds me, "It's important to keep in mind that Turkey is a resource-poor country. China isn't a resource-poor country. It produces huge amounts of coal, for example. Turkey has no resources at all. A Turkish politician can't count on foreign exchange from resources. We have to earn it. It forces certain qualities upon us. We don't have the curse of resources. A Vladimir Putin can do what he wants, because he can count on the foreign exchange from oil. We buy oil from him, and we sell Russia shirts, and socks, and ashtrays. And look at what the curse of oil did to Qaddafi!"

"Let's assume," Azat hypothesizes, "the current government decides to turn Turkey into Iran. The first thing is that $30 billion of foreign exchange from tourism will disappear—directly and indirectly, that's what Turkey gets from tourism. How are we going to buy oil? If foreigners don't want to come to Turkey, how are we going to sell shirts? Iran's oil is pumped out of the ground and piped out of the country by foreigners. Ahmadinejad just has to sit there and collect the money. We have to make the yarn, and then make shirts out of the yarn, and then sell them overseas. That's a very big constraint on us. We have a big current account deficit as it is. We are a net importer of food. We rely on the confidence of financial markets."

"If Turkey goes in the Iranian direction," Professor Azat concludes, "the financial markets will shut us out. The middle class will ship their money overseas, and many of them will move overseas, like Iran's middle class did after Khomeini's revolution. The country will collapse. The fact is that Turkey depends on globalization."

This paradox may account for some of Erdogan's frustration. From a cultural and religious viewpoint, his apocalyptic warnings against the "eradication of the Turkish nation" dictate a radical rejection of secularism and the embrace of Islam. Yet he cannot take that option—at least not quickly or openly—without destabilizing the Turkish nation, perhaps beyond repair. Erdogan is subject to Spengler's Universal Law #10: *There's a world of difference between a lunatic and a lunatic who has won the lottery.*

Turkey's only resource is human capital. Unlike the diploma mills of the Arab Middle East that grind out graduates qualified to do little more than stamp each other's papers, many Turkish universities uphold international standards. Kemal Atatürk founded the country's university system during the 1930s on the German model, and Turkey sheltered prominent academic refugees during the Second World War. Turkey has hired thirteen hundred foreign academics at competitive salaries, and its graduates compete successfully with their European and American peers. Turkey's elite educational venues are a bastion of secularism. They are the most Western of the country's institutions. And they are the goose that lays golden eggs for the Turkish economy. Privately, many Western-educated Turkish professionals have told me that they will emigrate if Erdogan tries to impose Islamic law. They have degrees from foreign universities, speak excellent English and other European languages, and compete effectively with their counterparts from other countries. Many of the educated have already left Turkey. According to one study, "The last few years have witnessed an increase in the number of highly qualified professionals and university graduates moving to Europe or the CIS countries. Today, it is estimated that there are approximately 3.6 million Turkish nationals living abroad, of whom about 3.2 million are in European countries, a substantial increase from 600,000 in 1972."[19]

The universities remain a bastion of the old Turkish elite, descended from the Westernized subjects of the Ottoman Empire. Westernization, though, has been their undoing, for the Turkish elite suffers from the same infertility and anomie as Western Europe. And they lost power to the small-town Anatolians like Erdogan. "Turkey had the same elite for eight hundred years," Professor Akat adds. "The bureaucracy of the Ottoman Empire became the bureaucracy of the republic. This elite was unable to offer reform. If you don't offer reform, someone else will do it. Now there's an Anatolian elite, and the old Western elite feels nervous. There was always a sense of an internal colony in which the 'White Turks,' the European-oriented elite, ruled a much larger population of natives. It was almost like South Africa: the natives were numerous, and we were scared of them."

The Anatolian "natives" are coming up in the world, to be sure. A 2005 report by the European Stability Initiative entitled "Economic Calvinists" claimed that the emerging businesses of central Turkey, the so-called "Anatolian Tigers," would match the economic miracle of East Asia: "Central Anatolia, with its rural economy and patriarchal, Islamic culture, is seen as the heartland of this 'other' Turkey. Yet in recent years, it has witnessed an economic miracle that has turned a number of former trading towns into prosperous manufacturing centers. This new prosperity has led to a transformation of traditional values and a new cultural outlook that embraces hard work, entrepreneurship, and development. While Anatolia remains a socially conservative and religious society, it is also undergoing what some have called a 'Silent Islamic Reformation.'"[20] But no one should confuse Turkey with South Korea. Comically, the case study for the "Anatolian Tigers" in the cited report is a sugar-beet processing plant in Kayseri, whose profitability "requires protection from imports. No northern hemisphere sugar-beet producer can compete with cane sugar from the tropics, produced at half the cost." Turkey, in short, makes its consumers overpay for sugar to protect a low-tech domestic industry. That's not a formula for long-term success.

Previous Turkish governments built universities in all the substantial provincial cities, and many of the farm boys and girls of earlier generations are now college students. "Wherever you have a university, soon enough you have a couple of discos, and a half-dozen Internet cafes," Professor Akat observes.

Despite Anatolian success in low-and-medium-tech industries such as furniture, fabrics, and food processing, the deep backwardness of the Turkish hinterland still presents an intimidating hurdle. Most of rural Turkey remains stuck in the thick mud of traditional society. A fifth of Turkish marriages are consanguineous (to first or second cousins), about the same level as in Egypt, despite the fact that Turkey's GDP per capita is double that of Egypt. Traditional prejudice, it appears, prevents most Turkish women from working outside the home. Turkish women have lost rather than gained ground in economic life: only 22 percent of Turkish women sought employment in 2009, down from over 34 percent in 1988, despite better female education and a sharp drop in fertility, that is, better qualifications and greater opportunity. By contrast, 54 percent of South Korean women work. As smallholding agriculture shrinks, women who no longer can work on the family farm simply sit at home.[21] Turkey's official unemployment rate stands around 10 percent; adjusted for the underemployment of Turkish women, the unemployment rate would be above 25 percent. Almost half of Turkish workers, moreover, find employment in the so-called informal economy. Forty-three percent of Turkish employment is off the books,[22] against a developed-country average of 18 percent.[23]

Turkey is holding its own, but just barely. It has made inroads in the lower end of the manufacturing spectrum, but largely abandoned earlier hopes of competing with the Asians in high-tech industries. Turkish construction companies are prominent in Russia. Erdogan, the former businessmen, travels with Turkish executives in tow and puts them in front of foreign leaders when they bid for construction work (those businessmen who support him politically, that is).

But Turkey's economic profile in no way resembles the East Asian success stories. A country with a fast-aging population is supposed to save more; individuals do this by foregoing consumption, and countries do it by exporting and saving the proceeds. Unlike China and the East Asians with their enormous export surpluses and savings rates, Turkey still runs a current account deficit at a dangerous 6 to 7 percent of GDP, and depends on short-term money markets to finance it. The current account deficit is matched by an enormous deficit in the state social security system, whose annual shortfall is about 5 percent of GDP. The social security problem reflects outlandishly generous terms offered to retirees by previous governments. But the fact remains that Turkey's population is aging and its fertility is falling almost as fast as Iran's. And the falling participation rate of Turkish women in the labor force is a warning signal that Turkey has failed to bring the population of its Asian hinterland into the modern world at a fast enough pace.

Unlike Iran, whose Persian population will shrink into the insignificant rump of a former empire, Turkey has means at its disposal to moderate its demographic decline. Counting the Turkic republics of the former Soviet Union—Uzbekistan, Turkmenistan, Tajikistan, Kyrgyzstan, and Kazakhstan—there are 60 million ethnic cousins of the Anatolian Turks with higher fertility rates. That is not to mention neighboring Azerbaijan, or for that matter the Turkish-speaking Azeri minority in Iran, who make up 30 percent of the Iranian population. Their ancestors migrated into the Anatolian peninsula, and many of them might do so in the future. Just as Spain draws on Latin American immigrants, Turkey may counterbalance the growth of its Kurdish population with immigrants from the Turkic peoples of central Asia. A great migration of sorts already is under way from central Asia into Russia: up to 12 million migrant workers (although estimates vary widely) now work in Russia, and half of them are Turkic peoples.[24] Many of them are Turkish citizens, and Turkish construction companies are recruiting labor in central Asia. Turkey's trade with Russia and the former Soviet Union exceeds $40 billion and is its most important source of foreign exchange. Russia fought Turkey for centuries over central Asia and the Caucasus; Erdogan is cautious enough to include Russia as a partner in Turkey's Central Asia interests.[25]

There are many reasons why Turkey might succeed: its geographical and cultural position and its comparative advantages in the regional market, for example, and its talented and energetic managerial caste. But there is one big reason why Turkey might fail: the Islamists' attempt to reverse the country's cultural direction of the past eighty years may provoke an open conflict between the Western and Asian readings of Turkishness and short-circuit the possible solutions. Erdogan is straddling a chasm between Western Turkey and the Anatolian hinterland, secular and religious, Turk and Kurd. His apocalyptic tone is not a symptom of a fragile personality, but rather of a fragile nation.

⟐⟐⟐

CHAPTER 6

THE END OF TRADITIONAL MUSLIM SOCIETY

Abnegation of child-bearing is the ultimate expression of nihilism. If no generation succeeds us, everything we do is in vain, for no one will be there to remember what we did, or to benefit from our labors. Great civilizations die because they choose to, and Muslim civilization is choosing decline and death—as Europe and Japan are also doing today, and as myriad civilizations that fell before it have done. All unhappy families are unhappy in a different way, as Tolstoy points out at the beginning of *Anna Karenina*. And all declining civilizations decline in their own fashion.

The Muslim world is going straight from adolescence to senility without ever passing through maturity. In the West, we have agonized over our crisis of faith for centuries. But we are accustomed to viewing Islamic countries as a reservoir of unshaken faith and blind belief. Most of the Christian (or formerly Christian) world has succumbed to secularism. But America, the leading nation in the West and the world's most powerful

superpower, retains a strong Christian majority, as well as a small but determined minority of observant Jews. Catholics, evangelical Christians, Orthodox Jews, and other Western people of faith see a challenge but not an
enemy in the modern world. That is not how Muslim scholars see the issue.
If we are surprised by Muslim demographics, it is because we have not
listened carefully enough to what Muslims themselves have been trying to
tell us. To make sense of the great changes sweeping the Muslim world we
must look at the world through Muslim eyes.

"The much heralded Islamic 'awakening' of recent times will not be a
prelude to the rebirth of an Islamic civilization; it will be another episode
in its decline. The revolt of Islam becomes instead the final act of the end
of a civilization."[1]

The above observation is from Ali A. Allawi—former professor at
Oxford University, former Iraqi minister of Finance, Defense, and Trade,
now a visiting fellow at Princeton University—from *The Crisis of Islamic
Civilization*, which the *Economist* called one of the best books of 2009.
Allawi argues that Islam is an all-or-nothing proposition: either Muslims
will make society conform to their religion—"live an outer life which is an
expression of their innermost faith"—and "reclaim those parts of their
public spaces which have been conceded to other world views over the past
centuries," or "the dominant civilizational order" will "fatally undermine
whatever is left of Muslims' basic identity and autonomy."[2]

Allawi fears that "Islam will simply be another motif in a consumer-
driven, self-obsessed, short attention-span global culture; another 'player'
in the marketplace for ideas and religions. The retreat of Islam into the
private, individual sphere will be complete." And it is striking that the Muslims who are educated, the ones who have joined "the marketplace for ideas
and religions," prove the least likely to bear children.

Muslim women do not make a transition to the modern world; they
tumble into it unprepared. Traditional life in the Muslim world envelops
the individual with relentless totality. The maintenance of Muslim traditional society requires the effacement of female identity, effected by strong

societal sanctions, up to and including the omnipresent threat of religiously approved violence. To escape this totalizing embrace demands a clean break. It would be a mistake to believe that Islam can be repaired by insisting on women's rights. The repression of women, on the contrary, is part of the warp and woof of Islamic society, the most obvious manifestation of its inextricable roots in tribal life. Muslim men and women make their culture together, as in Spengler's Universal Law #11: *At all times and in all places, the men and women of every culture deserve each other.*

Thus it is not surprising that once free of the constraints of traditional society, educated Muslim women turn their backs on traditional family life. Fertility does not simply decline; it crashes to the ground. This result has surprised demographers. But it should not have. The disintegration of traditional society in countries that were fervently Catholic in the 1960s led to a sudden decline of fertility in places such as Ireland and Quebec. And the gap between traditional religion and modernity is incomparably greater in the Muslim world than in any country of the Christian West. The worst that one can say of European Christianity is that it fought with tribalism and lost. And the most nearly tribal pockets of European culture had the most traumatic encounter with modernity. But Muslim culture is tribalism elevated to a universal principle. Islam presents itself as a universal religion, rising above tribe and nation. But in theology as well as practice, Islam sanctifies the petty tyranny of tribal society. This emerges most clearly in the Koran's defense of wife-beating in Sura 4:34.

Wife-Beating as a Religious Practice

It is not simply that the Koran explicitly encourages a husband to beat a disobedient wife. The Koran offers a well-articulated legal theory in support of wife-beating, and this theory presumes a society radically different from that of the Judeo-Christian West. All Western political theory places the individual in a social contract with the sovereign, just as biblical religion locates the individual in a covenant with God. The "inalienable rights" of the American Founding derive from a God who grants such rights to every individual by eternal covenant: no king, petty official, or family member can impair them. Islam's legal system is closer to the pagan model of ancient Rome: the paterfamilias is a "governor" or "administrator" of the family, a miniature sovereign within his domestic realm, with the right to employ violence to control his wife. Wife-beating is practiced widely in the Muslim world as well as among Muslim immigrant communities in the West. It is embedded too profoundly in sharia law to be extracted. Nowhere to my knowledge has a Muslim religious authority of standing repudiated wife-beating as specified in Sura 4:34 of the Koran. To do so would undermine the foundations of Muslim society.

Among the acts of cruelty routinely perpetrated against women in Muslim countries, only wife-beating has the explicit sanction of the Koran. But the concept of law and society expounded in the Koranic defense of wife-beating explains why related practices are ubiquitous in the Muslim world. These include honor killings, arranged consanguineous marriages, and female genital mutilation.

Westernized Muslim scholars not only defend wife-beating but elaborate on its broader legal implications. Muslim society is organized like a set of nested Russian dolls. The clan is an extended family, the tribe an extended clan, and the state an extended tribe. The family patriarch thus enjoys powers in his realm comparable to those of the state in the broader realm. That is the deeper juridical content of the Koranic provision for wife-beating in Sura 4:34:

> [Husbands] are the protectors and maintainers of their [wives] because Allah has given the one more [strength] than the other, and because they support them from their means. Therefore the righteous women are devoutly obedient and guard in [the husband's] absence what Allah would have them guard. As to the women on whose part you fear disloyalty and ill-conduct, admonish them first, refuse to share their beds, spank them, but

if they return to obedience, seek not against them means of [annoyance]: for Allah is Most High, Great.

An essay by two Michigan State University Law students, Bassam A. Abed and Syed E. Ahmad, is cited often on Islamic websites as a credibly modern interpretation of Sura 4:34.[3] Abed and Ahmad proceed from the underlying legal principal that sanctions wife-beating:

> The translator's use of the term "protectors" in the first line of the aforementioned quote is in reference to the Arabic term of *qawaamoon* (singular: *qawaam*). Qawaamoon has been defined in various manners by different scholars and translators. Abul 'Ala Maududi, has defined *qawaamoon* as "governors" and as "managers." Qawaam "stands for a person who is responsible for the right conduct and safeguard and maintenance of the affairs of an individual or an institution or an organisation."

Abed and Ahmad explain,

> The majority of jurists hold that the language of the "Discipline Passage" itself reveals a sequential approach to the discipline authorized. For them, the conjunction *wa* ("and") used between the various types of discipline signifies its chronological order. This approach guides a husband in disciplining his wife that is disobedient, regardless of how disobedience is defined. In following the disciplinary process, he must first admonish his wife, then desert her in bed, and finally physically discipline her as a last resort to marital reconciliation.

Beating is permitted, Abed and Ahmad add, but only if it is done in a spirit of reconciliation:

The greatest controversy and misunderstanding of the "Discipline Passage" is in the final stage of the disciplinary process—"spanking" the disobedient wife. The reconciliatory purpose behind the passage's "spanking" provision helps debunk the misconceptions surrounding this disciplinary stage. A husband is not to "spank" his wife if his motivation in doing so is other that [*sic*] such reconciliation. "Spanking" out of anger, for punishment, or for retaliation is prohibited, running contrary to the reconciliatory rationale. Similarly, a husband cannot "spank" his wife to humiliate her, cause in her fear, or to compel her against her will. Islam permits "spanking" to remind the wife of her disobedience and to bring her back to obedience so as to facilitate marital reconciliation.

Defending wife-beating sounds monstrous to Western ears. The fact that it is codified into sacred law underscores how utterly different Islam is from Judaism and Christianity. Decisive in Abed and Ahmad's parsing of Surah 4:34 is the analogy between the husband and the "qawaam" or head of a political subdivision or organization. The state in traditional society devolves its authority to the cells from which it is composed, starting with the family, which is a state in miniature, whose patriarch is a "governor" or "administrator." The relationship of citizen and sovereign is reproduced at each level—state, tribe, clan, family. Ties of blood are stronger than such metaphysical abstractions as "individual rights."

This principle of authority trumping individual rights makes Muslim society incompatible with the principle of law in modern liberal democracy, in which the state alone wields the monopoly of violence. Sharia in principle cannot be adapted to the laws of modern democratic states, for it is founded on the pre-modern notion that the family is the state in miniature and that the head of a family may employ violent compulsion just as the state does.

From the vantage point of Western family law, wife-beating is a crime, even if a devout Muslim wife were to accept a beating. Family courts in the

West would intervene to separate a wife-beater from his family in the interests of the children. Sharifa Alkhateeb, the president of the North American Council for Muslim Women, found in a 1998 study that physical violence occurred in about 10 percent of Muslim marriages in the United States. "The rates of verbal and emotional abuse may be as high as 50 percent based upon international studies and preliminary research in the US," Alkhateeb's website states.[4] It is no surprise that the efforts of Alkhateeb and other Muslim advocates for women's rights get little help from Muslim clergy. "Certainly, it is wise for our religious leaders to be cautious in not passing quick, superfluous [sic] judgment when counseling couples on domestic matters," the al-Muslimah website complains. "However, when a Muslim sister approaches the masjid [mosque] for help, in fear of her life and that of her children, our leaders need to seriously consider the repercussions, and possible legal implications, of their advice. It is never enough for sisters in abusive relationships to be told to 'be patient,' 'try harder,' or 'your reward is with Allah.'"

The Koran's justification for wife-beating is not merely a vestige of the ancient world, but a vestige of the ancient *pagan* world. Jewish law predates Islamic law by two millennia, and it has always prohibited injury or even insult to the person of a spouse. Apologists for the application of Muslim religious law, or sharia, in Western courts mistakenly cite the compatibility of Western law and Jewish religious law, or *Halakha*, as a precedent for accepting sharia. When the archbishop of Canterbury in February 2008 proposed to admit sharia into British courts on a limited basis, he mentioned the compatibility of *Halakha* with British Common Law three times.[5] Observant Jewish communities in the diaspora have submitted civil matters to rabbinical courts for two thousand years without any authority other than the religious loyalty of the litigants to make their judgments binding. But Jewish law never sanctioned wife-beating. The authoritative Jewish legal text, the Babylonian Talmud, mandates unconditional respect for the wife's person: "A man should not project excessive fear in his household" (Gittin 6b); "Rabbi Helbo said: A man should always be careful in respecting his wife, for any blessing found in his home is only on account of her." Not only the violence, but the humiliation of wife-beating is explicitly forbidden. The thirteenth-century sage Rabbi Moshe ben Yaaqov of Coury writes, "It is forbidden for a person to injure either himself or another; and not only to injure but also anyone who hits another Jew— whether child or adult, man or woman—to disgrace them, such a person transgresses a prohibition."[6]

Sharia, to be sure, superficially resembles *Halakha*, for the same reason the Koran resembles the Bible: Jewish and Christian law preceded Islamic law just as Jewish and Christian scripture came before the Koran, and portions of both were adapted to Muslim requirements. But the underlying principles of the two legal systems diverge radically. That is why Jewish observance of *Halakha* never has clashed with the legal systems of modern democracy, while sharia inevitably conflicts, in the most intractable and intimate way, in matters of family law. Jewish law requires no adaptation to modern Western law, for modern Western law ultimately derives from Jewish principles, as Harvard's Eric Nelson most recently showed in his 2010 book *The Hebrew Republic*,[7] and Michael Novak explained in his 2003 volume *On Two Wings*.[8] Jewish law proceeds from God's covenant with each member of the Jewish people. The notion of an intermediate sovereign, such as Islam's "governor" of the family, is inconceivable in Jewish law, for there is only one Sovereign, the King of Kings. The powers of the earthly sovereign derive from God and are limited by God's laws, for every individual stands in a direct covenantal relationship with the King of Kings.

The American founding notion of "inalienable rights" stems from the Hebrew concept of covenant: a grant of rights implies a Grantor, and an irreversible grant implies a God who limits his own sovereignty in covenant with mankind. From the vantage point of Islam, the idea that God might limit his own powers by making an eternal covenant with human beings is unthinkable, for Allah is absolutely transcendent, and unconditionally omnipotent. From a Hebrew, and later Christian, standpoint, the powers of the earthly sovereign are limited by God's law, which irreversibly grants rights to every human being. Islam, unable to make sense of such self-limitation of the divine sovereign, has never produced a temporal political system subject to constitutional limitations.

Honor Killings, Genital Mutilation, and Cousin Marriages

By extension, the power of the petty sovereign of the family can include the killing of wayward wives and female relations. In sharp contrast to biblical law, ancient Greece and Rome gave the paterfamilias power of life and death over children. Execution for domestic crimes, often called "honor killing," is not explicitly sanctioned by the Koran, but the practice is so widespread in Islam that it is recognized in the law of most Muslim countries. The United Nations Population Fund estimates that five thousand women and girls are murdered annually in the name of family honor. Writing in the *Independent* in September 2010, Robert Fisk cited estimates from women's advocacy groups four times as high.[9] Muslim courts either do not prosecute honor killings or prosecute them more leniently than other crimes. Article 340 of Jordan's penal code reads, "He who discovers his wife or one of his female relatives committing adultery and kills, wounds, or injures one of them, is exempted from any penalty." Syria imposes only a two-year prison sentence for such killings. Pakistan forbids them but rarely punishes them. Turkish courts regularly reduce sentences for perpetrators. Honor killing, to be sure, is a tribal rather than a Muslim practice, but Muslims are responsible for 84 percent of honor killings in North America and 96 percent in Europe, according to one recent study.[10] Hindu honor killings occur, but they number in the dozens per year rather than the thousands in the Muslim world.[11]

Female genital mutilation is nearly universal in certain Muslim countries but entirely absent in others. There is almost no practice of what is euphemistically called "female circumcision" in Iraq, Iran, Pakistan, Afghanistan, and Indonesia. Nonetheless, leading Islamic authorities defend this barbaric practice on the strength of the *Hadith* (the reported sayings of Mohammed's companions).

Percentage of Women Subjected to Genital Mutilation in Selected Muslim Countries

Country	Year	Estimated prevalence of female genital mutilation in girls and women 15 – 49 years (%)
Djibouti	2006	93.1
Egypt	2008	91.1
Eritrea	2002	88.7
Mali	2006	85.2
Mauritania	2007	72.2
Niger	2006	2.2
Nigeria	2008	29.6
Senegal	2005	28.2
Sierra Leone	2006	94
Somalia	2006	97.9
Sudan	2000	90
Yemen	2003	38.2

Source: World Health Organization[12]

Writing on the website IslamOnline, Sheikh Yusuf al-Qaradawi—the president of the International Association of Muslim Scholars—explains,

> The most moderate opinion and the most likely one to be correct is in favor of practicing circumcision in the moderate Islamic way indicated in some of the Prophet's hadiths—even though such hadiths are not confirmed to be authentic. It is reported that the Prophet (peace and blessings be upon him) said to a midwife: "Reduce the size of the clitoris but do not exceed the limit, for that is better for her health and is preferred

by husbands." The hadith indicates that circumcision is better for a woman's health and it enhances her conjugal relation with her husband. It's noteworthy that the Prophet's saying "do not exceed the limit" means do not totally remove the clitoris.[13]

Sheikh al-Qaradawi preached to crowds of more than a million in Cairo in March 2011 during the Egyptian uprising.

Finally there is the matter of arranged cousin marriages. Between a half and three-fifths of all Muslims, depending on the country, marry a first or second cousin. So-called consanguineous marriages pose a high risk of birth defects and naturally worry medical authorities. In the UK, the BBC reports, British Pakistanis—55 percent of whom have consanguineous marriages—account for 3.4 percent of all births, but for 30 percent of all birth defects.[14]

From the table below we observe that the majority of marriages are consanguineous in Muslim countries with low rates of literacy and economic development—Pakistan, Egypt, and the Sudan. But even Muslims with a high literacy rate have extremely high rates of cousin marriages. Israeli Arabs are 95 percent literate—the highest rate for Arabs anywhere in the Middle East—but 34 percent marry cousins. Jordan's literacy rate is 90 percent, but 40 percent of Jordanians still marry cousins.

Consanguineous (First or Second Cousin) Marriages as a Percentage of All Marriages, by Country

Country	Consanguineous marriage percentage
Afghanistan	55.4
Algeria	22.1
Egypt	29
India (Muslims)	33
Iran (Shi'a Persians)	38.6
Iraq	33
Israeli Arabs	34.2

Continued on next page

**Consanguineous (First or Second Cousin) Marriages
as a Percentage of All Marriages—*Continued***

Country	Consanguineous marriage percentage
Jordan	39.7
Kuwait	38.4
Lebanon	35.5
Morocco	19.9
Oman	36
Pakistan	61.2
Palestinian Territories	29.2
Qatar	45.5
Saudi Arabia (Riyadh)	45
Sudan	52
Syria	31.65
Tunisia	26.9
Turkey	21.1
United Arab Emirates	32
Yemen	33.9

Source: www.consang.net

Islamic religious texts do not explicitly encourage consanguineous marriage. "It seems the well-known Iranian proverb 'the first cousin's marriage
contract has been recorded in heaven' is merely a cultural and local custom
rather than a religious belief," concludes a study by two Iranian geneticists.[15]
What the universal practice of cousin marriage in the Muslim world makes
clear, though, is the primacy of blood ties over the mere abstraction of
Islamic universality. We observe the same power hierarchy in the practice
of consanguineous marriage as in the matter of wife-beating: the Koran
establishes the family as a miniature state with the paterfamilias as miniature caliph. The family, in turn, is nested within the clan, whence it derives

power and protection. And the clan within the tribe. And the tribe within the state. Muslims marry within their extended family as an expression of loyalty to blood relationships.

The Crisis of Criticism

Modernity came to revealed religion through biblical criticism. Judaism and Christianity have survived centuries of scholarly assault on biblical authority. But Koranic criticism is theology's most dangerous minefield. Academics who challenge the authority of the Koran publish at their own peril. The German philologist whose assertion that the seventy-two "virgins" promised to Jihadi martyrs were in fact raisins writes under the pseudonym "Christoph Luxenburg." And a Muslim scholar who published a 2008 paper suggesting that the Prophet Mohammed may not have really existed was whisked from his office at the University of Münster by German police to an undisclosed location, "on security grounds."[16] His offense was to assert that Mohammed had been invented in order to transmogrify Moses and Jesus into an Arab prophet.

Judaism and Christianity have both stood the test of biblical criticism. No archaeologist will prove that Moses did not receive the Torah from YHWH on Mount Sinai, or that Jesus Christ did not rise from the grave three days after the Crucifixion. To the extent that it reflects on the veracity of the Bible, archaeology tends to confirm scriptural accounts, most recently in unearthing evidence of the Davidic kingdom. But whether or not God revealed Himself as recounted in the Hebrew and Greek Bibles is a question not for forensics, but for faith. Devout Christians and Jews may acknowledge the authority of Scripture without repudiating the parallel claims of science, for the explicitly supernatural claims of the Bible lie hidden in the mists of time, or by metaphysical claims beyond proof or disproof. The Christian is not expected to prove that Jesus of Nazareth was resurrected from the dead; on the contrary, Christian salvation depends on faith in the Resurrection. The Gospels themselves are human reports of revelation; the

Christian revelation is Jesus Christ himself. To Orthodox Jews, the Torah is a more-than-human report ("from the mouth of God, by the hand of Moses"), but the written Torah is embedded within the Oral Torah also given to Moses at Mount Sinai.

In Islam, God's self-revelation took the form not of Mount Sinai, nor the Incarnation, but rather a book. *The Encyclopaedia of Islam* (1981) observes, "The closest analogue in Christian belief to the role of the Koran in Muslim belief is not the Bible, but Christ."[17] The Koran alone is the revelatory event in Islam. It is pointless to quarrel with Christians about the cadaver of Jesus Christ; one believes in the Resurrection, or not. But the Koran is available for study and subject to scrutiny. To be a Muslim is to accept that the Koran was dictated by the Archangel Gabriel to the Prophet Mohammad during the seventh century. To question any statement of the Koran—for example its defense of wife-beating—amounts to apostasy. Centuries of biblical criticism have left undamaged the faith of orthodox Christians and Jews; the first tentative steps towards historical criticism of the Koran have left Islam in rage and doubt.

Samir Khalid Samir, S.J., an Arab Christian who advises Pope Benedict XVI on Islamic matters, argues that the divinity of the Koran freezes Islam in time. Unlike the Magisterium of the Catholic Church, or the Oral Torah of observant Judaism, there is no human agency with the authority to interpret the text:

> The notion of the promise or covenant with Abraham, like that of the "history of salvation," which is common to Judaism and Christianity, is practically absent in Islam. For Muslims, the Qur'an can be compared to Christ: Christ is the Word of God made flesh, while the Qur'an—please forgive my play on words—is the word "made paper." If the Qur'an was indeed "sent down" by Allah, there is no possibility of a critical or historical interpretation, not even for those aspects that are evidently related to the customs of a particular historical period

and culture. In the history of Islam, at a certain point, it was decided that it was no longer possible to interpret the text.... The weight of the tradition and, above all, the fear of questioning the acquired security of the text have created a taboo: the Qur'an cannot be interpreted, nor can it be critically rethought.[18]

The scholarly assault on the Koran has barely begun. Western scholars outgun the resources of religious scholarship in Muslim countries as overwhelmingly as Western armies outgun the local militaries. Whether or not the Koranic critics can offer proof that the Koran is not a seventh-century document (for example), but rather was redacted by later writers, is beside the point: Muslims who wish to defend the divine authority of the Koran have no defense but dogma. Unlike Jews or Christians, a Muslim today cannot acknowledge the parallel authority of scholarly as well as traditional investigation.

It has long been known that variant copies of the Koran exist, including some found in 1972 in a paper grave at Sa'na in Yemen, the subject of a cover story in the January 1999 *Atlantic*. Before the Yemeni authorities shut the door to Western scholars, two German academics, Gerd R. Puin and H. C. Graf von Bothmer, made thirty-five thousand microfilm copies, which remain at the University of Saarland. Many scholars believe that the German archive, which includes photocopies of manuscripts as old as 700 C.E., will provide more evidence of variation in the Koran.

In 2005, Professor Puin published a collection of articles under the title "Die Dunklen Anfange. Neue Forschungen zur Entstehung und fruhen Geschichte des Islam" (published in English as "The Hidden Origins of Islam: New Research into Its Early History").[19] It drew on the work of "Christoph Luxenburg," who sought to prove that incomprehensible passages in the Koran were written in Syriac-Aramaic rather than Arabic. The Koran, according to the research of Puin and his associates, copied a great deal of extant Christian material. Apart from the little group at the University of Saarland and a handful of others, though, the Western Academy is reluctant to go near the issue. In the United States, where Arab and Islamic Studies rely on funding from the Gulf States, an interest in Koranic criticism is a failsafe way to commit career suicide.

The Islamic world is therefore forced to adopt an openly irrational stance, employing its power to intimidate scholars and frustrate the search for truth. It is impossible for Muslims to propose a dialogue with Western religions, as thirty-eight Islamic scholars did in an October 13, 2008, letter to Benedict XVI and other Christian leaders, and exclude the subject of text criticism from the discussion. Precisely for this reason, Catholic Church leaders see little basis for a dialogue with Islam. Jean-Louis Cardinal Tauran, who directs the Pontifical Council for Interreligious Dialogue, told the French daily *La Croix*, "Muslims do not accept discussion about the Koran, because they say it was written under the dictates of God. With such an absolutist interpretation, it's difficult to discuss the contents of the faith." That's the trouble with Islam and criticism in general—including even the implicit challenge that modernity itself poses. The Muslim understanding of revelation precludes textual or historical criticism, so that Islam must eschew all scholarly challenges. And then when it succumbs, it collapses altogether. A great gulf is fixed between Muslim self-understanding and modernity.

CHAPTER 7

THE ISLAMIST RESPONSE

Islamist jihad responds to fear of civilizational failure. In a 2006 volume of essays on modern Islamic thought, two Islamist academics, Suha Taji-Farouki and Basheer M. Nafi, observe, "Rather than being a development within cultural traditions that is internally generated, twentieth-century Islamic thought is constitutively responsive; it is substantially a reaction to extrinsic challenges."[1] Those challenges include the drastic transformation of Muslim life in modern times.

"In the Middle East of 1900 less than 10 percent of the inhabitants were city dwellers. By 1980, 47 percent were urban. In 1800, Cairo had a population of 250,000, rising to 600,000 by the beginning of the twentieth century. The unprecedented influx of immigrants from rural areas brought the population of Cairo to almost eight million by 1980. Massive urbanization altered patterns of living, of housing and architecture, of the human relation with space and land, of marketing, employment and consumption, and of the very structure of family and social hierarchy," the authors report.[2] Plus, "A Muslim sense of vulnerability and outrage is further exacerbated by the seemingly unstoppable encroachment of American popular culture and modes of consumerism, and the transparent hypocrisy of the American rhetoric of universal rights and liberties. It is also stoked by Western ambivalence towards economic disparities in the world."[3]

The Islamists are not throwbacks to the past, but products of Western education. Sayyid Qutb (1906–1966), the founder of the modern Islamist movement, formulated his theory while earning a master's degree in education at the Colorado State College of Education. In 1949, he wrote, "Islamic society today is not Islamic in any sense of the word.... In our modern society we do not judge by what Allah has revealed; the basis of our economic life is usury; our laws permit rather than punish oppression.... We permit the extravagance and the luxury that Islam prohibits; we allow the starvation and the destitution of which the Messenger once said: 'Whenever people anywhere allow a man to go hungry, they are outside the protection of Allah, the Blessed and the Exalted.'"[4]

In considering Taji-Farouki and Nafi's scholarly views on Islamism, it is worth keeping in mind that at least one of these professors may have a more than academic interest in jihad. Professor Nafi, who teaches history and Islamic studies at Birkbeck College, University of London, was indicted in Florida for "conspiracy to murder, maim or injure persons outside the United States." He was deported from the United States for visa violations in 1996 and was one of eight men, including three professors, indicted by a U.S. District Court in Florida in 2003 for providing material aid to the terrorist organization Islamic Jihad. Nafi was indicted along with Ramadan Abdullah Shallah, an adjunct professor of Middle East Studies at the University of South Florida.

Basheer M. Nafi is not the only Muslim intellectual to support violence in the cause of Islamic theocracy. Five years ago, *Time* magazine hailed the Geneva-based Professor Tariq Ramadan as one of the world's "spiritual innovators," for "creating a new kind of European Islam that bridges his

Islamic values and Western culture." *Time* enthused, "Ramadan's chosen task is to invent an independent European Islam.... With 15 million Muslims on the continent, Ramadan believes it's time to abandon the dichotomy in Muslim thought that has defined Islam in opposition to the West."[5] Ramadan's reputation grew so great that Notre Dame University offered him its Henry R. Luce professorship of "Religion, Conflict and Peacebuilding" in 2004. Before Ramadan could assume his position, however, the U.S. Department of Homeland Security revoked his work visa on the grounds of alleged terrorist association. Precise reasons were not given, but it turns out that the Department of Homeland Security was not alone in its evaluation of the Swiss Islamist. France had refused entry to Ramadan in 1996 because of alleged links to an Algerian terrorist then engaged in bombing attacks. In January 2010 the Obama administration reversed earlier American policy and announced that it would permit Ramadan to visit the United States.

Ramadan's most eloquent critic in American letters is the liberal writer Paul Berman. In his 2010 book *The Flight of the Intellectuals*,[6] Berman excoriates his fellow liberals for allowing Ramadan to get away with blatant deception. "Tariq Ramadan," Berman writes, " is nothing if not a son, a brother, a grandson and even a great-grandson—family relations that appear to shape everything he writes and does. The most famous member of his family was his grandfather. This was Hassan al-Banna, who is a giant of modern history."[7] In 1928 al-Banna founded the Muslim Brotherhood, the first organization of modern Islamism. The Egyptian government had him murdered in 1949, and the Brotherhood remains banned in Egypt. Its Palestine branch operates under the name of Hamas, which the United States and most Western governments list as a terrorist organization.

Ramadan does not explicitly endorse terrorism, but he slyly endorses terrorists. In his account, grandfather Hassan al-Banna was a man of "light-giving faith, a deep spirituality, personal discipline, gentle and soft with his fellow human beings.... The secret of Hasan Al-Banna was the quality of his faith and the intensity of his relationship with God. Anyone who had ever been in contact with him perceived and experienced this."[8] Paul Berman presents exhaustive evidence that Ramadan has covered up al-Banna's close connection to the Nazi state. University of Maryland historian Jeffrey Herf obtained access to thousands of pages of transcripts of wartime broadcasts from Berlin by Islamists. These reveal how much modern Islamism owes to Nazi ideology—in particular, its extreme hatred of Jews. But in Ramadan's account, the Nazi-influenced founder of a terrorist organization becomes a gentle and pious man.

A thin membrane separates the educated arguments of academic Islamists from the violent acts of terrorist organizations. This is an index of despair. Unlike their Western apologists, the Islamists know how fragile Muslim society has become and are willing to draw extreme conclusions—and act on them.

Can Islam Take the West Down with It?

Philip Jenkins, an authority on Christianity in the Global South, is one of a very few Western scholars to consider the strategic implications of declining Muslim demographics. In 2007, Jenkins wrote in *The New Republic*, "Iran is experiencing what you might call the reverse-*Children of Men* effect. Just like in the post-apocalyptic film, Iran is, increasingly, a society devoid of children. But the real-life outcome of this birth dearth is far less grim than the police state depicted onscreen. In fact, there's a good chance that declining fertility rates will usher in a new era of stability—an Iran that is bourgeois, secular, less like *Children of Men*'s bombed-out Britain and more like…Denmark."[9]

That might be true—sixty or seventy years hence. In the meantime, Iran's looming demographic disaster makes the country more dangerous. People stop having children when they lose faith in their future. Loss of faith may express itself in passive despondency—for example, in Iran's high rate of opium addiction, or in the casual decision of upwardly mobile Iranian women to prostitute themselves to pay university tuition. But it also may express itself in a desperation to achieve victory before the window of opportunity closes. That sense of urgency inspires the fanaticism of Iran's 125,000 Revolutionary Guards, which brutally suppressed Iran's democracy protests after the summer 2009 presidential elections. The Guards have been shipping men overseas to fight alongside terrorists from Lebanon to Afghanistan. According to a Council on Foreign Relations background paper,

> Military analysts say the guard began deploying fighters (NPR) abroad during the Iran-Iraq war of 1980 to 1988.... The Quds Force, a paramilitary arm of the Revolutionary Guards with less than a thousand people, emerged as the de facto external-affairs branch during the expansion. Its mandate was to conduct foreign-policy missions—beginning with Iraq's Kurdish region—and forge relationships with Shiite and Kurdish groups. A Quds unit was deployed to Lebanon in 1982, where it helped in the genesis of Hezbollah.... More recently, some experts say, the Quds Force has shipped weapons to the Lebanon-based Hezbollah, Gaza-based Hamas, and Palestinian Islamic Jihad, and is also supplying munitions to the Taliban in Afghanistan and Shiite militias in Iraq.[10]

Iran's main strategic objectives are the Iraqi, the Azerbaijani, and eventually the Saudi oilfields. But its preferred and most successful methods are infiltration and subversion through the Shi'ite majorities who inhabit oil-rich regions on its borders. A collateral objective is to keep pressure on Israel through Hezbollah in Lebanon, which has a stockpile of fifty thousand missiles, according to Israeli sources, including many that can reach any point in Israel and can be targeted with precision.

Ahmadinejad's generation of Iranians, who came to adulthood in the Islamic Revolution of 1979 and bled for their cause through the terrible Iran-Iraq War of the 1980s, is determined to secure Iran's greatness for the ages. And to achieve its long-term ambitions, Iran cannot do without nuclear capability. In the event that the United States and its allies (if it still has any) were to attack Iran to forestall a regional oil grab, nuclear weapons would be of great use to Iran, either as a way of attacking enemy staging areas or as a terrorist device. As long as Iran lacks nuclear weapons, the Western powers and Israel have the option to put a stop to its plans. Without nuclear capability, Iran must live under the constant threat of an attack against which it cannot defend.

Iran has failed as a society in the face of the modern world. It embodies a fatal combination of modern demographics—that is, a rapidly aging population—with a failure to assimilate modern productivity. Without military victory (in other words, without nuclear weapons), the forces that rallied to the banner of the Islamic Revolution can look forward only to a relentless pulverization of the traditional society whence they came. Such is the stuff of military strategy inspired by religious mysticism. When there is no retreat, nothing to which to return, Destiny beckons from the enemy's lines, and the army leaves its trenches and flies forward into the cannons.

Turkey's premonition of demographic doom, meanwhile, has inspired the Turks to make common cause with the Iranians. "Turkey is now more aligned to Iran than to the democracies of Europe. Whereas Iran's Islamic revolution shocked the world with its suddenness in 1979, Turkey's Islamic revolution has been so slow and deliberate as to pass almost unnoticed. Nevertheless, the Islamic Republic of Turkey is a reality—and a danger," writes American Enterprise Institute scholar Michael Rubin.[11]

In January 2009, Prime Minister Erdogan stormed out of a panel at the Davos World Economic Forum with Israel's courtly President Shimon Peres, after denouncing Israel for "murder" in the Gaza Strip. The Turkish leader declared that he never would return to Davos. When Kurdish rebels killed eleven Turkish soldiers in a June 2010 border raid, Erdogan warned that the Kurdish independence fighters "would drown in their own blood." Turkey's Islamist government, moreover, evinces a paranoid antipathy to the United States as well as Israel. Members of Erdogan's inner circle financed a 2006 action thriller, *Valley of the Wolves,* which portrayed American intervention in Iraq as a scheme by Jewish Americans to sell organs harvested from the dead bodies of Iraqis. The prime minister's wife urged all Turks to see the film.

In May 2010, a foundation associated with Erdogan's AKP sponsored a flotilla of boats intended to break the Israeli-Egyptian border controls over Gaza, imposed to prevent Iran from shipping weapons to Hamas. One boat, the *Mavi Marmara,* refused to unload its cargo at an Israeli port for transshipment to Gaza. When lightly armed Israeli commandos intercepted the *Mavi Marmara,* Hamas supporters on board tried to kill them. The Israelis fought back and killed a dozen axe-and-chain-wielding militants. Turkish-Israeli relations collapsed, and Erdogan declared that the Israelis were worse than gangsters: "Even despots, gangsters and pirates have specific sensitiveness, (and) follow some specific morals."[12]

None of these incidents impaired Erdogan's popularity among Turkish voters. On the contrary, the prime minister's public rages play to the disquiet among his constituents. Despite an economic performance that seems impressive to outsiders, there is an ugly undertone to the Turkish national mood, and Erdogan's spontaneous displays of paranoia resonate with it.

Hakan, we'll call him, prospers in a fast-track career in Istanbul, buoyed by an M.B.A. from a good English-language university. At a restaurant near the city's Taksim Square hub, he speaks enthusiastically about the trade coups of Turkish companies. But his voice falls as he changes the subject to the national mood. "After the *Mavi Marmara* incident things happened that I wouldn't have thought possible. Colleagues of mine were saying, 'Hitler was right,' and 'Hitler left us unfinished business with the Jews,' and things like that. And these weren't ignorant people off the street. They were professionals, with university degrees. Of course the loss of life was deplorable, but to talk about Hitler like that—what came over them?" Hakan adds in a whisper, "My wife is a Christian. When Turks get in that kind of mood they don't make fine distinctions." Almost every Turkish professional I know with a foreign spouse is considering emigration. So are most of the remaining members of Turkey's Jewish community—once a prominent part of Turkish society, now a fearful, marginalized minority.

In the long term, the great demographic freeze will leave the United States the only man standing among the industrial democracies. But population collapse in the Muslim world is more likely to aggravate security risks during the next generation than to attenuate them. A nuclear-armed Iran, and a follow-the-leader game of nuclear acquisition by its neighbors, drastically increases the likelihood of nuclear war as well as nuclear terrorism. America will prevail, provided the Muslim world does not take us down with it first.

PART TWO

THEOPOLITICS

CHAPTER 8

CIVILIZATIONAL FAILURE AND SUICIDE

Spengler's Universal Law #12: *Nothing is more dangerous than a civilization that has only just discovered it is dying.*

The Western world watched horrified as suicide attacks multiplied from a few dozen a year during the 1990s to a peak of more than 350 during 2007. Muslim radicals perpetuated virtually all of these. But there is nothing uniquely Muslim about terrorism in general, or suicide attacks in particular. Men hold their lives cheap when they cease to believe that their culture will endure—because the persistence of our culture makes it possible for our lives to have meaning beyond the brief span of our physical existence.

Consider this example from twentieth-century history:

A liberal publicist confirmed, "murders flooded the periphery and the center with blood." As they occurred daily, often many times a day, assassinations quickly ceased to provide sensation, and newspapers began to ignore them. Soon, acts of terror became more numerous than traffic accidents. From April 27 to July 9 [of one year], terrorists killed 177 people in 317 attempts. By [the following year], they claimed a rough average of 18 casualties each day, and then the editors no longer bothered to provide detailed reports on every occasion.... By the most conservative approximation, the terrorist exploits yielded over 16,800 killed and wounded [in a single five-year period].... All in all, in the last 17 years...about 17,000 individuals fell victim to the 23,000 terrorist attacks.

Sound like the past few years in Iraq? In fact, the above report is quoted from Anna Geifman's 2010 book *Death Orders*,[1] examining terrorism in the Russian Empire between 1900 and 1917. Scores of recent books portray a violence-prone Islamic world in contradistinction to the Christian West. But terrorism on the grand scale, including suicide bombing, began in the Christian world. It arose in revolutionary Russia under conditions comparable to those of the Muslim world today. In sheer scale, Russian terrorism of a century ago can be compared with the modern terror plague. Suicide bombers—almost all of them Muslims—killed more than 21,350 people and injured about 50,000 between 1983 and 2008, just slightly higher than the Russian toll.[2] Today's suicidal terrorism is not a Muslim problem as such, but a manifestation in the Muslim world of a general principle: there is no such thing as rational self-interest for people who believe that they have nothing to lose.

Geifman reports that Russia's "urban populace swelled from around 9 million people in the mid-19th century to about 25 million in 1913, with inhabitants of most major Russian cities increasing four- or five-fold," leading to a "breakdown of social values." All of Europe experienced political upheaval associated with urbanization. "Less prepared for the advent of modernization, the Russians were vulnerable to an even greater degree, increasingly prone to take an opportunity to release the bottled-up rage, especially when external circumstances stimulated the expression of distress." Self-destructive despair accompanied the abrupt shift from traditional to modern society, marked by an increase in the number of attempted and actual suicides from 557 in 1906 to 3,795 in 1910.

"Regardless of the espoused creed, be it secular, as among the Russian extremists, or religious, such as radical Islam, the terrorist cult practices a modern type of paganism," Geifman argues. She is referring to the apocalyptic messianism encountered in Islamism and Communism as well as at the heretical margins of Russian Orthodoxy. "The fatal attraction of Communism," she explains, "was that it was messianic. Its atheism notwithstanding, it contained an enormous potential of an avowedly scientific prediction championed as faith and venerated." Soon after its formation in 1902, [the Social Revolutionary Combat Organization] turned into a sect that cultivated reverence for the "holy terror" as a sacred thing. "For Mariia Benevskaia, an ardent Christian Orthodox who never parted with the Gospels, preparations for fatal acts were religious rituals. Kaliaev, nicknamed 'the poet,' composed prayers in verse exalting the glory of the Almighty. Sazonov believed that the terrorists continued the work of Jesus."

For a century the Russian Empire had strained its resources by pushing eastwards towards the Pacific, paying for its Siberian ambitions with tax revenues milked from its productive Western provinces—Poland, the Ukraine, the Baltic states. Expansion to the East opened up vast regions to the plough and the axe, but at a net cost to the Russian state. It depended on the enterprise and skills of its Western colonies, which rankled under Russian control. After Japan destroyed the Russian fleet and routed the Russian army in 1905, Moscow was compelled to send a quarter of a million troops—a force larger than had fought the Japanese—to crush rebellion in Poland.

Russia's humiliation at the hands of a new Asian power had exposed the folly of its imperial policy and the hopelessness of its predicament. Russia was stymied in the East and challenged in the West by Germany and Austria, and in continuous danger of losing its western colonies, the empire's only pocket of economic strength. Traditional Russia was disappearing into a morass that had no outlet. The revolutionary terrorists of pre-war Russia were mad and bad, but not stupid. Russia stood on the cusp of a dizzying decline, and the Russo-Japanese War had revealed the fecklessness of its leaders. Suicide may seem just as reasonable to individuals trapped in a failing civilization as it does to a terminal cancer patient.

Suicidal Resistance in War

Spengler's Universal Law #13: *Across epochs and cultures, blood has flown in inverse proportion to the hope of victory.* The so-called instinct for self-preservation is not an instinct at all, but an attitude that depends on the conviction that the self is worth preserving in the first place.

Primitive peoples typically fought to the death. Suicidal resistance is common where peoples believe that they are fighting for their existence. And Stone Age peoples forced out of their refuges into the white glare of modernity tend to behave as if they have nothing to lose.

We have records of a small number of existential wars—that is, wars in which the wealth and blood of civilizations are committed without reservation. With few exceptions, most of the actual killing occurred long after rational calculation would call for the surrender of the losing side. We observe this in most of the great wars of which we have adequate records. Germany knew that it had lost the First World War by 1918, but launched the Ludendorff Offensive as a final gamble. It cost over 300,000 German casualties, compared to 240,000 on the Marne in 1914; 170,000 in Champagne in 1915; and 170,000 on the Somme in 1916. During the Second World War most of the German army's losses occurred after Stalingrad on the Eastern Front and in the Battle of the Bulge in the West. Japanese losses, meanwhile, escalated in the desperate resistance on Pacific islands during the last year of the war, and would have reached even more horrific proportions had the United States not ended the Second World War with atomic weapons.

The same observation applies to the deadliest of conflicts in European history. The first half of the Thirty Years' War saw armies of then-unprecedented size. The Imperial generalissimo Count Albrecht von Wallenstein raised fifty thousand men to fight the Danish invasion in 1625, and a hundred thousand troops to repel the Swedes under King Gustavus Adolphus in 1630. During the second stage of the war, though, the French sent an army of two hundred thousand against the Austrian Empire, and the Spanish responded with a force of comparable size. The two contenders for the dominant position on the European continent literally depopulated large parts of their territory in the war's final, terrible phase. Most of the military as well as civilian deaths during the Thirty Years' War occurred during its last eleven years, when the original source of contention along with the original combatants had long been buried. One might add that Athens knew it was losing to Sparta—and was depleted of military-age men and short of money—when it mounted its maximum effort in the disastrous Sicilian campaign of 415 B.C.E., sixteen years into the Peloponnesian War.

Irrational Resistance in the American Civil War

It would be self-serving to dismiss the terrible events in Russia at the turn of the last century as the actions of mystical and melancholy Slavs. Americans are capable of the same kind of suicidal behavior. The highest casualty rates for military-age men in any war in modern history were registered for Southerners during America's Civil War, which claimed the lives of nearly 30 percent of adult males. (A qualified exception is the loss of Serbian life during the First World War, estimated at close to 50 percent. Otherwise no combatant population fought to the death with the utter abandon of the American Confederacy.) But the curious fact about Confederate casualties is that they rose in inverse proportion to the probability of Confederate victory.

Mut der Verzweiflung, as the Germans call it, courage borne of desperation, arises not from the delusion that victory is possible but rather from the conviction that death is preferable to surrender. Wars of this sort end long after one side has been defeated—only when enough of the diehards have been killed. The Southern cause was effectively lost after Major General Ulysses S. Grant took Vicksburg, splitting the Confederacy in two down the Mississippi River axis, and General George G. Meade repelled General Robert E. Lee at Gettysburg in July 1863 in the two decisive battles of the war, fought within the same week. The Confederacy faced inevitable strangulation by the vastly superior forces of the North. Nonetheless, the South fought on for another eighteen months. Between Gettysburg and Vicksburg, one hundred thousand men had died, bringing the total number of deaths in major battles to more than a quarter of a million. But another two hundred thousand soldiers would die before Lee surrendered to Grant at Appomattox in April 1865.

Civil War Cumulative Casualties

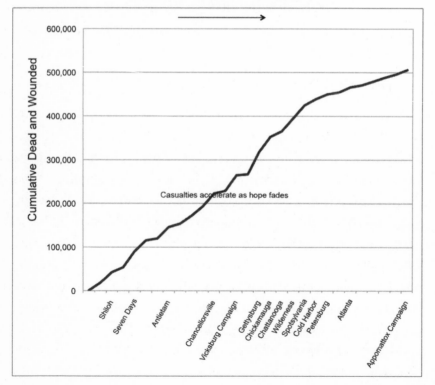

The chart above shows a jump in the rate at which casualties accumulated after Vicksburg and Gettysburg—through Spotsylvania, the Wilderness, and Cold Harbor. Confederate resistance became all the more determined once the tide had turned against the South. General William Tecumseh Sherman said, "There is a class of people [in the South], men, women and children, who must be killed or banished before you can hope for peace and order.... A people who will persevere in war beyond a certain limit ought to know the consequences. Many people, with less pertinacity than the South, have been wiped out of national existence." The South proved him right; it would rather die than give up the privileges (or the prospect) of slave-holding. The war did not end until the South no longer had enough men left to put into the line.

Preempting a Desperate Opponent

The most dangerous opponent is one who knows that he has nothing to lose and will fight to the death as a matter of pride. Is there any way to prevent such suicidal aggression? Humiliate your enemy, and he will have no pride to defend. A nation convinced that it is already too late to make a last stand is a much less dangerous nation than one that believes it has one final chance to redeem itself—or at least to go down in glory.

World War I is a case in point: by 1914, with a nearly perfect equilibrium of forces between the Allies and the Central Powers, a devastating war of attrition was the only probable outcome. Less than a decade earlier, though, it would have been easy to preempt the conflict. In fact, war between France and Germany nearly broke out in 1905 when Germany demanded an "open door" policy to Morocco in opposition to the colonial domination of France. Germany in turn demanded an international diplomatic conference to put France in its place, but in June 2005, France responded defiantly and cancelled all military leaves, an action just short of military mobilization—which would have been a *casus belli*. Germany would have been technically justified in initiating hostilities at that point. The German Chief of Staff,

Count Alfred von Schlieffen (author of the famous "Schlieffen Plan" that guided German strategy in the opening days of the subsequent war), urged Kaiser Wilhelm II to declare war on France. A Franco-German war in 1905 would have left Russia and Britain on the sidelines. Russia had just suffered a crushing defeat by Japan and was in the middle of a revolution. Britain had not yet signed a military alliance with France. The result probably would have been a repeat of the Franco-Prussian War, which Germany won in six weeks. If France had been decisively humiliated in 1905, Germany would have emerged as the dominant European power, and no world war would have ensued.

Preemption, in short, would have produced a far more merciful outcome than the dreary re-creation of the balance of power that each successive generation of European diplomats undertook. Kaiser Wilhelm II of Germany was no democrat, but neither was he a Hitler. It is hard to imagine that a Europe under imperial German hegemony would have been worse than a Europe devastated by Nazism.

A Case Study in Preemption: Russia and the Cold War

Uniquely among the World Wars of the past century, the Cold War was won by preemption—through the threat of massive military force. Thus little actual use of force was required outside a few proxy wars on the periphery of the major theaters. Nations are most dangerous at the cusp of weakness, when they still may have something to gain by fighting but see the present opportunity as their last. Once they have nothing to gain, they adjust to their fate with grumpy equanimity. Perhaps the closest analogue to Iran's position today is the predicament of the Soviet Union in the late 1970s and early 1980s. Starting with the invasion of Afghanistan in 1979, Moscow displayed an alarming degree of aggression, including overt and covert threats towards Western Europe. Russia sponsored Communist insurgencies in Nicaragua, Angola, and Mozambique.

According to Herbert Meyer, Vice-Chairman of the National Intelligence Council under President Reagan and an advisor to Reagan's CIA chief William J. Casey, "They were trying to neutralize Europe: that was the number one objective. They thought that if they could split NATO, they would win."[3] Sclerotic Russia could not compete with America economically, but if Russia were able to harness the European economic engine, it had a chance to win the Cold War. "The CIA's official position in 1981 was that the Soviet economy was growing at an annual rate of 3%," Meyer adds. "I wrote a series of reports arguing that the productivity gap between the U.S. and the Soviet Union was beginning to widen very rapidly. We were introducing the personal computer. We were learning words like software. The Soviets were increasing the production of shoes and steel. To an economist, the numbers looked the same, but the numbers weren't picking up the productivity gap. The military implications would be absolutely staggering."

Not only the CIA's Russian team (then led by Robert Gates, at this writing Secretary of Defense) but also America's most prestigious economists insisted that Russia's economy was a success. Ronald Reagan's belief that the Soviets were vulnerable seemed hallucinatory to respectable academic opinion. Today, the same respectable academic opinion insists that the Soviet economy would have collapsed on its own, with or without Reagan, Margaret Thatcher, or John Paul II. That, for example, is what we hear from the "dean of Cold War historians," Professor John Lewis Gaddis of Yale. He writes, "It was no source of strength for the USSR to be sustaining a defense burden that may well have been three times that of the United States by the end of the 1970s, when its gross domestic product was only about one-sixth the size of its American counterpart.... The USSR under [Leonid] Brezhnev's faltering rule had become incapable of performing the most fundamental task of any effective strategy: the efficient use of available means to accomplish chosen ends."[4]

What Gaddis and other liberal historians fail to grasp is that Russia's weakness made it aggressive. Meyer points out that the Soviets said in public that "history was on their side—except we knew at CIA that they didn't believe that. They're not stupid. They knew that the window of opportunity was beginning to close. If they couldn't beat us now, they couldn't beat us at all. There was a nuclear superpower who knew that their opportunity to win the Cold War was running out." The Reagan administration believed that if the U.S. convinced the Russians of American superiority, Communism would collapse. Dr. Norman A. Bailey, then head of plans for the National Security Council under National Security Advisor Richard Allen, told me in 1981 that America's economic recovery and military buildup would bring down Communism by 1988. He was a year off in his forecast.

"Strategic Defense Initiative," the so-called "Star Wars" missile defense program, "was the bullet between the eyes," Meyer recalls. "The Russian military gave up the next morning." The issue was not whether the United States would develop a fully operational missile shield in the next several years; SDI, rather, demonstrated the superiority of American military technology.

But the Soviets very nearly won, by holding a gun to the heads of the West Germans. Gaddis does not take into account that while military strength depends on economic power, economic power can flow out of the barrel of a gun. If the Soviet Union had effectively blackmailed West Germany and other European nations into meeting its economic requirements, its military expansion would have returned a dividend.

The Carter administration had showed no will to meet the Soviet challenge, so the Germans individually and collectively made their deals with Moscow. That was true of the circle around German chancellor Helmut Schmidt. Russia's proposed natural gas pipeline to Western Europe was to be the Trojan horse for economic integration of German industry with the weak Russian economy. German defeatism had rational grounds: Russian military strength on the European front dwarfed that of the North Atlantic Treaty Organization. If Russia had launched a conventional or nuclear attack on Germany, NATO doctrine called for the United States to retaliate with a nuclear strike against the Soviet Union. No such thing would ever have happened, of course, for no U.S. president would risk a strike against the American homeland to save Germany. Even if the U.S. had been willing to meet its obligation, the Germans would never have known who had won World War III—for all of them would have been dead. Thus Germany's ruling Social Democratic Party in 1982 saw little incentive to stick with the American alliance, and Russia had every hope of turning Europe into a satrapy.

Installing Pershing II nuclear missiles in Germany with a six-minute flight time to Moscow was a decisive act of preemption. The missiles turned the tables on the Soviets. Were Russia to attack Germany, the Pershings would strike Russia. If Russia were then to launch nuclear missiles against the United States, the response would be an annihilating counter-strike. No Russian premier would sacrifice the Russian homeland for Europe. Thus the Russians sponsored an enormous "peace movement" to prevent the deployment of the Pershings. Once the intermediate-range missiles were installed in 1983, and once the U.S. was embarked on the Strategic Defense Initiative, Russia had lost the Cold War.

The year 1983, therefore, was the moment of truth for the Soviet Empire: if it was going to choose to fight rather than bow to American superiority, that would have been the time. After Reagan launched the Strategic Defense Initiative on March 23 of that year, Russia's military knew that it could not ultimately compete, and U.S. disinformation succeeded in exaggerating in Russian minds the speed of prospective SDI implementation. Germany had just elected a new parliament, which voted for deployment of the Pershings on November 22, and the first missiles were operational by mid-December. That marked a point of no return for Russia: once Germany committed to deploy the Pershings, Russia's strategic advantage in Europe would necessarily disappear. That is the context for the war scare attending the 1983 "Operation Able Archer" exercises that began on November 2—a simulation of nuclear war.

The Russians let it be known that they suspected that under cover of the exercises, NATO actually was planning to launch a first strike during the Able Archer exercises. Some Russian nuclear forces were placed on alert. The controversy continues among military historians about what the Russians actually perceived. Robert Gates, then head of the CIA's Russia desk, afterwards wrote, "Information about the peculiar and remarkably skewed frame of mind of the Soviet leaders during those times that has emerged since the collapse of the Soviet Union makes me think there is a good chance—with all of the other events in 1983—that they really felt a NATO attack was at least possible and that they took a number of measures to enhance their military readiness short of mobilization. After going through the experience at the time, then through the postmortems, and now through the documents, I don't think the Soviets were crying wolf. They may not have believed a NATO attack was imminent in November 1983, but they did seem to believe that the situation was very dangerous."[5] The KGB defector Colonel Oleg Gordievsky reported, "In the tense atmosphere generated by the crises and rhetoric of the past few months, the KGB concluded that American forces had been placed on alert—and might even have begun the countdown to war.... The world did not quite reach the edge of the nuclear abyss.... But during Able Archer 83 it had, without realizing it, come frighteningly close—certainly closer than at any time since the Cuban missile crisis of 1962."[6]

Whether the Russians actually thought NATO was preparing an attack seems questionable. It is probably not a coincidence that the Russians gave serious consideration to an attack on the West only a month before the deployment of the Pershing missiles. Once the Pershings were installed, NATO was poised to win without a fight. But the story of a near-nuclear confrontation conceals a deeper truth. Some of the Russian leadership preferred a preemptive war against the West as an alternative to inevitable defeat. Fortunately, Andropov overruled them. Rather than fight to extinction, the Soviet Union chose to go quietly. To win the Cold War, the Reagan administration took a risk that seemed frightful in November 1983. But the likelihood that an aging and exhausted Russian leadership would sacrifice the Russian homeland in a nuclear exchange was small. Stalin had long since extirpated the apocalyptic messianism that had motivated the grandfathers of the Soviet leadership, the terrorists of 1900 to 1917. The Politburo of 1983 were not revolutionary fanatics but bureaucratic survivors of the Stalinist terror. Reagan's people were counting on it. CIA Director Bill Casey quipped at the time, "These guys must be exhausted over there. These damn Politburo meetings go on for hours—by the time the guy gets back to his dacha he just wants to have a drink. All they want to do is enjoy being at the top, and we're not letting them do it."[7]

The United States won the Cold War by presenting the Russians with convincing superiority in weapons (American dominance of the skies), the threat of even greater superiority (Strategic Defense Initiative), forward defense (installation of the Pershing medium-range missiles), and aggressive response to Russian insurgencies.

The Ambitions of the Persian Empire

Unlike the Soviet leadership, Iran's leaders warn openly that a rapidly aging population portends national extinction. And the depletion of Iran's aging oilfields has their undivided attention. Mass protests against election fraud during the summer of 2010, moreover, showed how fragile the regime has become. The aging ayatollahs recall the sclerotic Politburo. But there is one giant difference between the Soviet Union of 1981 and Iran of 2011: the United States could crush the capacity of Iran to make war within days with a couple of aircraft carriers anchored in the Persian Gulf. Iran's insistence on pursuing nuclear weapons in the face of an overwhelming deterrent is remarkable given its ultimate defenselessness.

Not only is Iran risking attack by attempting to develop nuclear weapons. It is threatening the United States directly by emplacing missiles in Venezuela, within range of Washington, D.C. The German daily *Die Welt* reported on November 25, 2010, that Iran planned to build a missile base in the Latin American nation as part of a broader agreement between Venezuela's anti-American strongman Hugo Chavez and the Tehran regime.[8]

Dore Gold, a former Israeli ambassador to the United Nations, warns, "The world's biggest supporter of international terrorism is about to get a nuclear umbrella, and that means that terrorist groups will have a protective umbrella over them." According to Ambassador Gold,

> Iran is not a "status-quo" country. There are countries in the world that are happy with what they have, that aren't interested in expansion or intruding on their neighbours and basically just want to be left on their own. Then there are states that are active, that are actively intervening in the affairs of their neighbours and have interests well beyond their own borders and Iran is really in that latter category. It is Iran that is engaged in the insurgency in Afghanistan, providing the Taliban, who were their enemies 10 years ago with weaponry and other forms of assistance to fight US and UK forces in that country. It is Iran that has been engaged in Iraq, particularly through the Shiite militias in southern Iraq. It is Iran which declared, earlier this year that Bahrain, an independent kingdom, is a province of Iran. And that came from individuals very close to the supreme leader, Ayatollah Khameini. Iran is active in Lebanon; it created and sustains Hezbollah. It's involved in the Gaza Strip, in Egypt, Sudan and Yemen.[9]

Iran's economic decline is irreversible—and so is its complete demographic collapse—unless Iran can conquer adjacent oil production in Southern Iraq, neighboring Azerbaijan, and perhaps northern Saudi Arabia on the other side of the Persian Gulf, where Shi'ite Arabs comprise a regional majority. Iran has already undertaken a symbolic occupation of Iraqi oil fields just over the common border. And what is now Azerbaijan had been for centuries the northern provinces of the Persian Empire; a nuclear-armed Iran could revive Persian claims on southern Azerbaijan. Iran continues to lay claim to a share of Caspian Sea energy resources under the Iranian-Soviet treaties of 1921 and 1940. A Heritage Foundation study warned, "The U.S. should strongly oppose Iran's threatening military actions to claim a large portion of the energy-rich Caspian Sea."[10]

"Geopolitics" that confines itself to the rational interests of nations is wholly inadequate to explain how the American South poured out its young men's lifeblood in defeat, or why Russia descended into bloody terror at the beginning of the twentieth century and risked nuclear annihilation near its end. How much less can conventional political science cope with the motivations and choices of Muslim nations that are currently living under existential threat? In order to address the dangers to our national security posed by the imploding Islamic world, we must study *theopolitics.*

What distinguishes Iran from France in 1914, the Confederacy of 1861, or the Soviet Union in 1981 is its apocalyptic eschatology. An Iranian high school textbook quotes Ayatollah Khomeini: "I am decisively announcing to the whole world that if the world-devourers [i.e., the infidel powers] wish to stand against our religion, we will stand against their whole world and will not cease until the annihilation of all them. Either we all become free, or we will go to the greater freedom which is martyrdom. Either we shake one another's hands in joy at the victory of Islam in the world, or all of us will turn to eternal life and martyrdom. In both cases, victory and success are ours."[11] The lessons of the First World War, the Civil War, and the Cold War point to the same conclusion: preemption with overwhelming force is the appropriate means to contain an adversary who knows that he has nothing to lose. The strategy most likely to avoid war in the Middle East is not to reach out to Iran but to humiliate it.

CHAPTER 9

FOUR GREAT EXTINCTIONS

We know of three Great Extinctions that cleared the earth of most of the cultures of the past. Islam has had the misfortune to be caught in the fourth Great Extinction.

Civilizations arose and vanished long before humankind had the ability to record the event—before the first Babylonian scribe poked a stylus into wet clay five thousand years ago, or the first Egyptian drew hieroglyphics a millennium later. The civilizations that matter most to the West, whose culture we in part inherit—classical Greece and Rome—died of moral inanition. With good reason the great classicist Gilbert Murray used the title "The Failure of Nerve" for the last section of his book *Five Stages of Greek Religion*.[1] The most reliable observers in the classical era itself complained of endemic infertility and infanticide. Ultimately, the city-states could not field enough soldiers to fend off their enemies.

By the nineteenth century, classical scholars had drawn an alarmed parallel between the decline of classical civilization and the first modern case of self-imposed infertility, in France. We are not as different from our remote ancestors as we might wish to believe. We sometimes indulge the complacent thought that historical tragedies occurred only because such clever people as we were not present to prevent them; if only those unfortunate folk had had the benefit of the wisdom of our preferred political philosopher, all would have worked out for the best. But the facts tell a different story.

We know of several great past waves of national extinction. There probably were more, but they lie buried so deep under the rubble that we cannot discover them.

Archaeologists tell us that every city in the Eastern Mediterranean burned between 1206 and 1150 B.C.E. The prehistoric Greek civilization of Mycenae, the Hittite Empire in Asia Minor, and the Egyptian Empire in Syria and Canaan disappeared into a Dark Age more than a millennium before the birth of Christ. We read of this first Great Extinction in the accounts of the fall of Troy, Mycenae, and Jericho. The Hittite Empire had already buried countless little cultures in the sands of Mesopotamia and Asia Minor. We hear a distant echo of Hittite and Assyrian conquests in the names of the nations that Rome absorbed or destroyed: the Illyrians, the Sicani, the Quadians, Sarmatians, Alans, Gepidians, Herulians, and Pannonians.

Of most of these dead cultures we know nothing at all; the very few of whose existence we are aware typically left nothing behind but a desiccated sandal strap or a pottery shard. Linguist David Crystal estimates that somewhere between 64,000 and 140,000 languages have been spoken over the course of human history.[2] That is not an actual count, of course, but rather a statistical estimate based on analysis of the rate of mutation of the few languages we know; we cannot count the vast majority of dead languages because no trace of them remains. We have written records of only seventy-five extinct languages which once were spoken between the Atlantic and the Black Sea: Bithynian, Cicilian, Phrygian, Sumerian, Hittite, and Elamite, among them. Most of these records are fragmentary. A single book survives from the rich literature of the Etruscans, the Italian people whom Rome conquered and absorbed, but it is unreadable, for we can decipher only a few words of their lost language.

The sadness of this circumstance is worth a moment's reflection. A hundred thousand times, perhaps, warriors' chants and mothers' lullabies, tales and songs handed down through generations, lovers' laments and sacred hymns, the hopes and memories of a people—all of these came to nothing. Human beings like us loved, fought, farmed, hunted, built, worshipped, raised their young, and buried their dead. But they have vanished into dust so fine that no trace of them sticks to the sieves of the archaeologists. The first Extinction destroyed the Bronze Age civilization of Ancient Greece and the petty kingdoms of Canaan, as well as the Hittite Empire in what is now modern Turkey and Syria. "The end of the eastern Mediterranean Bronze Age, in the twelfth century B.C.E., was one of history's most frightening turning points," according to Robert Drews. "For those who experienced it, it was a calamity.... Within a period of forty or fifty years at the end of the thirteenth and the beginning of the twelfth century [B.C.E.] almost every significant city or palace in the eastern Mediterranean world was destroyed."[3] That Israel was only one of many nations who arrived through a great and destructive migration remained in memory when the prophet Amos wrote, "Are ye not as children of the Ethiopians unto me, O children of Israel? saith the Lord. Have not I brought up Israel out of the land of Egypt? and the Philistines from Caphtor, and the Syrians from Kir?" (9:7). Israel was "a firebrand plucked out of the burning" (4:11).

The second Great Extinction destroyed Hellenistic civilization in the first two centuries B.C.E. The third made an end of ancient Rome. We are living through the fourth and most devastating, which perhaps only a tenth of all living languages will survive. Innumerable Great Extinctions must have occurred in a past so remote that neither tale nor artifact has survived. Of the first Great Extinction that we know any details of, at the end of the

Bronze Age, we have limited testimony from the ancient world—the biblical book of Joshua, the epics of Homer, the legends of Hesiod, and the
many-times-buried layers of burnt cities. Since Roman times, tourists have
visited the ruins of the prehistoric Greek city of Mycenae, sixty miles south-
west of Athens. It was burned around 1200 B.C.E., along with all the palaces
of southern Greece, presumably by the Hellene invaders whose descendants
built the splendid culture of the Greek golden age.

From the earliest literature that the West has preserved, to the philosophers of Greece and the geographers of Rome, to the historians and philolo-
gists and archaeologists of the nineteenth and twentieth centuries, the best
thinkers of the West have tried to make sense out of the extinction of their
antecedents. Why did these civilizations die? A too-simple answer is conquest
by other peoples, or the ravages of famine and disease. The foot soldiers of
invading tribes wielding the new iron swords and javelin-throwers, according to one theory, learned to defeat the expensively maintained chariot-
and-archer armies of Bronze Age cities. But the peoples of the ancient world
did not understand the matter so simply. The Hebrew Bible, the epics of
Homer, and the tragedies of Athens' sixth-century golden age, each in their
own way, offer a different explanation: these ancient civilizations destroyed
themselves from within before the conquerors came.

The invading Hellenes replaced the people who had built the palace at
Mycenae, but they kept their stories. What we now call Western literature
began in morality plays at a religious festival, which also offered a public
lesson in statecraft. Half a millennium later the tragic playwrights of classical Athens still retold the errors of the kings of Mycenae.

In the first surviving masterpiece of Western letters, Aeschylus staged
the fall of the House of Atreus, the legendary Mycenaean king whose son
Agamemnon led the war against Troy. Agamemnon's drive for vengeance
on the Trojan prince Paris, who had seduced Agamemnon's sister-in-law
Helen, led him to sacrifice his youngest daughter in return for a wind to
speed the Greek ships to Troy. His wife Clytemnestra avenged the butchered
child by murdering the king when he returned victorious to Mycenae ten

years later. Their son Orestes, in turn, murdered Clytemnestra, extending a chain of killings that ended only when the god Apollo convened a jury at Athens to render justice on Orestes. Thus the Greeks celebrated the founding of their polity on the ruins of the kingdoms that had preceded them, both to justify their conquest and as an object lesson not to emulate the evil ways of their extinct predecessors.

In the Hebrew Bible, God inveighs against the abominations of the Canaanite cities—including child sacrifice, temple prostitution, and witchcraft (Leviticus 18:11–12)—and tells the invading Israelites that "all that do these things [are] an abomination unto the LORD: and because of these abominations the LORD thy God doth drive them out from before thee." The matter of infanticide is a bright line separating ancient Israel and the later Christians from the pagan peoples that surrounded them. It is not until the third century B.C.E. that we have historical testimony from contemporary observers that infanticide brought down a great civilization: Greece. But the vehement prohibition against child-killing that runs from the most ancient portions of the Hebrew Bible (the Binding of Isaac in Genesis 22) to the later prophets (Jeremiah 19)—and the appearance of the same theme in the Mycenaean sources—underscores the terrible significance of this practice.

The Gods That Failed

The explanations that have come down to us for the first Great Extinction of peoples at the turn of the First Millennium B.C.E. belong to legend or revelation. The second Great Extinction—the collapse of the Hellenistic world—was witnessed and recorded by some of history's keenest thinkers, including the philosopher and polymath Aristotle, the father of empirical science in the West. It was Aristotle who first diagnosed a fatal weakness in a leading contemporary culture—a flaw that occasioned the decline of Sparta, the leading military power of the Greek golden age.

Spartan armies led the Greeks to victory against the Persian invasion of the early fifth century and afterward defeated Athens and her allies in the

Peloponnesian War from 431 to 405. Sparta was still around in the first century B.C.E. But the handful of remaining red-robed, oily-haired Spartan warriors had become a draw for Roman tourists, who visited the ancient town the way Kung Fu aficionados turn up at the Shaolin Temple in modern China. By that time the once-dominant power on the Greek mainland had not fought an important war for two hundred years.

Which points to Spengler's Universal Law #14: *Stick around long enough, and you turn into a theme park.*

Sparta's caste of citizen-soldiers, dedicated from childhood to military service, had once created armies that no force in the ancient world could withstand. But Sparta's hegemony was broken forever at the Battle of Leuctra in 371 B.C.E., by a Theban army under the command of Epaminondas. In his *Politics*, Aristotle says of Sparta's humiliation by a second-rate Greek power that the city-state "sank under a single defeat; the want of men was their ruin." Sparta once had ten thousand citizens, but by the middle of the fourth century B.C.E., Aristotle reports, the number had shrunk to only one thousand. Aristotle's observation is doubly remarkable. It is the first report in history of depopulation due to a reluctance to raise children. It is also the first time that the decline of a great power is blamed on depopulation.

The Spartans, Aristotle explained, concentrated wealth in the hands of an ever-narrower oligarchy, which raised fewer children the better to concentrate wealth in family hands:

> While some of the Spartan citizens have quite small properties, others have very large ones; hence the land has passed into the hands of a few. And this is due also to faulty laws; for, although the legislator rightly holds up to shame the sale or purchase of an inheritance, he allows anybody who likes to give or bequeath it. Yet both practices lead to the same result.... Hence, although the country is able to maintain 1,500 cavalry and 30,000 hoplites, the whole number of Spartan citizens fell below 1,000....

And from these facts it is evident, that this particular is badly regulated; for the city could not support one shock, but was ruined for want of men.[4]

Sparta had another distinction; it was (after the island of Crete) the first Greek *polis* to formalize the practice of pederasty.[5] The "Athenian Stranger" reproaches his Spartan and Cretan interlocutors in Plato's *Laws,* "This custom, which is long-standing, seems to have corrupted the life-style and pleasures of sex that are natural not only for humans but also animals. Someone might make these accusations first of your states and of whatever other states are particularly inclined to the gymnasium."[6] That this practice was no matter of idealized admiration, but explicitly sexual, is demonstrated by the hundreds of surviving vase-paintings showing explicit sexual acts between bearded men and beardless youths.[7]

Pederasty had a deep connection to Greek religion, which was above all a cult of youth. Not even Zeus was immune, abducting the boy Ganymede to be the gods' cupbearer. The older lover, or *erastes*, is the needy worshipper before the god-like object of his love, the *erômenos*. "Though the object of importunate solicitation, [the youth] is himself not in need of anything beyond himself. He is unwilling to let himself be explored by the other's needy curiosity, and he has, himself, little curiosity about the other. He is something like a god, or the statue of a god," explains Martha Nussbaum.[8] But chastity was not considered a virtue for an adolescent boy. In Greek legend the gods turned Narcissus into a flower to punish his pride in refusing male suitors; only the older lover, not the *erômenos*, is allowed to be a Narcissist.

The love of Greek men for adolescent boys embodies the same longing for immortality we observe in the cult of eternally youthful gods. No Greek would pray along with King David, "O Lord, thou hast brought up my soul from the grave: thou hast kept me alive, that I should not go down to the pit." Every Greek, even heroes beloved of the gods, expected to go down to the pit. The dead hero Achilles tells Odysseus in Book XI of Homer's

Odyssey that he would rather be a poor farmer's hired hand than king over the underworld. No Greek god would rescue his favorites from death (except on rare occasion by turning them into trees, brooks, flowers, or stars, which must have seemed tiresome even to the Greeks). Once in a very long while an extraordinary hero, Heracles for example, would be adopted into the Olympian family. But for everyone else—even the best, the strongest, and the cleverest—immortality was unattainable. Not even the immortal Zeus would enjoy a life that was properly eternal, for one day his successor would replace him, just as he had replaced his own father Chronos.

What becomes of a nation that foresees its own extinction? Pagans worship their own image in the person of gods who are like them, only better. Pagan faith is everywhere and always fragile, according to Spengler's Universal Law #15: *When we worship ourselves, eventually we become the god that failed.* The function of pagan gods is not to redeem us from death, but to bring us success. Pagan gods do not love men and women, although they may occasionally lust after them. Absent success, pagan societies lose their faith; the religion of the ancient world is a carnival-parade of new gods introduced by winners to replace the failed gods of the losers, as defeated tribes were absorbed into their conquerors.

An empire like fifth-century Athens, though, was not a tribe that could be assimilated into its neighbor. Which brings us to Spengler's Universal Law #16: *Small civilizations perish for any number of reasons, but great civilizations die only when they no longer want to live.* Athens could not be assimilated; it could only perish of disappointment and disgust. Loss of faith sooner or later sapped them of the will to live. As Sophocles wrote, under such conditions it is better to die, and better yet never to have been born. The most noxious exhalations of modern cultural pessimism in the West do not come close to the summary nihilism of the Greeks' most sublime tragedian. The richest culture of the ancient world reached its apogee with its epitaph.

Greek religion does not propose to overcome death, but only to flee from it for a while—into the arms of perpetual youth. If, as Rose Castorini said in *Moonstruck*, modern men chase women because they want to live forever, Greek men found that the search for eternity was served better by chasing a youthful version of themselves. The older lover worships his own youthful image in the form of his adolescent beloved. Where the Hebrew religion channeled the sexual impulse into marriage and procreation within a covenantal community, Greek religion linked the martial defense of the polis to the lover's vicarious return to youth through his *erômenos*. The separation of sexuality from procreation in Greek culture helps explain the terrible demographic decay that Greece would suffer during the fifth and fourth centuries B.C.E.

As the dominant city in the plains of Boetia, Thebes had been a second-rate power next to the martial Spartans to their south and the imperial Athenians to their north. Thebes, to the lasting contempt of its neighbors, had allied with Persia before the Athenian-Spartan alliance repulsed the Eastern invaders in the early fifth century B.C.E. The Oedipus trilogy of the great Athenian playwright Sophocles portrayed Thebes as a tragic example of monarchical arrogance, while the comedies of his younger contemporary Aristophanes made the Thebans the butt of the classical equivalent of hillbilly jokes. While Athens built an empire at sea and Spartan armies dominated the land, Thebes remained a rural backwater, a bystander at best during the sixth-century Greek defense against Persia, and a minor player during the Peloponnesian war.

But Thebes' apparent backwardness turned out to be a source of strength in the hands of a visionary leader like Epaminondas. A country of small-holding farmers, Boetia continued to raise children, as small-holding farmers always have throughout history. Victor Davis Hanson observes that the ten thousand farms of the Boetian plains could each produce one or two heavily-armed Hoplites, while the low property requirements for Theban citizenship yielded a large militia.[9] Epaminondas brought nine thousand men to confront a marginally greater force of Spartans and allies at Leuctra, according to ancient sources, but the Spartan professionals who stood in the phalanx opposite the Theban spearmen likely numbered fewer than a thousand, of whom four hundred died in the charge of the Theban phalanx. Modern historians speculate about the contribution of Epaminondas' generalship, especially his use of an oblique formation that concentrated maximum force upon the critical point in the enemy line. But the decisive fact remains that there were too few actual Spartans facing the Thebans in the opposing phalanxes at Leuctra, and too many of Sparta's unmotivated auxiliaries. Aristotle, the most astute contemporary observer, rightly blames the Spartan collapse on the hollowing-out of its ruling caste.

The Thebans liberated the Spartan hinterland and assisted the Helots in fortifying their own cities. Bereft of its serfs, Sparta began its irreversible decline. The depopulation of Sparta and its environs continued until the Greek geographer Strabo in the first century B.C.E. characterized it as "a country the most of which is now deserted; in fact, Laconia too is now short of population as compared with its large population in olden times, for outside of Sparta the remaining towns are only about thirty in number, whereas in olden times it was called, they say, 'country of the hundred cities'; and it was on this account, they say, that they held annual festivals in which one hundred cattle were sacrificed."[10]

Nor did Thebes enjoy its success for long; as a "reactionary" agrarian society (in Hanson's description), it could not withstand the globalization of its time, the empire of Alexander of Macedon. And that's because of Spengler's Universal Law #17: *If you stay in the same place and do the same thing long enough, some empire eventually will overrun you.* Thirty years after Leuctra, Thebes refused to join Alexander's puppet Greek coalition. The eighteen-year-old Macedonian ruler butchered six thousand men, women, and children, sold thirty thousand into slavery, and razed the town. A traditional society of smallholding farmers never long resisted the encroachment of empire.

But great empires are also subject to decline and death. Slave labor and tribute from conquered provinces relieved a great deal of the population of Athens—and, later, most of the population of Rome—of the need to work for food. In place of smallholding farmers, the fifth-century Athenians and the first-century Romans became soldiers and slave-masters. Half of Periclean Athens' food supply was imported and paid for with tribute from subject cities.[11] And as soon as the constraints of traditional society fell away, the Athenians stopped raising children. Within an oligarchy, families jostle for control, and their chances of maintaining power depend on concentration of wealth. As Aristotle observed of Sparta, the oligarchical model—in contrast to the system of free-holding farmers elsewhere in Greece—led gradually to depopulation. Athens' own mode of corruption was slower and more insidious. Under Pericles, Athens' democratic empire expanded to the point that the Athenians no longer fed themselves but exacted their sustenance as tribute.

It is common to juxtapose a good democratic Athens to a bad oligarchical Sparta. The pro-Athens bias is understandable; as Victor Davis Hansen once told an interviewer, "The war pitted two antithetical systems—cosmopolitan, democratic, Ionic and maritime Athens at its great age versus parochial, oligarchic, Dorian, and landlocked Sparta—and thus became a sort of referendum on the contrasting two systems."[12] Athens is often seen as a model for American democracy—especially by those who would like to find a *secular* precedent for America's success.

But Athenian democracy was voraciously imperialist. Athens died of a fatal addiction to living off the labor of others, by majority vote. The Athenians themselves understood the rapacious nature of their democratic imperialism. "We have forced every sea and land to be the highway of our daring, and everywhere, *whether for evil or for good*, have left imperishable monuments behind us," declared Pericles, the greatest of Athens' democratic leaders, at a funeral of the Athenian dead after the first battles of the war with Sparta. "Such is the Athens for which these men, in the assertion of their resolve not to lose her, nobly fought and died; and well may every one of their survivors be ready to suffer in her cause."

The defenders of traditional Athenian mores despised the imperialist democratic party—no one more so than the great comic playwright Aristophanes. A character in his comedy *The Wasps* warns bitterly that Athenians may cease to work altogether: "We have now a thousand towns that pay us tribute; let them command each of these to feed twenty Athenians; then twenty thousand of our citizens would be eating nothing but hare, would drink nothing but the purest of milk, and always crowned with garlands." Aristophanes excoriated the greed and sloth of the Athenian mob:

> They are the men who extort fifty talents at a time by threat and intimidation from the allies. "Pay tribute to me," they say, "or I shall loose the lightning on your town and destroy it." And you, you are content to gnaw the crumbs of your own might. What do the allies do? They see that the Athenian mob lives on the tribunal in niggard and miserable fashion, and they count you for nothing, for not more than the vote of Connus; it is on those wretches that they lavish everything, dishes of salt fish, wine, tapestries, cheese, honey, chaplets, necklets, drinking-cups, all that yields pleasure and health. And you, their master, to you as a reward for all your toil both on land and sea, nothing is given, not even a clove of garlic to eat with your little fish.[13]

Thucydides, the chronicler of the Peloponnesian War, tells the same woeful story as Aristophanes. He blames the catastrophic Athenian campaign in Sicily during 413–415 B.C.E., and his city's ultimate humiliation, on the Athenians' desire for imperial booty. Athenian democracy voted to attack a fellow democracy, the Sicilian city of Syracuse, "on a slight pretext, which looked reasonable, [but] was in fact aiming at conquering the whole of Sicily.... The general masses and the average soldier himself saw the prospect of getting pay for the time being and of adding to the empire so as to secure permanent paid employment in the future."[14] Athens lost its fleet and forty thousand men in the adventure, along with most of its empire.

Spengler's Universal Law #18: *Maybe we would be better off if we never had been born, but who has such luck? Not one in a thousand.* In 401 B.C.E. the citizens of Athens assembled at the foot of the Acropolis for the Festival of Dionysus to hear the last work of Sophocles, perhaps the greatest playwright in classical history. The author had died four years earlier, just short of his ninetieth birthday. Three years before the premiere of his final play, *Oedipus at Colonus*, his exhausted city had accepted a humiliating peace, ending the two-generation war with Sparta. Athens had lost its empire and its maritime preeminence in the Aegean Sea, as well as three-fifths of its military-age population—an unimaginable toll by modern standards—in the just-concluded Peloponnesian War. Sophocles' protagonist, the ruined King Oedipus who wandered the earth after gouging out his own eyes, was a synecdoche for Athens herself. As the chorus circled the stage in the stately dance of ancient tragedy, it sang the saddest words in the high literature of the West:

> Not to be born at all
> Is best, far best that can befall,
> Next best, when born, with least delay
> To trace the backward way.
> For when youth passes with its giddy train,
> Troubles on troubles follow, toils on toils,
> Pain, pain for ever pain; And none escapes life's coils
> Envy, sedition, strife,
> Carnage and war, make up the tale of life.[15]

Better to be dead than alive; even better never to have been born. In this posthumous utterance, Sophocles captured the Athenian mood. The war had ruined Greek civilization. Its great historian Thucydides wrote, "Never had so many cities been taken and left in ruins—some by barbarians, others by Greeks themselves as they warred against each other. Indeed several of those cities captured suffered a change of inhabitants. Never had so many human beings been forced into exile or had there been so much bloodshed—either as a result of the war itself or the resulting civil insurrections."[16] It was, to Greece, what the Thirty Years' War of 1618–1648 or the twentieth century's conflict from 1914 to 1945 was to Europe. Wars of this ilk last for thirty years in order to consume two generations. First you kill the fathers, and then, when they grow old enough to fight, the sons. Usually there are not enough grandsons to continue fighting.

Greek civilization lost its will to live, prefiguring the condition of Europe today. Western historians and philosophers who reject religious faith in the Jewish or Christian tradition and seek a secular model for rationality and political freedom—as, for example, the late Leo Strauss—usually look for a spiritual home in classical Greece. The contributions of Greek civilization are beyond dispute. But in a more decisive way, ancient Hellas presents a cautionary model of civilizational suicide. Which brings us to Spengler's Universal Law # 19: *Pagan faith, however powerful, turns into Stygian nihilism when disappointed.*

And Spengler's Universal Law #20: *Democracy only gives people the kind of government they deserve.* If the people are evil, the expression of their will through democracy may produce an evil government. The crowning achievements of Greek classical culture occurred in the aftermath of Athens' ruin at the hands of Sparta. Thucydides, Socrates, Plato, and Aristotle all sought to identify the systemic flaws that ruined Athens, and failed. Plato's dystopic vision of a polis governed by philosopher kings repels us, whether we read *The Republic* as prescription or (as some suggest) a reduction to absurdity. Socrates ridiculed Athenian fecklessness, but offered no cure. As Søren Kierkegaard put it, he was an ironist, not a prophet: he looked backward but not forward, and offered a diagnosis but not a cure.[17] The democratic party condemned Socrates to death by a 360–140 jury vote. And Aristotle in his *Politics* saw only an endless swing of the pendulum between democracy and oligarchy. Some of the policies he recommended—killing deformed children, for example—contributed to Athens' later population decline and set a precedent for the epidemic infanticide that would be the curse of Greece for the next two centuries. Aristotle wrote, "As to the exposure and rearing of children, let there be a law that no deformed child shall live, but that on the ground of an excess in the number of children, if the established customs of the state forbid this (for in our state population has a limit), no child is to be exposed, but when couples have children in excess, let abortion be procured before sense and life have begun; what may or may not be lawfully done in these cases depends on the question of life and sensation."[18]

We are accustomed to consider Western civilization as the confluence of Greek philosophy and biblical revelation, of Athens and Jerusalem. Athens, unlike Jerusalem, failed of its desire to live, which should undermine the perception of an equal share in the subsequent founding of the West.

Sparta's was the first instance of self-inflicted demographic death in recorded history, unusual enough in the fourth century B.C.E. for Aristotle to single it out. But the Spartan disease had become the norm in the rest of Greece a century and a half later, before Rome conquered the enervated and depopulated Greek cities. A team of modern archaeologists notes "the disappearance in the [eastern Peloponnese], by about 250 B.C.E., of the dense pattern of rural sites, and of the intensive agriculture that implies." This rural depopulation was associated with "a growing divide between a small class of wealthy individuals and an increasingly impoverished free lower class of citizens, declining in numbers relative to slaves and immigrants."[19]

Our best source on the declining Greece that failed to resist Rome is Polybius (220–146 BCE), a prominent Greek general who became the tutor to the future Roman conqueror of Carthage. Meditating on the cause of his nation's fall to Rome, Polybius blames the Greeks' refusal to raise children:

> In our time all Greece was visited by a dearth of children and generally a decay of population, owing to which the cities were denuded of inhabitants, and a failure of productiveness resulted, though there were no long-continued wars or serious pestilences among us. If, then, any one had advised our sending to ask the gods in regard to this, what we were to do or say in order to become more numerous and better fill our cities,—would he

not have seemed a futile person, when the cause was manifest and the cure in our own hands? For this evil grew upon us rapidly, and without attracting attention, by our men becoming perverted to a passion for show and money and the pleasures of an idle life, and accordingly either not marrying at all, or, if they did marry, refusing to rear the children that were born, or at most one or two out of a great number, for the sake of leaving them well off or bringing them up in extravagant luxury. For when there are only one or two sons, it is evident that, if war or pestilence carries off one, the houses must be left heirless: and, like swarms of bees, little by little the cities become sparsely inhabited and weak. On this subject there is no need to ask the gods how we are to be relieved from such a curse: for anyone in the world will tell you that it is by the men themselves if possible changing their objects of ambition; or, if that cannot be done, by passing laws for the preservation of infants.[20]

Numerous contemporary sources attest to the destruction of female children. The third-century Macedonian poet Poseidippus of Pella wrote, "Even a rich man always exposes a daughter." A 200 B.C.E. survey of seventy-nine families in Miletus, an ancient Greek colony on the Western Turkish coast, show a combined total of 188 sons but only 28 daughters.[21] Another survey at Eretria in central Greece reports that only one of twelve families had two sons, and almost none had two daughters. A rare exception that proves the rule was Philip V of Macedon, who in the second century B.C.E. outlawed any form of family limitation and thereby increased his military manpower by half in thirty years.[22] The Greek geographer and historian Strabo (63 B.C.E.–21 C.E.) described Greece as "a land entirely deserted; the depopulation begun since long continues. Roman soldiers camp in abandoned houses; Athens is populated by statues." Plutarch observed that "one would no longer find in Greece 3,000 hoplites [heavy infantrymen]."

The seemingly inexhaustible manpower of the Roman Republic prevailed over the depopulated Greek city-states. And yet, by the second century B.C.E., Polybius reported, the Roman republic already had contracted the Greek disease of creeping population decline. "Some of my readers," he wrote of Rome's enormous commitment of naval power against Carthage in the Punic Wars, "will wonder what can be the reason why, now that [the Romans] are masters of the world and far more puissant than formerly, they could neither man so many ships, nor put to sea with such large fleets. Those, however, who are puzzled by this, will be enabled to understand the reason clearly when we come to deal with their political institutions."[23] The implication is that Rome already was growing short of manpower.[24]

Roman demographics in the late Republic and early Empire are the source of longstanding scholarly squabbles. More than two hundred theories about the causes of the Decline of Rome are in print, ranging from lead poisoning caused by Roman plumbing to the spread of venereal disease. But the Romans themselves became alarmed about their own fertility as early as the first century B.C.E. The first Roman Emperor, Augustus, promulgated laws punishing childlessness, divorce, and adultery among the Roman nobility during the first century B.C.E. in response to plunging fertility.[25] Modern demographers confirm the ancient sources. "Classical literary sources, tombstone inscriptions, and skeletal remains have been used by classicists to show that there was probably a decline in the population of the Roman Empire caused by the deliberate control of family numbers through contraception, infanticide and child exposure. This finding is important as it appears to demonstrate that the fertility transition associated with the modern Industrial Revolution is not unique and may have had predecessors," writes John C. Caldwell.[26]

Classical Extinction in a Nineteenth-Century Mirror

Some of today's academics, to be sure, consider it politically incorrect to speak of a Decline in the first place. The deserted, illiterate, violent, and impoverished Italian peninsula of the eighth century C.E. was just differently abled.[27] But the nineteenth-century consensus as to the cause of

Roman decline was clear. The century's outstanding classicist, Theodore Mommsen, wrote a *History of Rome* that earned him the 1902 Nobel Prize for literature. No academic historian before or since has dominated a field with Mommsen's authority. And he had no doubt as to what ailed ancient Rome. "In the largest and most important part of Italy," Mommsen wrote, "the Italy of the Ciceronian epoch resembles substantially the Hellas of Polybius," for "the population was visibly on the decline":

> Celibacy and childlessness became more and more common, especially among the upper classes. While among these marriage had for long been regarded as a burden which people took upon them at the best in the public interest, we now encounter even in Cato and those who shared Cato's sentiments the maxim to which Polybius a century before traced the decay of Hellas, that it is the duty of a citizen to keep great wealth together and therefore not to beget too many children. Where were the times, when the designation "children-producer" (proletarius) had been a term of honor for the Roman? In consequence of such a social condition the Latin stock in Italy underwent an alarming diminution, and its fair provinces were overspread partly by parasitic immigrants, partly by sheer desolation. A considerable portion of the population of Italy flocked to foreign lands.[28]

Rome worked its slaves to death and required fresh supplies through new conquests (unlike the American South, where the slave population rose through natural increase). A high proportion of recently captured slaves came from the same barbarian tribes that were about to invade Rome, and they deserted their Roman masters to join the invading Germanic tribes. As archaeologist Brian Ward-Perkins reports, "Even as early as 376-8 discontents and fortune-seekers were swelling Gothic ranks soon after they had crossed into the empire—the historian Ammianus Marcellinus tells us that their numbers were increased significantly, not only by fleeing Gothic slaves, but also by miners escaping the harsh conditions of the state's gold mines and by people oppressed by the burden of imperial taxation." Ward-Perkins cites a contemporary Roman source who observed that during the Goths' siege of Rome in the winter of 408–409, "Almost all the slaves who were in Rome, poured out of the city to join the barbarians."[29]

The ruin of the free-holding farmer was the beginning of the end, Mommsen believed. "There was nothing to bridge over, or soften the fatal contrast between the world of the beggars and the world of the rich.... The wider the chasm by which the two worlds were externally divided, the more completely they coincided in the like annihilation of family life."

Rome's demographic decline commanded the attention of Mommsen and other classicists because they feared a similar decline in Europe as the old agrarian society dissolved into the modern industrial world. They already had before them the example of one great European nation that had lost interest in child-rearing—namely post-Revolutionary France. In 1840 the distinguished French historian Bureau de la Malle published his *Economie Politique des Romains*, a study in Roman decline. The *Edinburgh Review* summarized de la Malle's account, "Southern and central Italy, instead of being tilled by a race of hardy active farmers, themselves freemen, and working on their own land, was divided into plantations cultivated by slave labour. This was the true nature of the change which Pliny considered the ruin of Italy. It was the diminution of the free class in the country, and the substitution of the comparatively wasteful and unprofitable labour of slaves, which he justly thought to be so disastrous.... Where the increase of wealth leads to the consolidation of landed property, to the extinction of small proprietors, and the substitution of slave for free labour, it may cause depopulation, or, what the ancients considered as the same thing, a diminution in the number of the citizens."[30]

Writing during the reign of King Louis-Philippe, De la Malle reported that in Paris, "the average number of children per marriage is $3^1/_3$, which is insufficient to maintain the population at a constant level, for half of children die before the age of twenty, that is, before they can marry. And among the 200,000 electors [qualified to vote for Louis-Philippe], [the birth rate] is even lower."[31] A British historian, citing de la Malle in 1857, wrote that the infertility "observed with regard to the oligarchies of Sparta and Rome had its effect even on the more extended citizenship of Athens, and it even affected, in our times, the two hundred thousand electors who formed the oligarchy of France during the reign of Louis Philippe."[32]

So the first frost of the coming demographic winter was already felt in the France of 1840, just two generations after the French Revolution. Not gradual attrition of traditional society by modernization, but the sudden upheaval of revolution and war had transformed France from a country of peasants. The French Revolution was the world's first attempt to found a society upon reason rather than religion. Specialists still debate the causes of the great French fertility decline in the nineteenth century. The usual factors such as urbanization and literacy do not explain it. Some demographers argue that the contraceptive methods employed by a licentious aristocracy at Europe's most hedonistic court were adopted by the population at large.[33] Perhaps Napoleon's defeat at Waterloo and the national humiliation France suffered in its aftermath played a role. Perhaps the secularism of the French Revolution eroded the fertility of the earlier traditional society.

Whatever the cause, during the second half of the nineteenth century, the population of France simply ceased to grow. In 1800 there were 29 million Frenchmen and only 21 million Germans; by 1900 there were 40 million Frenchmen and 56 million Germans. England in 1800 had fewer than 9 million inhabitants; by 1900 it had 31 million. French married couples simply had fewer children than their German or English counterparts.[34] Mommsen, de la Malle, and other scholars observed the slow decline of France, once Europe's most populous country and now a second-rate power, in an era when general staffs wrote battle plans on the basis of manpower tables. In French infertility, they saw a repetition of the closing of the classical womb, as empire and oligarchy displaced the traditional society of subsistence farming.

In 1800, city-dwellers made up a quarter of the population of France and Germany and two-fifths of the British population; by 1914, four-fifths of Britons and three-fifths of Germans lived in cities, along with nearly half of Frenchmen. Only a tenth of Eastern Europeans were city-dwellers in 1800, compared to three-tenths on the eve of the First World War. By the outbreak of that war, the triangle of farm, family, and church was broken. Napoleon had already trampled down the old aristocratic order on the European continent; by 1870 the unification of Italy and Germany under secular governments had destroyed the political power of the Catholic Church.

The declinists of the early twentieth century saw in the French example the future of Europe. No English writer attacked social convention and the sanctity of family life with more venom than George Bernard Shaw, and no writer better understood how dangerous it was to tamper with the foundations of the traditional world. In 1903, Shaw wrote,

> The day is coming when great nations will find their numbers dwindling from census to census; when the six-roomed villa will rise in price above the family mansion; when the viciously reckless poor and the stupidly pious rich will delay the extinction of the race only by degrading it; whilst the boldly prudent, the thriftily selfish and ambitious, the imaginative and poetic, the lovers of money and solid comfort, the worshippers of success, of art, and of love, will all oppose to the Force of Life the device of sterility.[35]

During the First World War, a German high school teacher named Oswald Spengler saw in the enervation of the ancient world the same infertility that had begun to afflict his contemporaries, and composed a massive tome that sought to explain why all civilizations must fail of their will to live. Spengler's *The Decline of the West* appeared in 1918, at a moment when cultural pessimism hung over Europe in thick clouds. Absent the compulsions of traditional society, he declared, people simply would cease to raise children:

The primary woman, the peasant woman, is mother. The whole vocation towards which she has yearned from childhood is included in that one word. But now emerges the Ibsen woman, the comrade, the heroine of a whole megalopolitan literature from Northern drama to Parisian novel. Instead of children, she has soul-conflicts; marriage is a craft-art for the achievement of "mutual understanding." It is all the same whether the case against children is the American lady who would not miss a season for anything, or the Parisienne who fears that her lover would leave her, or an Ibsen heroine who belongs to herself—they all belong to themselves and they are all unfruitful.[36]

Spengler and Shaw both, in their different ways, were biological determinists. Spengler argued that civilizations follow a biological life cycle of rise and decay, while Shaw believed in a mystical "life force" that prompted people to reproduce. It never occurred to them that people might bring children into the world as an act of faith. They were half-right and half-wrong—that is, right about some people, and wrong about others. Certain populations seem to be immune to the demographic collapse that comes with modernity. Most of the world's developed nations validate these century-old warnings. But America refutes them.

Only its unique religious history and culture explains America's apparent exemption from the life and death cycle of nations. And only Islam's very different theology explains the Muslim world's extreme vulnerability to the demographic effects of modernization.

CHAPTER 10

ISLAM: THE ARABS AS CHOSEN PEOPLE

In 2008 a Muslim theologian at Germany's University of Münster scandalized his co-religionists by asserting that the Prophet Mohammed was a figment of myth rather than an historical personality. Sven Muhammed Kalisch was a convert to Islam who held one of the most important positions in Islamic studies—the first German university chair for teaching Muslim religious instructors in German public schools. His paper, "Islamic Theology without the Historical Mohammed,"[1] was the first work by a Muslim academic to dispute the Prophet's existence. Professor Kalisch since has apostatized and repudiated the Muslim faith, but the damage was done. As he told a German newspaper, "It might be that the Koran was truly inspired by God, a great narration from God, but it was not dictated word for word from Allah to the Prophet."

In Kalisch's account, the invention of the historical Mohammed transformed the Christian message into a declaration that the Arabs were God's chosen people. The Koran accomplishes this theological feat, Kalisch argues, by casting Mohammed as an Arab prophet who embodies the characteristics of Moses as well as Jesus.

"We hardly have original Islamic sources from the first two centuries of Islam," Kalisch observes. "And even when a source appears to come from this period, caution is required. The mere assertion that a source stems from the first or second century of the Islamic calendar means nothing. And even when a source actually was written in the first or second century, the question always remains of later manipulation. We do not tread on firm ground in the sources until the third Islamic century [the ninth century C.E.]." This substantial lag between the time Mohammed is supposed to have lived and the first historical evidence of the religion he is purported to have founded is extremely suspicious, Kalisch observes. How can a world religion have erupted in a virtual literary vacuum? He quotes Patricia Crone and Martin Hinds: "It is a striking fact that such documentary evidence as survives from the Sufnayid period makes no mention of [Mohammed] the messenger of god at all. The papyri do not refer to him. The Arabic inscriptions of the Arab-Sasanian coins only invoke Allah, not his rasul [messenger]; and the Arab-Byzantine bronze coins on which Muhammad appears as rasul Allah, previously dated to the Sufyanid period, have now been placed in that of the Marwanids. Even the two surviving pre-Marwanid tombstones fail to mention the rasul."[2]

The trouble with the Muslim version of the religion's early history lies not in the absence of evidence, but rather in an abundance, including a large number of coins and inscriptions on monuments during its first two centuries that fail to refer to the Prophet Mohammed. "Coins and inscriptions are incompatible with the Islamic writing of history," Kalisch concludes, citing the monograph *Crossroads to Islam*, by Yehuda Nevo and Judith Koren.[3] The oldest inscription with the formulation "Mohammed Messenger of Allah" is found in the sixty-sixth year of Islamic reckoning. But there also exist coins found in Palestine, probably minted in Amman, on which the word "Muhammed" is found in Arabic script on one side and a picture of a man holding a cross on the other. Kalisch cites this and a dozen other examples of evidence that contradicts official Muslim history. Citing Nevo and Koren among other sources, Kalisch also argues that the Islamic conquest as reported in much later Islamic sources never happened—instead, there was a gradual migration into depopulated Byzantine lands by the Arab auxiliaries of the Eastern Empire.

"To be sure," Kalisch continues, "various explanations are possible for the lack of mention of the Prophet in the early period, and it is no proof for the non-existence of an historical Mohammed. But it is most astonishing, and begs the question [sic] of the significance of Mohammed for the original Muslim congregation in the case that he did exist." The numismatic and archeological evidence against the received version of Islamic history confirms the source-critical case that the Koran is based on earlier Christian sources and was originally written at least partly in Syriac-Aramaic, not Arabic. This compelling case has been assembled by scholars who swam against the current of Islamic studies—for example Patricia Crone, Martin Hinds, Karl-Heinz Ohlig, and John Wansbrough. Kalisch, though, was the first Muslim scholar to argue against the authenticity of the Koran.

If the Mohammed story was invented, then by whom was it invented, and to what end? The answer, Kalisch explains, is that the new Arab empire wanted to conflate the figures of Moses and Jesus into an Arab prophet. Neither the Jews nor the Christians as people of God, but the Arabs, instead, would become the Chosen People under Islam. "No prophet is mentioned in the Koran as often as Moses, and Muslim tradition always emphasized the great similarly between Moses and Mohammed," Kalisch writes. "The central event in the life of Moses, though, is the Exodus of the oppressed Children of Israel out of Egypt, and the central event in the life of Mohammed is the Exodus of his oppressed congregation out of Mecca to Medina.... The suspicion is great that the Hegira appears only for this reason in the story of the Prophet, because his image should emulate the image of Moses." Furthermore, the image of Jesus is also seen as a new Moses. The connection of Mohammed to the figure of Jesus is presented in Islamic tradition through his daughter Fatima, who is identified with Maria.... The Line Fatima-Maria-Isis is well known to research. With the takeover of Mecca, Mohammed at least returns to his point of origin. Thus we have a circular structure typical of myth, in which beginning and end are identical. This Gnostic circular structure represents the concept that the soul returns to its origin. It is separated from its origin, and must return to it for the sake of its salvation.... In the Islamic Gnosis, Moham- med appears along with [his family members] Ali, Fatima, Hasan and Hussein as cosmic forces...the Gnostic Abu Mansur al Igli claimed that God first created Jesus, and then Ali. Here apparently we still have the Cosmic Christ. If a Christian Gno- sis gave birth to Islam, then the Cosmic Christ underwent a name change to Mohammed in the Arab world, and this Cosmic Mohammed was presented as a new edition of the Myth of Moses and Joshua (=Jesus) as an Arab prophet.[4]

The Theology of Submission versus the Theology of Love

We cannot understand societies driven by a religious impulse without considering their religion as such. In this regard theology is the elder sister of political philosophy. But theology is helpless if it offers nothing better than a catalogue of ritual and belief. Theology must instead look at ritual and belief through the eyes of the committed believer. Our knowledge of the Transcendent is existential, not objective. There is never a "reasonable" ground for martyrdom, let alone suicide (except perhaps at the point of capture by the Gestapo). Yet Christians and Jews have offered their lives rather than apostatize. To make sense of what a religion teaches and what

the faithful actually believe, we must understand its theology both objec-
tively—as a statement about God and the world—and also existentially,
that is, as the members of the religion live it in ordinary life.

In chapter 6 we reviewed Islam's deep roots in tribal society. Unlike
Judaism and Christianity, in which every individual participates directly in
the covenant with God, Islam retains the hierarchy of pre-biblical traditional society, in which the head of a family is a miniature head of state. If
the Muslim womb is closing because of a failure of faith, we must look more
deeply at the faith that has failed in its encounter with modernity.

Judaism and its daughter-religion Christianity sought to distinguish
themselves from paganism. But what does "paganism" actually mean? In
Franz Rosenzweig's sociology of religion, the animal ties of common ances-
try define the pagan order. Individuality in the Judeo-Christian sense is
inconceivable, for every member of society must bear the same identity of
blood and soil as every other member, and the single member of society
can be nothing other than an expression of collective blood and collective
will. For this reason every institution of pagan society, emphatically including
family and clan, must collapse into the totality. Here is how Rosenzweig
described the absence of individuality in pre-modern society:

> In the thoroughly organized State, the State and the individual do
> not stand in the relation of a whole to a part. Instead, the state is
> the All, from which the power flows through the limbs of the
> individual. Everyone has his determined place, and, to the extent
> that he fulfills it, belongs to the All of the State.... The individual
> of antiquity does not lose himself in society in order to find him-
> self, but rather in order to construct it; he himself disappears. The
> well-known difference between the ancient and all modern con-
> cepts of democracy rightly arise from this. It is clear from this why
> antiquity never developed the concept of representative democ-
> racy. Only a body can have organs; a building has only parts.[5]

As we have seen, the family is a miniature clan, the clan is a miniature tribe, and the tribe is a miniature nation. All the layers of society stand in relation to each other like nested Russian dolls, identical except for their size.

Ancient Israel, and later Christianity, constituted an alternative to pagan social order. The covenant between Abraham and the biblical God applies not only to the Hebrew nation but to every individual member of that nation. Through his covenant, God establishes the rights of every individual—emphatically including the weakest members of society—beyond the claims of tribe and clan, and provides laws, judgments, and ordinances which stand above the whim of any human magistrate or chieftain. No longer can the Roman paterfamilias command the death of his own children in the little empire of his home; the covenant protects every member of society directly. And no longer can a husband be justified in beating his wife because he acts with the legal authority of a head of state in miniature, as in Sura 4:34.

It is common to speak loosely of "three Abrahamic religions" and assume an underlying commonality among Christianity, Islam, and Judaism. But the defining experience of Judaism and Christianity is alien to Islam. That is the love of a personal God. The founding premise of Judaism is that God's love for Abraham, "God's lover," extends by covenant to each and every one of his descendants, as well as those who are adopted into Israel by conversion. Christianity proposes to extend this grace to all who believe in the Resurrection of Jesus Christ. Each morning, the observant Jew enacts a wedding ceremony with God, forming a wedding band with the leather strap of his phylacteries and reciting the words of Hosea: "And I shall espouse you to Me eternally; I shall espouse you in mercy and loving-kindness, in righteousness and justice, and you shall know The Lord." The personal God of Judaism who loves the faithful soul with the ardor of the Divine Lover in the Song of Songs is unimaginable in Islam, for Allah does not condescend to enter into a relationship of love with mere mortals. Allah cannot bind himself to covenants that he himself cannot alter out of love for his Chosen people, as the biblical God did with Abraham and his descendants; much less can Allah become incarnate as a human being, as Christians believe God did, to offer salvation to all humankind.

Jews and Christians worship a God who cannot be like them, for their God is perfect and incapable of doing evil. For Christians, the incarnate God Jesus Christ is without sin. God is thus wholly Other, for we are imperfect: frail, mortal, and prone to sin. God does nothing without a reason, and his reasons always are good, even if they surpass our understanding.

Allah, by contrast, is beyond good and evil. His cosmic caprice determines everything, and if he so wishes he can make us commit acts of evil, even the ultimate evil of idolatry. Covenant is a concept alien to Islam. For by definition a God of covenants places a limit on his own power and enters into a partnership with a human society. Unlike YHWH of the Hebrews, the all-transcendent Allah does not stoop to make agreements with mere human beings.

Allah usually is described as "absolutely transcendent," but in comparison to the God of the Bible, he is rather more like us. That is what Rosenzweig meant when he called Islam a pagan parody of Judaism and Christianity, and Allah the "colorful panoply of the pagan Olympus rolled up into one," that is, "a monistic paganism." Rosenzweig's use of the term "paganism" is not a reproach but a diagnosis. There is a pagan purpose to the reconfiguration of Christian and Jewish concepts in the Koran: the election of the Arabs in place of the Jews, as Professor Kalisch explains.

A God of Love Is a God of Laws

What is it that unites Catholic Thomists and evangelical Biblicists—as well as observant Jews—but separates all of them from Muslims? It is the biblical belief that God loves his creatures. A loving God, the Bible asserts, places man in a world that he can comprehend, which is to say that God establishes order in the universe out of love for humankind. We live in a world sufficiently comprehensible for us to adapt nature to our needs. Heavenly bodies do not act capriciously (either as pagan deities, or at Allah's arbitrary whim); rather, they are lamps and clocks placed in the sky for the benefit of humankind. If God were not good, the world might not be as hospitable to humans as it is. Such a state of affairs is unimaginable to Christians or Jews. But not to Muslims, who believe that Allah can make any sort of world he wants—or indeed a different world from one day to the next.

A God of love is also a God of laws. For man to survive and prosper in the natural world, he must be able to understand enough of the laws of nature to plant crops and smelt iron and split atoms. This is not only a statement about nature but about the rightly constituted state. The biblical God places limits on his own powers by granting to man what the politicians later called inalienable rights. No one in a position of power, from kings and presidents down to the cop on the beat, may act arbitrarily, for the Covenant establishes a bond between God and every individual, whose rights are protected by laws that no earthly authority can disregard.

Allah is not a God of laws because he is not a God of love. It is possible for Muslims to love Allah, but nonsensical to imagine that God loves Muslims, declared Abu Hamid al-Ghazali (1058–1111), still the dominant authority in normative Islam. A leading Western historian of Islam calls him the most influential figure in Islam since the Prophet Mohammed,[6] and such putative updaters of Islam as Tariq Ramadan still base their theology on al-Ghazali. "When there is love, there must be in the lover a sense of incompleteness; a recognition that the beloved is needed for complete realization of the self," al-Ghazali wrote. But since Allah is perfect and complete, this notion of love is nonsensical. "There is no reaching out on the part of God...there can be no change in him; no development in him; no supplying of a lack in Himself."[7]

Allah is beyond love and has therefore has no need to favor humankind with laws of nature. As al-Ghazali argues,

> The connection between what is habitually believed to be a
> cause and what is habitually believed to be an effect is not

necessary, according to us. For example, there is no causal connection between the quenching of thirst and drinking, satiety and eating, burning and contact with fire. Light and the appearance of the sun, death and decapitation, healing and the drinking of medicine…and so on to include all that is observable in connected things in medicine, astronomy, arts and crafts. Their connection is due to the prior decree of God, who creates them side by side, not to it being necessary in itself, incapable of separation…the philosophers offer no other proof than the observation of the occurrence of the burning, when there is contact with fire, but observation proves only simultaneity, not causation, and, in reality, there is no other cause but God.[8]

In this mainstream Muslim view of things, Allah personally and immediately controls the motion of every molecule by his ineffable and incomprehensible will, directly and without the mediation of any laws of nature. This philosophy is called occasionalism—all things happen merely because Allah decides that they should happen on each separate occasion. Unlike the biblical God of covenants, who is bound forever to his pledge to humankind, Allah may do whatever he pleases. As Pope Benedict XVI observed in his September 2006 address at Regensburg University, the eleventh-century Muslim theologian Ahmad Ibn Said Ibn Hazm taught that Allah was not bound even by his own word, and should Allah desire it, we must become idolaters.

The Judeo-Christian notion of divine love is what makes possible the rational ordering of human existence: as an act of love towards humankind, God made nature sufficiently intelligible for us to cope with it. For Jews and Christians, the rationality of everyday life proceeds from the biblical concept of covenant. Islam eschews reason. Muslim life is arbitrary because it rejects the concept of divine love as expressed in the covenant between God and man.

It might be argued that al-Ghazali in some way corrupted the true faith of Islam, which in earlier centuries included some rationalists. But the

Koran itself is consonant with al-Ghazali's position. The phrase "Allah loves" occurs in the Koran only sixteen times; the remote and absolutely transcendent God of Islam loves "those who do good," "those who purify themselves," "those who trust," "those who act equitably," "the doers of justice," and above all "those who fight in His way in ranks as if they were a firm and compact wall." Allah, in short, loves those who do him service. The Judeo-Christian notion that God has a special love for the weak and defenseless—let alone that God loves the sinner—is entirely absent in Islam. As Franz Rosenzweig wrote, "Unlike the God of faith, Allah cannot go before his own [people] and say to their face that he has chosen them above all others in all their sinfulness, and in order to make them accountable for their sins. That the failings of human beings arouse divine love more powerfully than their merits is an impossible, indeed an absurd thought to Islam—but it is the thought that stands at the heart of [Jewish and Christian] faith."[9]

For Jews and Christians, it is God's love that exalts the individual, who is created in God's image and thus is a fitting lover for the Maker of Heaven. Islam, by contrast, propounds a collective identity, for Allah loves "those who fight in His way in ranks as if they were a firm and compact wall."

Failure and Faith

For Christians and Jews, prayer is first and foremost communion with a God of love, whom Christians see in Jesus Christ, and whom Jews anthropomorphize as the divine spouse of Israel. To attribute recognizably human emotions to Allah is unimaginable within Islam. The Judeo-Christian belief that the Maker of Heaven has a personality that in some way can interact with human personalities, including through prayer, is deeply repugnant to Islam. Muslims do not seek the love of a personal God. The muezzin who summons them to prayer makes clear why Muslims pray. He calls, "Come to prayer! Come to prayer! Come to success! Come to success! Allah is Great!" Allah is a remote sovereign who loves those who faithfully serve him and hates the slacker; he may have pity on the weak and powerless but is under no obligation to do so. He rewards the faithful with success.

Islamic culture, though, has been singularly unsuccessful during the past seven centuries. A religion that abolishes cause and effect does not naturally incline to innovations in natural science, and it is not an exaggeration to say that the previous fecundity of Islamic science dried up within a generation after the twelfth-century triumph of al-Ghazali's occasionalist view of creation. That philosophy gives rise not to scientific achievement and technological advance, but to the mad, *jinn*-haunted "science" of Turkish Islamist-in-exile Fethullah Gülen.

Which poses a paradox to Islam. Allah is a god who offers not succor, but success. Yet the full acceptance of Allah's capricious power over every occurrence at every instant hardly promotes success in a science-driven world. Successful cultures produce people whose contributions resonate through the world—scientists, poets, musicians, entrepreneurs, or philosophers. One great individual can transform a nation: Finland with just 5 million people became a force in the world of classical music thanks to the example of the composer Jan Sibelius, the father of Finnish national culture. Apart from political leaders, the average reader of a quality newspaper in the West is hard put to name a single Muslim distinguished in any field of human endeavor. Excluding the politically skewed Peace Prize, Muslims have won only three Nobel prizes since the establishment of the prizes more than a century ago, or one for every 450 million Muslims alive today. By contrast, there have been 169 Jewish Nobel Laureates (excluding the Peace Prize), or about one for every 89,000 Jews alive today. During the past century, a Jew was 5,000 times more likely to win the Nobel than a Muslim.

Only one Muslim writer today is mentioned as a frontrunner for the literature prize: the Syrian poet Adonis (the pen-name of Ali Ahmad Sa'id). Adonis is a man whom the world should know better. He has almost single-handed created a modernist poetic style in Arabic that vividly conveys the terror of the Muslim encounter with the modern world. Adonis calls his work an "obituary" for the Arabs, and depicts his people as a sort of Living Dead. "We have become extinct," he told Dubai television on March 11, 2007. "We have the masses of people, but a people becomes extinct when it no longer has a creative capacity, and the capacity to change its world.... The great Sumerians became extinct, the great Greeks became extinct, and the Pharaohs became extinct." Islam itself destroys the creativity of Muslims, Adonis argues: "Because Islam—the last message sent by God to mankind—has placed the final seal on the Divine Word, successive words are incapable of bringing humankind anything new. A new message would imply that the Islamic message did not say everything, that it is imperfect."

Nothing less than the transformation of Islam from a state religion to a personal religion is required for the Arabs to enter the modern world, Adonis told Dubai television: "I oppose any external intervention in Arab affairs. If the Arabs are so inept that they cannot be democratic by themselves, they can never be democratic through the intervention of others. If we want to be democratic, we must be so by ourselves. But the preconditions for democracy do not exist in Arab society, and cannot exist unless religion is re-examined in a new and accurate way, and unless religion becomes a personal and spiritual experience, which must be respected."[10] The trouble, he added, is that Arabs do not want to be free.

Asked why Arabs glorify dictatorships, Adonis responded,

> I believe it has to do with the concept of "oneness" [*tawhid*], which is reflected—in practical or political terms—in the concept of the hero, the savior, or the leader. This concept offers an inner sense of security to people who are afraid of freedom. Some human beings are afraid of freedom.
>
> Interviewer: Because it is synonymous with anarchy?
>
> Adonis: No, because being free is a great burden. It is by no means easy.... When you are free, you have to face reality, the

world in its entirety. You have to deal with the world's problems, with everything.... On the other hand, if we are slaves, we can be content and not have to deal with anything. Just as Allah solves all our problems, the dictator will solve all our problems.

Tawhid and Totality

The cause of Muslim backwardness, Adonis contends, lies in the concept of *tawhid*, or "oneness," of Allah. *Tawhid* connotes not just monotheism, but the exclusion of all forms of thought except Islamic doctrine. It refers more to totality than to unity. As the leading European Islamist Tariq Ramadan explains *tawhid*, for a right-thinking Muslim, it is literally inconceivable to raise doubts about God. A Muslim, Ramadan explains, might forget Allah, but he cannot doubt Allah. A religion that permits no doubt—unlike Christianity, of which Pope Benedict XVI said that "doubt is the handmaiden of faith"—becomes an all-or-nothing proposition. Either Islam regulates the totality of life and thought, so that no questioning may intrude into its magic circle, or it becomes nothing.

Even in the most intimate human setting, the nuclear family, the collectivity consumes the individual: Muslim wives exist to placate their husbands ("because Allah has given the one more strength than the other") on pain of corporal punishment. Children are obliged to sustain the family's position within the clan by marrying first or second cousins, on pain of honor killing. The same totalizing principle that Adonis sees in Islamic society today was also discerned by Franz Rosenzweig in the ancient political order, as noted above.

On the surface, Islam and Judaism have much in common, for example, regular prayer times; Muslims pray five times a day, and the Jews thrice, the former facing Mecca, the latter facing Jerusalem. One doesn't need to know a word of Arabic or Hebrew, though, to detect a radical difference in the way Jews and Muslims pray. A cacophony of individual voices makes up most of a Jewish service; worshippers pray at their own speed, sometimes singing out loud a few lines of a Psalm before returning to the rapid undertone of

Jewish prayer. The Eighteen Benedictions, Judaism's definitive daily prayer, is recited in silence by every worshipper; and when the prayer-leader repeats the Benedictions, the individual worshippers are expected to chant the most important phrases before the leader does. Stylized gestures, for example a slight bow, accompany some parts of the basic prayer of Judaism, but each congregant executes them when ready, and a latecomer will do so while the rest of the group has moved on to another part of the service. Jewish prayer has defining moments of collective response, but at its core is a personal audience between the individual Jew and the King of Kings.

Jewish prayer covers a vast amount of text; the daily morning service alone consists of a hundred pages of closely printed Hebrew. Most of Muslim prayer, by contrast, is found in the first seven lines of the Koran, repeated thirty-two times a day:

> In the name of Allah, the Beneficent, the Merciful
> Praise be to Allah, the Lord of the worlds,
> The Beneficent, the Merciful,
> Master of the Day of Requital,
> Thee do we serve and Thee do we beseech for help,
> Guide us on the right path,
> The path of those upon whom Thou hast bestowed favors,
> Not those upon whom wrath is brought down, nor those who
> go astray.

In correctly executed Muslim prayer, worshippers display the coordination of a close-order drill. Gestures in Muslim prayer cannot be separated from uttering the right words. Prayer is measured in a basic unit, the *rak'a*, which consists of stylized gestures (raising hands to ears, placing hands over the breast, bowing, touching the forehead to the ground) as well as specific phrases. The experience of Muslim worship is inherently collective; the experience of Jewish prayer—which begins each morning with Hosea's nuptial declaration—is profoundly individual as well as communal.

Vicarious Sacrifice versus Personal Sacrifice: The Eucharist and Jihad

But it is in the matter of sacrifice that we encounter the most radical distinction between Islam on one hand, and biblical religion on the other. Religion is not so much a reflection of the life of a community, as it is the means by which the community seeks a life beyond its temporal existence. At the heart of religion is the encounter with mortality. Secular political science reduces religion to a belief-structure. But to people of faith, religion is not an ideology, but a life-or-death commitment. The believer stakes his or her life on the hope of conquering death. Religious communities that forget this—mainline Protestants, Reform Jews, and liberal Catholics—fade away in a generation or two. These questions seem primitive to the modern profession of political science, whose experts consider themselves superior to the obscure debates of the theologians and the enthusiasm of the faithful. Despite the political scientists, though, communities and nations continue to define themselves by what they hold sacred, and when nothing more is sacred, they lose their reason for being.

The bond of love between God and the individual Christian or Jew answers the question of mortality before which secularism stands mute. God in his love offers the Christian and Jew the gift of eternal life. But the love of the maker of heaven and earth is an overwhelming and consuming love: it requires of Christians and Jews that they offer up their whole being ("to love the LORD your God with all your heart, all your soul, and all your might"). If not for God's grace, his love would consume us. That is why the biblical God offers a sacrifice in place of the life of the beloved individual, so that we can approach God without destroying ourselves in the act. The Christian concept of sacrifice proposes to universalize the purpose of Jewish sacrifice: Jesus becomes the victim that God substituted for Isaac, and the Pascal lamb whose blood guarded Jewish homes from the plague that killed the first-born of Egypt.

To Christians and Jews, these are not boxes to be checked on an ideological clipboard, but a matter of life and death, the means that God has provided to commune with God and attain eternal life. Catholic, Orthodox, and Anglican Christians participate in this sacrifice through the Lord's Supper, partaking of what they believe to be the real presence of God in the Eucharist. The phylacteries whose strap is curled into a wedding band in Jewish morning prayers enclose a parchment with the biblical verses declaring that every first-born male belongs to God. Every Jewish father must redeem his first-born son in an ancient ritual in which the infant is presented to a representative of the *Kohanim*, Israel's ancient caste of priests. This "re-enacts the drama of Abraham offering Isaac to the Lord, of the knight of faith (using Kierkegaard's term) giving unreservedly away his son to God. The presentation of the child to the kohen is symbolic of Abraham's performance when he bound Isaac and placed him on the altar," wrote Rabbi Joseph Dov Soloveitchik.[11] Observant Jews recite daily the *Akedah*, the verses from Genesis 22 recounting the binding of Isaac.

God's covenant with Abraham is singular in world history. A universal and eternal God makes an eternal pact with a mortal that can be fulfilled only if Abraham's tribe becomes an eternal people. But the price of this pact is self-sacrifice, an existential act beyond all ethics, as Søren Kierkegaard tells us in *Fear and Trembling*. In our modern complacency, we do not like to recall that the sacraments of revealed religion are a substitute for human sacrifice: the biblical God in his love for humankind spares the victim, just as God provided a ram in place of the bound Isaac on Mount Moriah. Christians believe that a single human sacrifice spared the rest of humankind. Among Jews the covenant must be renewed in each male child through a substitute form of human sacrifice, namely circumcision.[12] Each individual Christian and Jew must die to this world to gain the Kingdom of God.

Islam offers no expiatory sacrifice, no substitute: the victim that the Muslim must sacrifice is himself. As a *fatwa* from the authoritative website Islam Online explains,

> Sacrifice is not a pillar of Islam.... Not only did the pagan Arabs
> sacrifice to a variety of gods in hopes of attaining protection

or some favor or material gain, but so, too, did the Jews of that day seek to appease the One True God by blood sacrifice and burnt offerings. Even the Christian community felt Jesus to be the last sacrifice, the final lamb, so to speak, in an otherwise valid tradition of animal sacrifice (where one's sins are absolved by the blood of another). Islam, however, broke away from this longstanding tradition of appeasing an "angry God" and instead demanded personal sacrifice and submission as the only way to die before death and reach *fana* or "extinction in Allah."[13]

Although the Muslim feast of Eid commemorates the post-Koranic legend of the Binding of Ishmael (rather than Isaac, as in the Bible), the custom of slaughtering a sheep for the feast has no ritual significance. It takes from Judaism the outward form of sacrifice, but not its content, that is, the manifestation of God's grace that provides a substitute for our own life. Each Muslim must be his own Christ.

The one form of sacrifice that all branches of Islam acknowledge as a failsafe guarantee of Allah's grace is death in battle on behalf of the faith.[14] Jihad is the exemplar of Islamic self-sacrifice, and it is not vicarious: God provides no ram to substitute for Isaac, let alone dies on the cross to take away the sins of the world. He who serves Allah so faithfully as to die in the violent propagation of Islam goes straight to paradise. Islam admits no substitutionary sacrifice, no grace that supplies another victim so that the individual Muslim may live. Everyone must carry his own spear.

Sacramental self-sacrifice in war is not a Muslim invention, or a practice in any way unique to Islam. On the contrary, it is the fundamental religious act of pagan (and neo-pagan) society. For it is only by the sacrifice of the young men of the tribe that the tribe can be sure of survival among a forest of enemies. The individual dies so that the tribe may live. Jihad universalizes that pagan principle by applying it to the tribe-writ-large, the *Ummah*, the whole Muslim world envisioned as a single nation.

According to Franz Rosenzweig, jihad is the supreme Muslim act of sanctification precisely because war is the most sacred act of pagan society in general:

> The concept of the Path of Allah is entirely different than God's path. The paths of God are the disposition of divine decrees high above human events. But following the path of Allah means in the narrowest sense propagating Islam through holy war. In the obedient journey upon this path, taking upon one's self the associated dangers, the observance of the laws prescribed for it, Muslim piety finds its way in the world. The path of Allah is not elevated above the path of humankind, as far as the heaven stretches above earth, but rather the path of Allah means immediately the path of his believers.[15]

Islam, in sum, is a religion in which personal self-sacrifice is rewarded by success, just as a soldier is rewarded for bravery in battle by a king. Death in jihad is the exemplary form of self-sacrifice which Islam offers its adherents, in place of the Judeo-Christian concept of vicarious sacrifice which gives life rather than takes it. And in the absence of success—in the face of spectacular economic and military failure over the past two generations of the Muslim encounter with modernity—Islam faces a crisis of faith from which it cannot recover, a crisis expressed most vividly in the closing of the Muslim womb.

And, as we shall see, population collapse in the West is not unrelated to pagan religion, either—including even the pagan principle of self-sacrifice in holy war (as opposed to vicarious sacrifice in light of God's love). By the turn of the twentieth century, the Europeans subordinated Christianity to their own inclination towards self-adoration, and a neo-pagan strain of nationalism overwhelmed the universal impulse in Christian churches. At the time of World War I, the words "holy war" were pronounced more often by Europeans than by Arabs. The catechism distributed to German military chaplains spoke of a "great, holy war" against "evil."[16] When the German army conquered Brussels in August 1914, the newspaper *Der Tägliche Rundschau* enthused, "The great times of heroes, which had almost become a legend, have returned. So, too, did our sons and brothers march off into the holy war."[17] And in England, in 1915, the Bishop of London indulged in this dumbfounding conflation of the sacrifice of Christ on the cross with British war aims: "The Church can best help the nation first of all by making it realize that it is engaged in a Holy War. Christ died on Good Friday for Freedom, Honour, and Chivalry, and our boys are dying for the same thing.... MOBILIZE THE NATION FOR HOLY WAR."[18]

European civilization—and European demographics—have never really recovered from the 1914–1918 war. But how and why did what used to be Christendom succumb to pagan religious impulses, and eventually to the demographic decline that has been the fate of pagan societies since ancient Sparta? The failure of Christianity in Europe is a story that begins in the Dark Ages but does not reach its terrible denouement until the seventeenth century.

CHAPTER 11

HOW CHRISTIANITY DIED IN EUROPE

In *The Rise of Christianity*, Rodney Stark observes that Christian prohibition of abortion and infanticide contributed to the success of the new religion. "Christian and pagan subcultures must have differed greatly in their fertility rates," Stark argues, so that "a superior birthrate also contributed to the success of the early church."[1] Europe's great recovery from the post-Roman depopulation began with its final Christianization in the ninth century C.E. Its modern depopulation began with the failure of Christianity a millennium later.

To make sense of Europe's tragedy in our own day, we must start even earlier than the French Revolution, with the unraveling of Christendom during the seventeenth century. Europe's descent into savagery during the 1618–1648 Thirty Years' War ultimately prepared the way for what Winston Churchill would call "another Thirty Years' War" of 1914–1945.

The first Thirty Years' War was far worse in proportion to population than the second one. The number of Germans declined from 21 million to perhaps 13 million, mostly due to starvation. The population of Castile, the home province of the Spanish monarchy, fell by a quarter, and large stretches of France became depopulated. Not since the decline of Rome had Europe suffered on this scale—and never afterward. "Executed malefactors were cut down from the gibbets to serve as butcher's meat, and the recently bereaved were forced to guard the cemeteries against the ghoulish activities of body-snatchers," explains Aldous Huxley.

> After [the 1634 battle of] Nordlingen, many thousands of the defeated Protestants' camp-followers went wandering in great troops, like foraging baboons, desperately looking for something to eat. Unprotected villages were overrun and looted; the larger towns closed their gates and sent out troops of soldiers to drive them away. Strasburg left its gates open, and thirty thousand of the almost sub-human creatures entered the town and, having exhausted the charity of the burghers, began to die by hundreds in the streets. Thereupon the city fathers had the survivors herded out at the point of the pike to die in the country.[2]

Repeated a thousand times, such exercises killed more than 8 million people, most of them civilians, and most of them horribly.

This was the definitive disaster in modern European history, the sad end of a millennium of Christian striving for universal empire and enduring peace—and the template for the great European conflicts to come: the Napoleonic Wars and the World Wars of the twentieth century. Most of subsequent European history consists of failed efforts to avoid a repetition. The subject is so unrelentingly dreary that English-speaking culture has avoided it. In contrast to the other great wars, not a single studio film recounts its major events. That is a shame, for Europe's history cannot be understood apart from the Thirty Years' War, and from the motives of its great actors. Ultimately it was a war of contending claims to divine election, the tragic result of the failure of the Church to fully convert the nations of Europe.

In the first years of World War II, Huxley—who had warned with such prescience of a technological dystopia with human cloning and designer babies in his 1931 novel *Brave New World*—probed the Thirty Years' War for the causes of Europe's plunge into self-destruction. And he discovered that the depopulation of Germany was not collateral damage in a war fought for other purposes. It was the objective of the war. Most of the victims, writes Huxley, "knew nothing of those two men, hundreds of miles to the West, in Paris, one dressed in scarlet, the other in tattered grey, and both of them working, working all day long and far into the night, to make quite sure that there should be no peace, that the soldiers should go on marching and the nightmare be prolonged."[3]

The man in scarlet was Cardinal Richelieu, head of Louis XIII's Council of State; the man in gray was the Capuchin Father Joseph du Tremblay, Richelieu's "Grey Eminence." Any college survey course on modern European history will tell you that the rise of the nation-state was the main event of the seventeenth century. It will explain that the religious wars arising from the Reformation of the previous century turned into dynastic wars fought under the false flag of religion. That conventional narrative tells a partial truth. The Thirty Years' War did overstep the Catholic-Protestant divide. It lasted for a generation because Catholic France supported the Protestants in order both to destroy Germany as a contender for hegemony on the European continent and to ruin its rivals, Catholic Austria and Spain.

Then, according to the conventional narrative, out of the terrible Wars of Religion rose the Enlightened modern nation-state of which France was the exemplar. Only later, in the nineteenth century, did the nastier forms of nationalism creep in.

Here the truth is quite different from the conventional story. Religious mystics built the French nation-state on the ruins of Europe—mystics of a fervor that exceeded even that of the Dominican crusaders (who slaughtered up to a million residents of Provence to crush the Albigensian heresy in the thirteenth century) or the Spanish inquisitors (who tortured and burned perhaps ten thousand heretics and "Judaizers" during the fifteenth and sixteenth centuries). The crusaders and inquisitors killed on behalf of a spiritual vision, a universal Catholic Church. The scarlet- and gray-clad clerics who governed France on behalf of the feckless Louis XIII worshipped something of their own blood and bone. They worshipped France herself.

Two rival versions of Christianity fought to the death in the Thirty Years' War: the Catholic concept of universal empire, and the obsession of the French that they, among all the nations of Christendom, were chosen by God as his proxy on earth. Both of these were religious passions, and thus the Thirty Years' War was a religious war. But it was not the Catholic-Protestant war about which we have all been taught. It was a war between Christianity and neo-pagan national idolatry, and Christianity lost.

The project of universal Christian empire that began with St. Augustine's *The City of God* died with the Thirty Years' War. In place of universal empire, the Treaty of Westphalia that ended the war established nation-states, and the Catholic Church delegated its authority to Europe's Catholic dynasties. As the Catholic intellectual historian Russell Hittinger explains:

> In 1648, Innocent X declared the treaties of Westphalia "null, void, invalid, iniquitous, unjust, damnable, reprobate, inane, empty of meaning and effect for all time." The new system of sovereign states caused the slow decline of the twin international colossi of papacy and Holy Roman Empire. But what choice was there except to adapt to what were de facto national churches? The Vatican was dependent on Catholic sovereigns to politically and militarily hold the line in the Counter-Reformation and to supply the material infrastructure for the ever-growing missions in the Americas and Asia. For their part, Catholic sovereigns understood that they needn't do anything so radical as Henry VIII's schism to enjoy a functional supremacy in matters religious.[4]

We should be surprised not by the disappearance of Christianity in Europe, but by its tenacity. For centuries Christianity was burned, tortured, and starved out of the European peoples. It is a testimony to the tenacity of their faith that it took so long to kill.

How did Christianity ultimately fail in Europe? The short answer is that the neo-paganism of national idolatry hatched like a cuckoo's egg in the nest of Christendom.

We need to remember that Christianity presented itself to the world, after the fourth-century conversion of the Roman Emperor Constantine, as the first universal religion of the West—backed by the authority of universal empire—at a moment when the lives of the peoples of the world had become desperately fragile. The Hellenistic and Roman empires had already leveled the tribal divisions of the ancient world. Rome had absorbed the competing kingdoms and cultures of the Italian peninsula just as Alexander of Macedonia had unified the Greek city-states into his empire by force. Their conquering armies had created the first two universal languages— with Latin or Greek spoken from the Irish Sea to the Black Sea, and from the Elbe River to North Africa.

Greek and Roman universalism, to be sure, had been achieved at hideous cost. The small peoples of the classical world were killed or enslaved; the smallholding farmers of Italy were replaced by latifundia worked by slave labor; the rural population that had manned the Greek and Roman armies became a dependent urban proletariat and gradually ceased to reproduce. A relatively tiny force of barbarians entered Italy in the fifth century B.C.E. and overthrew the rotten remnants of the Roman Empire, in part because the Roman armies themselves long had become dependent on foreign conscripts, and in part because the vast slave population of the Italian peninsula flocked as free men to the new army.

Back in the far reaches of the ancient world, before the triumphs of Alexander and Caesar, there existed an old pagan confidence that blood and tradition would bear the identity of the individual into an indefinite future. The decaying ancient situation dominated by imperial Rome, however, created a world of terrible uncertainty, during which the half-life of a small people might be measured in decades rather than centuries. That old pagan confidence began to fray. If, as Franz Rosenzweig said, the love of the peoples of the world for their own nationhood is pregnant with the presentiment of death, by the time of Constantine's conversion, this presentiment seemed all too urgent, not a hint of some indefinite future. Then, between the conversion of Constantine in 325 C.E. and the crowning of Charlemagne as Holy Roman Emperor in 800 C.E., the population of Europe fell by half or more; the great engineering, manufacturing, and trading network of Rome disappeared; cities were abandoned; and the great culture of the classical world was for the most part lost.

The bonds of blood and tradition that gave cohesion to the peoples of the ancient world disintegrated. The Christian message—that every individual must undergo a second birth, to replace his sinful Gentile nature with a rebirth into a new people (the "tribe of Christians" and "the race of those who honor God" in the words of Eusebius)—resonated through the rubble of ancient paganism. Obstacles to evangelization had been torn down by circumstance.

The conversion of the ancient world did not proceed mostly by baptizing individuals ready to abandon their pagan roots, however. Christianity became a state religion by imperial edict, and the peoples of the Greek and Latin worlds accepted the new cult in more or less the same way that they had accepted other cults before it.

After the fall of Rome, the Church stood as the only cohesive entity between the Atlantic Ocean and the Black Sea—even if it held on in just a few remote islands of faith and learning in a sea of anarchy. The Church did not have the means to evangelize individual souls. Instead it recruited kings, who could make their peoples Christian. And it enlisted these kings to conquer their neighbors who might resist. From the Gothic invasion of Italy in 401 C.E. to the defeat of the Magyars at Lech in 955 and the conversion of St. Vladimir in 1015, the barbarians entered Christian life not as individuals adopted into the new People of God, but as tribes incorporated into Christendom through conquest or alliance.

Charlemagne earned his title "Holy Roman Emperor"—which, in fact, meant simply emperor of the German peoples—by conquering the pagan

Saxons. Six thousand Saxon nobles who refused the cross were slaughtered on a single day in 782. The Europe that emerged from the alliance of throne and altar was a different entity, settled by different people, from the Rome whose authority and symbols it continued to invoke. Christianity created Europe. Indeed, Hilaire Belloc's old saw that "Europe is the faith, the faith is Europe" applies literally: the Church taught illiterate tribal chieftains to read and made them kings of nations under the unifying sign of the cross. The nations took letters, culture, statecraft, and authority from the Church, but they joined Christendom with their traditions, customs, and superstitions intact. As Franz Rosenzweig noted, Christianity allowed the pagans to continue to worship their own image. Germans worship a blond Jesus, Spaniards worship a dark-haired Jesus, Mexicans venerate the dark Virgin of Guadalupe, and so forth. The result, wrote Franz Rosenzweig, is that Christians "are forever torn between Jesus and Siegfried [the medieval pagan hero]."[5]

Christianity offered the promise of immortality to European nations for whom the prospect of extinction was a fact of daily life during the great depopulation of the Dark Ages. *Beowulf*, the one surviving epic in Anglo-Saxon, offers a window into the terrible fears of small peoples—the little tribe of Spear-Geats probably will not long survive the death of its hero. The epic concludes at Beowulf's funeral pyre, with a woman's lament for her people, who will perish without their leader: "A dirge of sorrow was sung for Beowulf by a woman; with hair braided up, she repeatedly said that she dreaded the evil days to come—days full of death, bloodshed, the horror of warriors, and captivity."[6] From the dawn of time the peoples of the world had lived under the shadow of extinction. In primitive society some two-fifths of the male population typically died in war. "A typical tribal society lost about 0.5 percent of its population in combat every year," reports Nicholas Wade. "Had the same casualty rate been suffered by the population of the twentieth century, its war deaths would have totaled two billion people."[7]

The ancient pagan's hope for immortality rested in the blood and culture of his tribe. But the peoples of the ancient world knew that no tribe could last forever, that one day a more powerful enemy, or the vagaries of drought and disease, would end its stay on earth. Franz Rosenzweig observes, that is why the gods of ancient peoples are immortal—in that their lifetimes exceed many human lifetimes—but not eternal, for even the gods will face a reckoning one day. In all the recorded myths of the ancient world, gods are born, fight for power, and die. Zeus wrested power from his father Chronos, who had killed his own father Uranus. The demigod Prometheus, impaled on a rock for the crime of stealing fire from the gods as a gift for man, bargained his freedom by warning Zeus not to mate with the nymph Thetis, who would bear a son greater than his father. The Norse gods will die at the Ragnorak, the end of the world.

Among all the peoples of antiquity, only Israel believed in a God who was not only immortal but also eternal—who was not part of the perishable natural world, but stood outside it, who would replace the universe when it wore out like a suit of clothes, but would "establish his servants forever" (Psalm 102). "Precisely through Christianity the idea of Election has gone out among the individual nations, and along with it the claim upon eternity that goes with Election," according to Rosenzweig. But the notion of eternal life beyond this world remained beyond the ken of the lightly baptized European tribes. They did not want to be adopted as individuals into a new "tribe of Christians"—that is, into Israel, as the Church promised. Instead, they want to *replace* Israel and become the uniquely chosen nation. That is, they wanted to be eternal in their own skins—to be the Chosen Nation among nations that, like ancient Israel, would enjoy eternity in its own flesh. From the beginning of the seventh century onward, jealousy over Israel's election inspired hatred of the Jews. Christianity made a fatal compromise with national idolatry, and the lightly baptized peoples who coveted the Election of Israel proceeded to persecute the original chosen people of God.

Genocidal nationalism was not a twentieth- or even a nineteenth-century invention. The unquiet urge of each nation to be chosen in its own skin began with the first conversion of Europe's pagans; it was embedded in European Christendom at its founding. Christian chroniclers cast the newly baptized European monarchs in the role of biblical kings, and their nations in the role of the biblical Israel. The first claims to national election came at the crest of the early Dark Ages, from the sixth-century chronicler St. Gregory of Tours (538–594), and the seventh-century Iberian churchman St. Isidore of Seville.

St. Gregory's *History of the Franks* conflates the deeds of the Merovingian dynasty in Gaul with biblical events, in a salvation history intended to persuade the Frankish kings of their divine calling as leaders of Christendom. "One can see in the historico-theological drama in Book II of the *Histories* Gregory's conception of Gaul as a holy land, a New Israel," writes Notre Dame University historian Phillip Wynn. "Here the author comes to grips with events central to his contemporary society, the establishment by Clovis of a Frankish kingdom in Gaul ruled by the Merovingian dynasty. How this happened within the framework of a divinely-actuated history and what lessons this past had for Gregory's present explain many of the peculiar aspects of his narrative in Book II, including its disordered chronology and historical errors."[8]

And the historian René Rémond notes, "It was perhaps in France that the identification of religion with national destiny was oldest, because it was one of the oldest nations. At a very early date, a tradition accredited by the abbey of St. Denis presented the kingdom of France as the chosen nation, called upon, after Christ's coming, to be the one to carry on the Israel of the Old Testament; hence the adage *Gesta Dei per Francos*—the deeds of God through the Franks."[9] The election of the Frankish king Charlemagne as Holy Roman Emperor in 800 C.E. provided a foundation for the French claim to chosenness.

If the Franks were the first European nation to discover their own national election in the manner of biblical Israel, the Spanish were not far behind. Seventh-century Spain was ruled by the Visigoths, "who considered themselves to be a chosen people with all the associated privileges and obligations. And in support of this proposition, the great Visigothic chroniclers such as St. Isidore, St. Julian, and Juan Biclarense argued that the

Visigothic people was God's instrument on earth," literary critic Jack Weiner writes in his study of the theme of the "chosen people" in medieval Spanish poetry.[10] It's no accident that the Visigoth King Ricared I (586–601 C.E.) promulgated the first anti-Semitic laws on the European record, prohibiting circumcision, preparation of kosher food, observance of the Jewish Sabbath and festivals, and other forms of observance, on pain of death by burning. The nations that sought to replace Israel—rather than seek adoption into Israel—always viewed the continued presence of the Jewish people as a stumbling-block to their own pretensions to Election.

The contending French and Spanish claims to national election—as we shall see below—were fought out at catastrophic cost much later, during the Thirty Years' War of the seventeenth century.

The tragedy of the Catholic Church was to believe that it could turn such patriotism to its own purposes. As recently as the 1913 edition of the *Catholic Encyclopedia*, we find this benign view of the French claim to national election: "The idea that the Franks were a people chosen by God arose soon after their conversion to Christianity, and finds expression many times in the traditions relative to Clovis, which Gregory of Tours transmits to us. We read in one of the prologues of the Salic Law: "Glory to Christ, who loves the Franks! May He preserve their kingdom! May He replenish their leaders with His grace, for this is the strong and brave nation which has richly covered with gold the bodies of the holy martyrs."[11] (One wonders at such "deeds of God through the Franks" as the 1204 sack of Constantinople by Frankish crusaders under Venetian leadership, which hastened the Eastern Empire's fall to Islam.)

The conceit of national election remained embedded in French Catholicism well into the twentieth century. "Some of the most eloquent writing which the Catholic revival produced [in the interwar years] were on the special destiny of France," writes John Hellman in his biography of the philosopher Simon Weil, an impassioned opponent of religious nationalism. "Not only the more 'pagan' nationalists such as Maurras and Barrès, but deeply serious Christians such as Bernanos, Léon Bloy, Paul

Claudel, and the young Jacques Maritain believed in a special relationship between their beloved country and Divine Providence. And this group was not exclusively right-wing; perhaps the most powerful poetry with this inspiration flowed from the pen of the Dreyfusard, socialist, and Catholic, Charles Péguy...[who] went so far as to describe God Himself as French."[12]

Not until the Second Vatican Council did the Church repudiate this kind of claim for earthly power and style itself instead the "People of God," under the influence of the great Jesuit Henri de Lubac, the founder of *Ressourcement*, that is, a return to the original sources of the Christian fathers. De Lubac wrote, "It is said in St. Matthew that the Kingdom 'shall be given to a people bringing forth the fruits thereof,'" not "to the Gentiles" but "to a new people" of God:

> To St. Paul the Church is the People of the New Covenant. Israel according to the Spirit takes the place of Israel according to the flesh; but it is not a collection of many individuals, it is still a nation albeit recruited now from the ends of the earth, "the tribe of Christians," says Eusebius, for instance, "the race of those who honor God"...and as YHWH bestowed adoption on no individual as such, but only insofar as he bestowed universal adoption on the people of the Jews, so the Christian obtains adoption only in proportion as he is a member of that social structure brought to life by the Spirit of Christ.[13]

The Church's new attitude towards the Jews, crystallized in John Paul II's declaration that the "Old Covenant" between God and the Jewish people remained in force, should be understood in this broader context. As the nations of Europe contended for the crown of divine election, they viewed the Jews with hostility—for how could France, or any other nation, claim to be the chosen people without denying the claim of the original chosen people? A truly universal Church had in theory an interest in supporting the Jews' claim to election, in order to suppress nationalist heresies, and insist that people of all other nationalities could be saved only through rebirth into the People of God.[14] But from the bloody wholesale conversions of the pagan tribes in the Dark Ages, through the compromise with modern nationalism in the seventeenth century, up to modern times, the Church made its peace with pagan nationalism. And welcome as was this message of John Paul II, and its reiteration by Benedict XVI, the damage that national idolatry had inflicted upon European Christianity could not be undone.

Contending Understandings of Election, and the Ruin of Europe

The Catholic project of universal empire founded on a universal Church had always been a vision, never a reality. Charlemagne's empire embracing France and Germany endured less than a century; the later Holy Roman Empire was only a federation of German states. But at the end of the fifteenth century, that empire came close to ruling Europe. Through astute diplomacy and lucky dynastic marriages, the Hapsburg family ascended to the thrones of Spain and Austria as well as Burgundy (including Holland). As Holy Roman Emperor, moreover, Maximilian I was the nominal sovereign of the Germans. His grandson the Emperor Charles V inherited the Spanish throne of the Catholic Kings Ferdinand and Isabella through their granddaughter, Juana "the Mad." A single dynasty allied to the Church in effect controlled all of Europe's major countries except England and France. Never had the prospect of unified Church and Empire appeared so close to fruition. The Church's sense of triumph occasioned the rebuilding of Rome during the late fifteenth and early sixteenth centuries as a symbol of imperial authority.

Under the surface, however, the poisoned legacy of the pagan conversions remained intact. Instead of uniting under the expanded reach of the empire, Europe exploded. The German princes, resisting the new hegemony of the Hapsburgs, turned a reform movement within the Church into a schism. Germany fractured along the old border between Rome and Germany; the Roman south and west remained Catholic, and the lately Christianized north and east became Protestant. Where Charlemagne had beheaded 4,500 pagan Saxon nobles in 782 to establish his new Christian empire, the Saxon King Frederick the Wise gave protection to the dissenting monk Martin Luther and fostered a competing Christian religion. The challenge to the authority of the Church teased to the surface the old national ambitions that the Church never had purged from among its Gentile converts. The Reformation in Germany and the English break with Vatican authority under Henry VIII served the political aims of the princes, and French Catholicism itself was eventually reduced to an instrument of Gallic ambitions.

In 1534, Henry VIII of England broke with Rome and made himself head of the Church of England—and it should not surprise us that such sixteenth-century apologists as John Foxe in his *Book of Martyrs* defended Henry's schism with the claim that England was a "peculiar" nation chosen by Providence for its purposes.[15] The trope continued for hundreds of years. John Milton wrote in his 1644 *Areopagitica* that England is a "nation chosen before any other … a nation of prophets, of sages, and of worthies." In 1719, the dissenting Protestant minister Isaac Watts published a popular edition of the Psalms in which he substituted the name "Great Britain" for every instance of the word "Israel."[16]

The Church's compromise with the Gentile nations it brought into Christendom could only have a tragic outcome. Of all the manifestations of national idolatry in Europe, the most virulent strain was French. Religious wars consumed France during the sixteenth century; the country achieved political stability only when the Protestant Henry IV of Navarre ended the conflict by converting to Catholicism on taking the throne in 1589. When war broke out between Catholic Austria and Germany's Protestant princes, France determined to prolong the conflict until the Germans had bled out. Not merely the temporal interests of the French state but the impassioned belief in the Election of France motivated Richelieu and

Tremblay to prolong the religious wars of the 1620s for thirty years, killing a vast proportion of the population of central Europe. It is hard to believe French interests were merely dynastic, as in the standard account. King Louis XIII, who reigned 1610–1643, was incapable of ruling; he was a puppet, handicapped by a congenital speech impediment and a propensity to homosexual masochism. Richelieu governed France until his death in 1642, when his picked successor, the Italian adventurer Cardinal Mazarin, succeeded him. (The historian Anthony Levi has presented convincing documentary evidence that Mazarin was the father of Louis XVI.)[17]

If the Thirty Years' War was genuinely a Catholic-against-Protestant religious war, France as the most powerful Catholic country should have supported Catholic Austria. But the French could not abide the claim of the Austrian and Spanish Hapsburg dynasties to the imperial title and the claim to represent Christendom. France set out instead to ruin Austria and Spain and establish the French claim to be God's proxy on earth. To modern ears it sounds mad, and improbable. But the madness of the conflict itself, which dragged on for fifteen years after the Protestants were defeated and reduced huge stretches of Europe to cannibalism, testifies to the mad national mysticism that motivated the contending leaders.

The French clerics bribed and manipulated Protestant and Catholic alike to extend the conflict, intervening directly when suitable proxies were not handy. In 1625 the Austrian Emperor Ferdinand II engaged a minor Bohemian nobleman, Albrecht Wenzel Eusebius von Wallenstein, to raise an army which grew to an unprecedented one hundred thousand men that would pay itself by living off the land. Wallenstein's mercenary army recruited adventurers from Scotland to Croatia and overwhelmed the Protestant resistance. It also caused mass starvation within Austria and among its Catholic allies. At the 1630 Imperial Congress at Regensburg, France's Father Joseph de Tremblay persuaded Austria's allies, including Bavaria, which had suffered horribly from Wallenstein's scavengers, to force Ferdinand to dismiss Wallenstein in 1630 in order to give his Swedish proxies a free hand.

"While the Imperial Diet was in session," Huxley notes in his biography of Father Joseph, "there had poured into Ratisbon, from every corner of Germany, an unending stream of supplicants.... Among these supplicants was a group of delegates from Pomerania.... In the preceding year, Wallenstein's armies had stripped the country so effectively that the people had been starving ever since. Since...those who survived were eating grass and roots—yes, and young children and the sick and even the newly buried dead. This seems to have been one of the first occasions, during the Thirty Years' War when public attention was called to the enforced cannibalism which was to become so horrifyingly common in Germany of those disastrous years. And yet du Tremblay and Richelieu pursued the war for nearly two more decades. With full knowledge of what had already happened in Pomerania, du Tremblay continued to advocate a course of action that must positively guarantee the spread of cannibalism to other provinces."[18]

By 1635, Austria—at terrible cost—had crushed the Protestant resistance once again. But then Richelieu sent two hundred thousand troops into Germany to fight on the Protestant side. Spain responded with its own forces, and the second half of the Thirty Years' War turned into a war of attrition between Catholic Spain and France, fought mainly on German soil. Huxley wondered how a Capuchin monk who awoke daily at four a.m. for two hours' worth of spiritual exercises in "self-annihilation" could justify "pursuing, patiently and with consummate skill, a policy which could only increase the sufferings of the poor he had promised to serve."

For Richelieu and du Tremblay, patriotic fervor "had been rationalized into a religious principle by means of the old crusading faith in the divine mission of France and the divine right of kings...."[19] "One wonders what went on in the friar's mind during those daily periods of recollection when, examining his thoughts and actions, he prepared himself for what his master in mysticism called the 'passive annihilation of mental prayer.' First, no doubt, and all the time, he reminded himself that, in working for France, he was doing God's external will. *Gesta Dei per Francos* was an axiom, from which it followed that France was divine, and those who worked for French greatness were God's instruments, and that the means they employed could not but be in accord with God's will."[20]

The Spaniards of the seventeenth century were men of high intelligence, profound culture, and religious passion. They believed with conviction that they were doing God's work. Spain's Prime Minister, the brilliant Count-Duke of Olivares, had Velasquez paint his equestrian portrait and the surrender of Breda. The sublime love-poet Francisco de Quevedo, whose sonnets compare to Petrarch's, served as private secretary to King Philip IV during the final and most destructive phase of the Thirty Years' War. Philip IV spoke five languages and made his own translations of Renaissance political theorists. These were brilliant and courageous men—whose defining flaw was the same sort of national megalomania that possessed Cardinal Richelieu and Father Joseph du Tremblay.

Like the French, Olivares and the Spanish court believed that Spain was the nation chosen by God as His proxy on earth. The monk and political theorist Juan de Salazar wrote in his 1619 treatise *Política Espanola* that "the Spanish were elected to realize the New Testament just as Israel had been elected to realize the Old Testament. The miracles with which Providence had favored Spanish policy confirmed this analogy of the Spanish people to the Jewish people, so that 'the similarity of events in all epochs, and the singular fashion in which God has maintained the election and governance of the Spanish people, declare it to be his chosen people by law of grace, just as the other was his elect in the times of Scripture.... From this it is proper to conclude from actual circumstances as well as sacred Scripture that the Spanish monarchy will endure for many centuries and will be the last monarchy.'"[21] According to Stanley Payne, this reflected "a not uncommon attitude at court and among part of the Castilian elite."[22]

The passion that drove Richelieu and Olivares was the mad, bad conviction that unspeakable and inhuman actions were justified by the goal of building a New Jerusalem where the gendarmes spoke French or Spanish, as the case might be.

Under Olivares, Spain's war policy sought to crush Dutch Protestantism at all costs. Spain might have overrun the Dutch except for one circumstance: underneath its gilded exterior, Spain was rotten. The population of Castile, the center of Spain and home province of the Spanish Queen, had shrunk by a quarter during the first two decades of the seventeenth century because of plague, emigration, expulsion of the Moriscos (converted Muslims), and war. Holland's smaller but better navy, meanwhile, cut off the maritime resupply of Spanish land forces and raided the Spanish treasure fleets from the New World. And all the time Spain was spending its last strength in a ferocious duel with Catholic France; the German Protestant cause had been crushed by 1634, but the Thirty Years' War dragged on until 1648 as the French and Spanish continued to fight over the corpse of central Europe.

The old regime of Church and Empire had disintegrated into a Catholic-on-Catholic religious war within which Europe's nations pursued their own grandeur to the point of mutual annihilation. Ultimately it was a war not between the Catholic and Protestant wings of Christianity, but between the respective ambitions of the French and Spanish to be the chosen people of God. And Europe's one successful experiment in republican government and religious toleration was crushed under the pressures of war. Holland was simply too small a platform on which to launch such a radical experiment. The Pilgrims made the peril-fraught decision to decamp to the New World. The seed-crystal of a different kind of Christianity made its way to America. It now has the better part of a billion adherents around the world.

Within the Protestant camp, a radical fringe had rankled at the princes' cooption of the reform movement into a vehicle for secular ambitions. The radicals espoused a primitive Christianity that they believed to hark back to the early Church before Constantine. They emphasized the conversion of the individual soul as a matter of conscience, rather than the imposition of Christianity from the top down. That is why the issue of adult baptism so preoccupied the Protestant radicals. The Anabaptists objected to child baptism on the grounds that only an individual of the age of reason could make a personal decision to follow Christ.

The theology of adult baptism had its parallel in ecclesiology. If the Catholic Church, as it professes, holds the key that can unlock what is locked in heaven, then its power to save lies in the authority of St. Peter as handed down by apostolic succession to his successors, the bishops and their priests. The individual is not saved by an inexplicable act of grace in direct relation to God (Calvin) or by an act of will to accept that grace (Arminius), but by education and instruction within the Church, and by the performance of sacramental acts by priests who hold the keys. The Protestants insisted that each individual must undergo a personal rebirth into the community of Jesus Christ; they denied that any earthly institution can pronounce a person free of sin.

Two modes of Christian life were in contest. One subordinated the peoples incorporated into Christendom to the authority of a unifying empire, leaving intact much of their pagan heritage; the other attempted to create an entirely new people from *individuals* called from out of the nations. Ultimately this bifurcation in Christianity does not fit into the simple categories of Catholic versus Protestant. No Christian churches were more tainted by nationalism than the Protestant state churches of Germany that became established after the Treaty of Westphalia. Germany's official Protestant churches, despite the dissension of a minority that included Karl Barth and Dietrich Bonhöffer, folded themselves into the Nazi regime in 1933. In the vision of the Gospels and the early Church Fathers, Christianity was the people Israel, into which Gentiles were adopted as individuals, through water and the Holy Spirit.

As long as it coincided with their dynastic ambitions, the Hapsburgs kept their commitment to a universal Catholic Church and a single Christian empire, self-serving as it may have appeared to the enemies of the Austrian-Spanish alliance. But until its fall in 1918, the Austro-Hungarian rump of the old empire remained only a fragment of multinational governance in reduced circumstances.

It took the Russians and the Germans until the nineteenth and twentieth centuries, respectively, to conclude that they were God's chosen nation.

The roots of Russian national messianism go back to 1510, when the monk Philoteus of Pskov proclaimed to the Russian royal house, "Two Romes have fallen. The third stands. And there will be no fourth. No one shall replace your Christian Empire!" Not until the middle of the nineteenth century, though, when Russia began its long duel with Germany over control of the failing Ottoman territories, did Russia's supposed divine election become a political factor. Russian Orthodox Slavophiles persuaded themselves that Holy Russia was chosen by God to save the world during the middle of the nineteenth century. In *The Demons,* Dostoyevsky puts his own Slavophile view into the mouth of his character Shatov, who insists that Christ was Russian. Accused of making God a mere "attribute of nationality," Shatov replies, "On the contrary, I raise the nation up to God…. The nation is the body of God…. If a great nation does not believe that it alone is able and called to resurrect and save everyone with its truth, then it at once ceases to be a great nation and becomes just ethnographic material…. It is Russia's mission to save the world: The only God-bearing nation is the Russian nation." Catholicism, Shatov added, "is worse than atheism."

Germany was the last European nation to stumble on the idea of its own election, but the Germans took to national self-idolatry with a vengeance. Leading German Lutheran theologian Ernst Tröltsch proclaimed in 1903, "The great religious movement of modern times, the reawakened need for religions, develops outside the churches, and by and large outside theology as well…. The German faith is a faith in the inner moral and spiritual content of Germanness, the faith of the Germans in themselves, in their future, in their world mission."[23] If Germany was to be the chosen people, then of course the Jews could not possibly be. As Michael Geyer and Hartmut Lehmann observe, "If the Jews were the people that the Germans wanted to become under Protestant leadership, then they could hardly be included as an integral component of the nation."[24]

Germany fought the First World War under the banner of its own *Kultur*. "On October 4, 1914, two months into the Great War, ninety-three German intellectuals published ... the Manifesto of the Ninety-Three, addressed 'An die Kulturwelt' (To the Civilized World), in which they ... made it clear they viewed the war not as a campaign against German militarism but above all as an assault on German culture," historian Peter Watson recounts. Among the ninety-three signatories were physicist Max Planck, the painter Max Liebermann, and William Wundt, the founder of experimental psychology. This exaggerated sense of cultural importance—and affliction—had wide currency in Germany. Also in 1914, Thomas Mann enthused about Germany's "indispensable role as missionary," defending German *Kultur* against the superficial *Zivilisation* of the West. Two years later Max Weber wrote, "It would be shameful if we lacked the courage to ensure that neither Russian barbarism nor French grandiloquence ruled the world. That is why this war is being fought."[25] This sad conflation of *Kultur* with national greatness condemned German intellectuals to perdition. In a 1933 play, the future Nazi poet laureate Hans Johst had his stage protagonist declare, "When I hear *Kultur* I release the safety catch on my Browning." Once German *Kultur* had become an ersatz religion, the way was clear for the Nazis to substitute the idolatry of blood for the idolatry of mind. Hitler's "Master People" (*Herrenvolk*) caricatured the idea of Israel's Chosen People. Hitler used biblical imagery in his speeches to evoke the notion of German election.[26]

After two World Wars, the Europeans had failed at being Christians and failed at being pagans. Their culture failed tragically—which is to say that the flaws built into European culture at its founding ultimately brought it to ruin.

CHAPTER 12

WHY SOME RELIGION FAILS IN THE MODERN WORLD

Islam at the beginning of the twenty-first century offers the most extreme illustration of a crisis of faith brought on by the confrontation with modernity. But Islam is hardly unique in this respect. A few pockets of the industrial world resisted the twin trends of secularization and infertility shift until the 1970s or 1980s—and then imploded. These anomalies bear close scrutiny as exceptions that reinforce the rule. Ireland, Spain, Poland, and Canada's Quebec province identified their Catholic faith with nationalist resistance to external (and sometimes internal) enemies. When the passions associated with the national cause dissipated, these pockets of faith and fertility made the transition to modernity in a remarkably brief interval. In fact, the demographic experience of these pockets of Catholic resistance is the closest thing that we have to a precedent for the demographic freeze in the Muslim world today. Religion founded on ethnic identity failed in the face of the new freedom, while faith sustained by individual conscience survived the transition to modernity and continues to flourish.

That is the substance of Spengler's Universal Law #21: *If you believe in yourself, you're probably whoring after strange gods.*

The fertile pockets were outliers in the Catholic world, where the conceit of ethnic election lingered on until the last quarter of the twentieth century. Patriots in countries resisting external oppression had long made the Catholic Church a bastion of national resistance, and the heroism of their political martyrs was equalled by the quiet courage of the womb. Canada's French-speaking province of Quebec, annexed by Britain a decade before the American Revolution, clung to its Catholicism in defiance of the Anglophone Canadian majority. In its long struggle for independence from Protestant Britain, Ireland found solace and solidarity in its Catholic faith, as did Poland in its fight to cast off the yoke of Orthodox Russia. A special case is Spain, whose 1936–1939 Civil War saw a Russian-supported leftist government that persecuted the Catholic Church opposed by a clerically supported nationalism allied to fascist Germany and Italy. The Catholic resistance succeeded—and in each case, political victory begat national failure. The downward spiral of fertility in the rest of the industrial world overtook the little tide pools of faith, and religious observance fell to the minimal levels observed elsewhere in the industrial world.

Secular scholars note the close correlation between fertility and faith. But faith is a moving target. Faith rooted in blood and soil weakens when people step out of traditional society into the modern world. By contrast, faith based on individual conscience can and does thrive in modernity— although in the industrial world, it thrives in the social mainstream today only in the United States and Israel.

Fertility in Strongly Catholic Countries

	Ireland	Spain	Poland	Europe
1965	4.0	2.9	2.7	2.6
2010	2.0	1.4	1.3	1.5
Change	-2.0	-1.5	-1.4	-1.1

Source: United Nations World Population Prospects

The European woman bore two or three children during the 1950s, but now has one or two. Europe's fertility rate, that is, fell from around 2.5 to around 1.5. That's one child fewer per woman. But Irish fertility has dropped by two children per woman, Polish fertility by 2.5 children per woman, and Spanish fertility by 1.5 children per woman—much farther than the European norm.

Quebec: The Final Bastion of French Messianism

Gesta Dei per Francos, the French credo of national chosenness, rang hollow in the France of 1927. With 5 million dead and wounded in the First World War, the worst toll of any Western European combatant, France had lost the will to fight. But the dream was not everywhere extinguished. "Tell our cousins that on the shores of our great river, you have seen the heart of France. We want to keep our language and our rights because we hope for the future, for the day for which we sigh, when we will have a state, not only autonomous, but independent. Who knows whether one day, we in America will not be called to continue the French tradition, 'Gesta Dei per Francos'!"[1] The speaker was Monsignor Alfred-Odilon Comtois, bishop of

Three Rivers in Quebec City from 1934 to his death in 1945. During his tenure and well afterwards, Quebec was more Catholic and more fecund than any province in the industrial world. In 1960 attendance at mass was 88 percent, the highest in the Catholic world, and the average Quebecoise had four children. By the 1980s the fertility rate had fallen to just 1.5, and Mass attendance to 20 percent.

Quebec's "Quiet Revolution" shows the fragility of ethnic faith encountering modernity. Father Lionel Groulx (1878–1967), the father of Quebec nationalism and the editor of its journal *Action Française,* "was not only a believer but a priest," writes Gilles Gougeon. "Religion, for him, was the highest value; it ranked at the top of his scale of values. Religion was more than simply one factor among others—Groulx was convinced that God was the master of history. Religion illuminated everything else; it was the norm, in a way; and it served as the measuring stick for his nationalism. Groulx always wanted to situate his nationalism within Catholic orthodoxy."[2] Groulx's faith was founded on the Frankish messianism of Richelieu. To be French, he wrote, "is in essence to be a Crusader country"; the French Canadian pioneers who cleared the northern forests were imbued with the "Crusader spirit." French Quebec would wield the same "dazzling sword brandished bravely by Roland," on behalf of "Catholic faith and French language," the vehicles of "the Apostolic mission that conquers and civilizes."[3] French-Canadians of the 1930s may have scratched out a living from half-frozen land and slathered maple syrup on their bacon, but they produced big families and turned up unfailingly to Mass, and Groulx saw in them the heirs of the Frankish Crusaders. A recent monograph cites Groulx's "belief in the alleged role of Apostolic French-Canadians as a people chosen by God to spread the Catholic faith on the North American continent," a form of "French messianism."[4]

In retrospect, Groulx's grandiosity sounds delusional. But Quebec *was* unique. "For almost one and one-half-centuries, between 1711 and 1850, the crude birth rate in Quebec stayed above 50 per thousand. Such levels of fertility are nowhere to be found in the history of European societies—or even among contemporary developing nations. Although by the early part of the 1900s, there had been some fertility declines, the fertility rate of Quebec still exceeded that of Canada by a notable margin," reports a recent study. High fertility stemmed in part from the fact that "until 1960, Quebec remained an essentially rural and traditional society...with the exceptions of Montreal and Quebec City, Quebec remained largely rural-agrarian well until before the outbreak of the Second World War."[5] Even more important is the Quebecers' loyalty to the Catholic Church, their bastion against an Anglophone Canada into which they were incorporated by conquest. "The Church had a central role in promoting a pronatalist agenda."[6]

When the French-Canadians emerged from the cocoon of traditional society during the last quarter of the twentieth century, it all fell apart—and in less than one generation. Not only did fertility fall by nearly two-thirds. "By 1982, more than 42 percent of Quebec men and women still in their reproductive ages had undergone voluntary sterilization. Moreover, in the period 1978-1998, abortion increased from 17.9 per 100 live births to 41. The 1998 figure is in fact much higher than the ratio for the same year in Canada as a whole."[7]

Quebecois nationalism died hard. In 1968, even as Quebec's fertility collapse was becoming apparent, the pro-independence Parti Quebecois (PQ) headed by René Lévesque formed out of a merger of independence movements. The PQ formed Quebec's provincial government in 1976 and dominated provincial politics until the late 1990s. In 1980, the PQ introduced a referendum on the subject of Quebec sovereignty, but it was rejected by three-fifths of the voters. Brought to a vote again in 1995, independence lost by a single percentage point. That was the high tide of French-Canadian nationalism. By the end of the nineties, voter sentiment had shifted decisively away from the PQ, whose percentage of the popular vote fell from 43 percent to only 33 percent in 1998. The people of Quebec no longer care.

Poland, "The Christ Among the Nations"

When Pope John Paul II kissed the tarmac at Warsaw Airport in 1979 on arrival for his historic papal visit, Polish families still had between two and three children, a decline from the three-to-four-child average of the 1950s, but still one of the highest birth rates in the industrial world. A generation later, the average Polish woman has 1.25 children, among the very lowest rates in the world.

The newly elected pope spoke of his love for the land of his birth, "Poland, which throughout the course of history has been linked with the Church of Christ and the See of Rome by a special bond of spiritual unity."[8] John Paul II, to be sure, eschewed the national martyr complex that prevailed in some parts of the Polish Church, and his personal circle warned sharply against reading Poland's story as a form of salvation history.[9] Nonetheless Polish nationalism had inextricable messianic roots.

Polish Catholics indulged in a different sort of messianism from the triumphalist French. The Poles were God's martyrs, rather than His conquerors.

> Poland, according to this view, is a place of especially brazen attacks of evil, but she was made fit for martyrdom by special favors. Just as it suffices to be a Christian to expose oneself to persecution (Matthew 10:17–33; 24:9), so it suffices to be a Pole to suffer various torments.... Poland is "Golgotha" or the "Christ of nations."... Golgotha was the condition of Resurrection; the martyrology of the Poles has the same end—it will lead to a new life. This will be a new life for all of Europe: "And on the third day the soul will return to the body, and the nation will rise up from the dead and liberate all of the peoples of Europe from captivity.... And just as bloody sacrifices on earth came to an end with the Resurrection of Christ, so wars in Christianity will cease with the resurrection of the Polish nation," wrote Adam Mickiewicz (1798-1865), the Poles' national poet, in 1832.[10]

At the climax of the Cold War, Poland seemed to fulfill Mickiewicz's dictum, "Polska Chrystusem narodów" ("Poland is the Christ of the nations"). In the struggles of the free trade unions and the Church against Communist occupation, the Poles seemed to be Europe's martyrs. Today they are Europe's plumbers, and each man sits unafraid beneath his own vine and fig tree, unencumbered by children.

Soviet domination had imposed alien cultural patterns and an open battle with religion. As John Paul II's biographer George Weigel writes, "The Communist regime was not satisfied with dominating every aspect of Poland's political and economic life. Its broader cultural agenda was to inculcate an atheistic ideology and a rereading of Poland's national history that severed the link between Polish nationalism and Polish Catholicism."[11] In the common thinking, "to be a Pole" meant "to be a believer," most often "to be a Catholic." The stereotype "Pole-Catholic" functioned as a safeguard of national identity.[12]

"The formal resumption of Polish statehood [after World War I] began in church," writes Neal Pease, as "the fledgling Second Polish Republic marked the convocation of its first parliament, or Sejm, with an inaugural Roman Catholic high mass.... In its symbolic union of church and state, this set piece of official pageantry neatly echoed the litany of historical axioms that commentators habitually cited—and cite to this day, for that matter—to prove the indomitable Catholicity of the Poles throughout the ages and the natural affinity of Catholicism with Polish patriotism."[13] Polish resistance centered in the Catholic Church was decisive for Western victory in the Cold War. But Poland's Catholic culture—and fecundity—did not long survive that victory.

In 1994, just after the fall of Communism, Poland was miserably poor, with per capita GDP of about $2,700, about the same as present-day Egypt—and the average Polish woman still bore two or three children. Today Poland has joined the ranks of the modern industrial world with per capita GDP nearly ten times as high—and the average Polish woman has one child. With fertility at only 1.25 children, Poland has become one of the most child-hostile countries in the world. At present rates the Polish population will fall by nearly a quarter between now and the middle of the century, and two-fifths of Poles will be over the age of sixty. Put another way, Poland will have only half as many women of child-bearing age in 2050, which means that its population will fall catastrophically through the remainder of the century. By 2100, the nation whose faith and heroism won the Cold War may have ceased to exist as a viable state.

The only case comparable to Poland's might be that of Hungary, whose Catholic Church remained a beacon of resistance during the long Soviet occupation, and whose uprising in 1956 was the first crack in Communist control of Eastern Europe. Officially Hungary's fertility rate is 1.4 children per woman, but unpublished government studies indicate that the Roma (Gypsy) minority, now just a tenth of the overall population, accounts for between 30 and 35 percent of all Hungarian births.[14] If so, the fertility rate for ethnic Hungarians would be less than one, the lowest in the world.

The Wearing Out of the Green

Ireland's struggle for independence was inseparable from the struggle of the Catholic Church for emancipation. "The Catholic Church is a national church, and if the people rally with me they will have a nation for a Church," said the nineteenth-century leader Daniel O'Connell, the father of Irish independence. An historian comments, "The identification of Catholicism with Irish nationalism had arisen in Ireland during the late eighteenth and early nineteenth centuries. The movement that consolidated that identification was Daniel O'Connell's campaign for Catholic emancipation from civil disabilities in the 1820s and his crusade in the 1830s to repeal the Act of Union which had incorporated Ireland into the United Kingdom by abolishing the Irish legislature. In part, the connection between this movement and Catholicism was a natural result of the parish clergy's active role as local organizers in both the emancipation and repeal movements."[15] There were other, non-sectarian visions of Irish nationhood, from the Marxist universalism of James Connelly to the Celtic mysticism of William Butler Yeats, but the Irish state formed after 1922 was founded on the Church. The former revolutionaries who formed the first governments of the Irish Free State after independence were eager to establish their Catholic credentials and gave the Church a dominant role in primary and secondary education.[16]

Mary Eberstadt notes that the faith of the Irish is flagging, with Mass attendance down from 91 percent in 1973 to only 34 percent in 2005. "Numerous familiar explanations have been offered for this especially speedy collapse in religiosity: rising prosperity, lowered taxes, urbanization, and the rest of the secularization script," she wrote in 2007. "But what these explanations overlook is perhaps the most obvious contributing cause of all. Not only has Irish religiosity been anomalous in the speed of its collapse; so too was Irish fertility. Essentially, the Irish stopped having babies and families—and shortly afterward stopped going to church."[17] Just as in Quebec and Poland, the fertility of Catholic-nationalist Ireland dropped precipitously. In 1965 Irish women had four children. By 2010, that number had been halved.

The Sudden Death of Spanish Religion

Of all modern states, Spain under Francisco Franco most openly melded nationalism and Catholic faith. "The synthesis of nationalism and Catholicism was accomplished in a continuous, solemn, and repetitive fashion by the civil and military authorities of the regime," writes Rafael Gómez Pérez.[18] "The identification of the regime in terms of direct continuity with the Crusaders did not seem an arbitrary construction. It was grounded in the historic fact of the religious persecution against Catholic individuals and institutions unleashed during various periods of the Second Republic and during the Civil War. On the other hand, the Franco regime from its inception joined the tasks of national and Catholic reconstruction." Spanish fertility began its plunge from the highest level in Europe to among the lowest in 1975, the year Franco died.

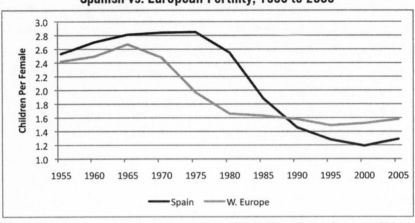

Spanish vs. European Fertility, 1955 to 2005

Source: United Nations Population Division

Most striking about Spain's fertility transition is the extreme suddenness with which it transpired. Until the mid-1970s, Spanish women still bore nearly three children on average, while the rest of Western Europe had already shifted to the one-child family. After Franco's death, Spain's fertility fell to the highest by far in Western Europe to the lowest in Western Europe in just twenty years, the most extreme turn away from family life observed anywhere in the world—until Iran's population plunge of the past fifteen years.

The fortresses of faith of the 1960s all disintegrated, as the late Cardinal Avery Dulles told the *Atlantic*'s Paul Elie in January 2006. "The breakdown of traditional societies and the indifference of modern people to religious faith have left us with a burden of re-evangelization. Quebec is a desert. Ireland is very nearly lost to posterity.... With [American] society's freedom of choice come our selfishness and competition, which are now being exported all over the world. We are not immune to the forces of secularization that are being felt in Europe. Is the Christian residue in America strong enough to resist them? I worry that it is not."

It may seem unfair to blame American sensibilities for the erosion of traditional society, but there is a great deal of truth to Cardinal Dulles' view.

Globalization—the integration of the most remote populations of the world into a single economic web—began with America's economic resurgence during the 1980s.

PART THREE

WHY IT WON'T BE A POST-AMERICAN WORLD

CHAPTER 13

PASSING THE ACID
TEST OF MODERNITY

Among the large industrial countries, there is one great exception to the declinist story: the United States. If a single characteristic makes America exceptional, it is the fact that American fertility has stabilized at replacement. In other words, as Europe and Japan reach the point of no return on the road to senility and depopulation, America will maintain its population, along with a healthy balance among age cohorts. In the second half of this century most of the great powers of the past—Germany, Spain, Italy, Russia, and Japan, among others—will cease to function. A century later they will have ceased to exist. What makes America utterly and completely exceptional among the industrial countries, in short, is that it will still be here in a hundred years.

It is not that Americans in general are having children, but that Americans of faith are having children, and there are more Americans of faith than citizens of any other industrial country. According to a 2002 survey by the Pew Research Institute, 59 percent of Americans said that religion was important to them, against 11 percent in France, 21 percent in Germany, 27 percent in Italy, 33 percent in Great Britain, and 36 percent in Poland.[1] In both Europe and America, people who practice a religion have far more children than those who do not. It's just that there are far more Americans than Europeans practicing a faith.

Thomas Frejka and Charles Westoff of Germany's Max Planck Institute[2] observe that half of American women in their childbearing years (ages 18–44) say that religion is "very important" to them, against fewer than one out of six European women. The close link between faith and fertility applies to Europeans as well as Americans, Frejka and Westoff report. The table below is adapted from their research:

Mean Number of Children Born to Women Aged 18–44 by Frequency of Religious Observation

Attend Religious Services:	U.S.	Europe
More than once a week	2.34	2.74
Once a week	2.17	2.23
One to three times a month	2.12	1.93
Less than once a month	1.86	1.83
Never	1.7	1.79

Surveys of individual attitudes throughout Europe make clear that religious commitment explains a great deal about fertility. That is one way to slice the data. Another is to compare the degree of religious commitment among European countries with their respective fertility rates. In 2007 the Gallup Poll asked more than one thousand individuals in each of forty European countries whether religion was important in their lives. Religious commitment does not explain all of the fertility differences among these countries. Other factors are important, including the presence of immigrant populations from developing countries with a cultural propensity for larger families, government subsidies to encourage fertility, and so forth. Nonetheless, religious differences explain a great deal of the variation among the European countries (and the explanation is statistically significant at a very high level of confidence).

European Countries:
Fertility vs. Importance of Religion[3]

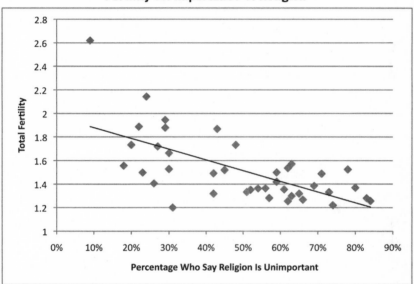

Source: World Church Database; CIA World Factbook

If we look more closely at the sources of American fertility, it is clear from available data that Americans of faith are far more likely to raise large families than secular Americans. Each year the General Social Survey (GSS) at the University of Chicago interviews thousands of Americans and compiles the results. It records family and employment characteristics, and—among many other variables—religious attitudes and practice. GSS allows researchers to compare a demographic variable, for example, number of children per individual, with religious attitudes:

- One of three families with no children says it is "not religious." The proportion falls to just one out of eight among families with four children.

- Among American families with no children, 41 percent say grace before meals. But 62 percent of families with four children say grace, and 86 percent of families with eight or more children.

- Forty-five percent of Americans with no children "strongly agree" that there is a "God who watches over me." But 80 percent of adults with four children "strongly agree" with this belief.

- Half of families that never take part in religious activities have no children, but only a third of families with three children do not practice a religion.[4]

Religion and American Fertility

Almost as extreme as the fertility gap between religious and secular Americans is the one between members of mainline Protestant denominations and evangelicals. "White fundamentalist Protestants" who attend services weekly show a fertility rate 27 percent higher than the national average,[5] that is, about 2.7 children. Episcopalians and Presbyterians average only 1.3 children per female. Why evangelical Protestants of European stock have large families while their cousins in mainline Protestant denominations have small families or none at all cannot be explained by differences in their respective gene pools.

There is so much migration among Protestant denominations—largely out of the old mainline churches into more devout evangelical denominations—that statistics cannot produce a freeze-frame of Protestant fertility. But the Global Social Survey data encompassing all religions make the case plainly enough.

When children become a cost rather than an asset, prospective parents must identify with something beyond their own needs in order to sustain child rearing. Given modern pension and social security systems, raising children is an economic cost to the parents and an economic benefit only to society at large. In the modern welfare state, child rearing is an act of altruism. Secular culture tells us to dedicate our lives to meeting our own needs. The therapeutic view of the human character has no way to explain altruism, unless, of course, in the case that helping others happens to make us feel better about ourselves. Pragmatic philosophy has nothing to say on the subject. Richard Rorty, the most prominent of modern pragmatists, famously said, "There is no answer to the question, 'Why not be cruel?' There is no noncircular theoretical backup for the belief that cruelty is horrible."[6] There is also no answer to the question, "Why have children?" Why not spend the nearly quarter of a million dollars that it costs to bring the average American child to the age of seventeen on the pursuit of perpetual youth—on vacations, fashion, and plastic surgery?

Church Membership

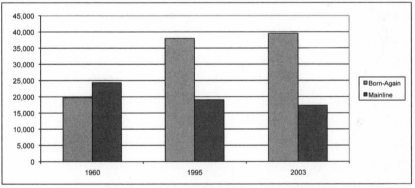

Source: 2005 Yearbook of American and Canadian Churches

Plainly, societies cannot exist without altruism. In the extreme case they could not defend themselves against external threats unless some of their members were willing to die in order to preserve their society. Richard

Dawkins and other self-styled New Atheists postulate that humankind evolved a genetic predisposition to altruism. This assertion is something of a flying spaghetti monster. Among all American ethnic groups, Jews share the most consistent gene pool—as studies have established beyond question—the result of two thousand years of marrying within the same community. Yet secular Jews show the least altruism—at least in the form of willingness to raise children—of any group of Americans, while religious Jews show one of the highest degrees of altruism by the same measure. A religious explanation of altruism, not a genetic one, fits the facts. People of faith believe that God loves them as a father loves his children, and that they should love their children as God loves us. They believe that God created us out of love, and that by bringing more human beings into the world, we imitate God and act as his partners in creation.

On *average*, pessimists like Oswald Spengler were right. Most of the denominations that once defined American Protestantism in particular and American religion in general—Presbyterians, Methodists, Episcopalians, Lutherans, Baptists—have declined, and their remaining members are less committed to religion as well as to family life. Nine-tenths of American Jews belong to the liberal denominations (Reform and Conservative) or to none at all. A generation ago, the Orthodox Jews seemed like a vanishing remnant of old country life. An observer looking at the configuration of American religion circa 1970 well might have forecast the end of faith in America, for the churches and synagogues that embodied faith at that moment in time were in decline. But the fervor of the evangelical Protestants, Pentecostals, and others has filled the vacuum left by the mainline denominations, and Jewish Orthodoxy is growing rapidly, in part by attracting adherents from liberal denominations, but mostly through its own fecundity. Although traditionally observant Jews remain a small minority in terms of overall numbers, a third of synagogue-going Jews below the age of thirty attend Orthodox services.

That is why the world's population outlook is not as bleak as the forecasts make it appear. Two cultures are contending at the family level throughout the world: secular modernity and renewed faith. Secular families have few children and religious families have many. That means that in each generation, religious families will increase in number and secular families will diminish. We do not know how many children raised in religious families will cleave to the faith of their parents, to be sure; the blandishments of hedonism will always be there. But it is possible that self-selection will reverse the fertility collapse of the industrial world at least in those countries that have not passed a demographic point of no return.

According to one school of thought, America is only the leper with the most fingers. America's overall fertility rate of 2.1 children per female remains at replacement. Among the non-Hispanic white population, some critics claim, falling fertility will lead to shrinking numbers, while Hispanic fertility of 3.0 will lead to changes in the composition of the American population. The Census Bureau projects that Hispanics will rise from 15 percent of the U.S. population in 2010 to 24 percent in 2050, while the non-Hispanic white population will fall from 65 percent of the population to 50 percent over the same period.

Assimilating Hispanic immigrants is a challenge, to be sure; whether it is a greater challenge than assimilating past waves of immigrants remains to be seen. Even without the Hispanics, though, the American population would continue to rise. According to the Census Bureau, the non-Hispanic white population of the U.S. will rise from 201 million in 2010 to 210 million in 2050. Compare that to a 25 percent drop in the Japanese population and a 10 percent drop in the European population between 2010 and 2050, which the United Nations data base projects under the assumption of unchanged fertility. And that doesn't take into account the increasing proportion of people of faith in America, and the snowball effect which will likely lead to larger family size among the non-Hispanic white population.

Number of Women Aged 15–49 Years (Year 2000 = 100)

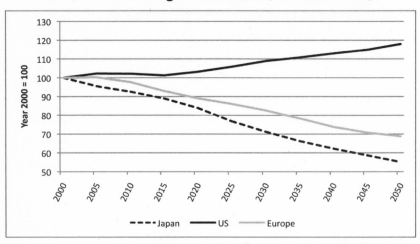

Source: United Nations Population Program (Constant Fertility Scenario)

America faces challenges. Europe and Japan face a point of no return. By the middle of this century, we see in the chart above, the number of prospective mothers (women aged 15 to 49 years) will have fallen by a third in Europe and by half in Japan. No matter what Europe and Japan do afterwards, their populations must continue to decline (except through immigration), because there simply will not be enough women in the population pool to produce babies. Even if the fertility rate of Japan (for example) were to recover by some miracle to the replacement level of 2.1, there will still be half as many Japanese women in 2050 as in 2010. If the fertility rate remains low, of course, there will be still fewer babies.

If America fails to fix the glaring weaknesses of its present immigration regime, to be sure, the country will be poorer and weaker. But America's demographic momentum offers a generation's grace period in which to fix these problems. No matter what Europe and Japan do today, they probably cannot reverse a downward trend whose inertia will take them into hitherto uncharted demographic territory. Europe has lost a third of its population to plague in the past, to be sure. But no plague ever wiped out the young people and preserved the old people. America faces difficult choices about the cost of supporting an aging population. But the proportion of Americans over sixty will stabilize at about 30 percent, while Europe's will rise to 40 percent and Japan's to over half.

Proportion of Population Over 60

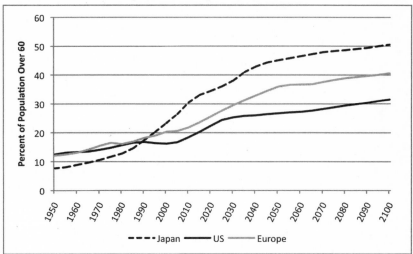

Source: United Nations Population Division (Constant Fertility Scenario)

Exceptional Israel

America was founded by radical Protestants who sought to emulate Israel's mission in the wilderness and succeeded in creating the only Christian nation that would survive the great wave of secularization and demographic decline of the past two generations. Remarkably, the only other advanced country to sustain high fertility rates is the modern State of Israel.

The late Yassir Arafat can take credit for the worst demographic forecast of the twentieth century. "The womb of the Arab woman," the late Palestinian strongman averred, "is my strongest weapon."[7] By this he meant that the Arabs of Israel and the occupied territories would outbreed and overwhelm the Jews. A generation of Israeli politicians believed him, fearing that a "ticking demographic time bomb" threatened the integrity of the

Jewish state. In 2001, for example, a report to the Knesset, Israel's parliament, said, "In the whole area west of the Jordan—including Israel, the West Bank, and Gaza—Jews last year represented 50.5 percent of the population; the Arabs, 49.5 percent. Testifying before the Knesset Foreign Affairs and Defense Committee, Prof. Arnon Sofer of Haifa University projected that with their higher birthrate, Arabs would constitute 58 percent of this population by the year 2020 and Jews, 42 percent. Without final borders and a clear separation between states, he said Israel faces an existential crisis."[8]

The supposed demographic threat loomed behind the late Yitzhak Rabin's celebrated Rose Garden handshake with Arafat in 1994. It motivated then Prime Minister Ehud Olmert to offer the Palestinians half of Jerusalem and almost all of the West Bank in return for a peace agreement in 2007. In October of that year, Olmert warned the Knesset of "a demographic battle, drowned in blood and tears,"[9] if Israel did not achieve peace through concessions of land. A month later Olmert predicted "the end of the State of Israel" by demographic exhaustion. "Mr Olmert," reported the BBC, "said it was not the first time he had articulated his fears about the demographic threat to Israel as a Jewish state from a faster growing Palestinian population. He made similar comments in 2003 to justify the failed strategy of unilateral withdrawals from Israeli-occupied land which holds large Palestinian populations."[10] Israeli concessions in the first decade of the twenty-first century were motivated by fear that Arab fecundity would swamp Israel's Jewish population.

In actuality, quite the opposite was occurring. The Jewish birth rate was rising steadily, and the Arab birth rate was falling. According to a June 2010 study by the American-Israeli Demographic Research Group, the fertility gap between Jews and Arabs had nearly converged by 2009, to a difference of only 0.7 births per woman, from six more births per Arab woman in 1969. The proportion of Jewish births in Israel has risen steadily, from 69 percent of the total in 1995, to 75 percent in 2008. Most remarkable is that today's "secular" Israeli women show a fertility rate of 2.6, far and away the highest in the industrial world. Their own mothers had a fertility rate of only 2.1. In the fifteen years from 1994 to 2009, the study adds, the number of Arab births in Israel remained stable at around 39,000, while Jewish births rose from 80,000 to 120,000. The Haredi (ultra-Orthodox), Jews who comprise about 8 percent of Israel's population, have a fertility rate of 8.5, bringing the overall Israeli fertility rate up to 2.9 births per woman.

An Israeli fertility rate of nearly three births per woman exceeds the industrial nations' norm by such a wide margin that Israel—assuming fertility remains unchanged—will have a larger population than Poland by 2085.

Polish vs. Israeli Population under Constant Fertility Assumption

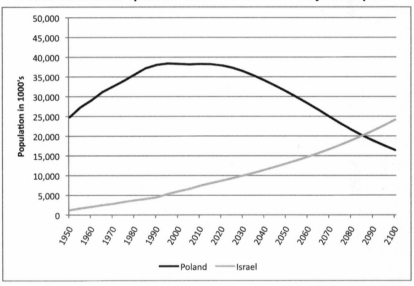

Source: UN Population Division

Poland's median age, moreover, will be 57, an outcome impossible for the Polish state to manage (because the majority of Poles in that case would be elderly dependents), while Israel's median age will be only 32. Even more remarkable is that Israel will have more young people than Italy or Spain and as many as Germany by the end of the century if fertility remains unchanged. A century and a half after the Holocaust, that is, the Jewish State will have more military-age men, and will be able to field a larger land army, than Germany.

Population Aged 15–24 Years in Israel and Selected Countries

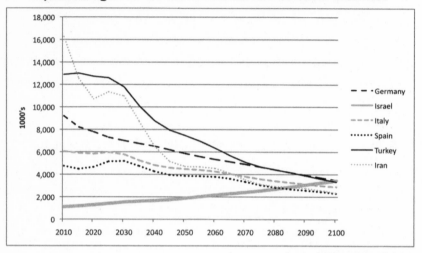

Source: UN Population Division

Secular sociologist Eric Kaufmann complains of the "Haredization" of Jewish life—a shift towards ultra-Orthodoxy—but the numbers tell a different story. In Israel, the so-called secular (a designation that in actuality covers a wide spectrum of religious belief and practice) account for Israel's uniquely high fertility rate. In fact, the line between "secular" and "religious" is blurred in the Jewish state. Fifty-six percent of Israelis light Sabbath candles every Friday evening (and a further 22 percent light them sometimes), according to the most comprehensive survey of Israel's religious practice. Fifty-five percent believe that Moses received the Torah at Mount Sinai. And 69 percent observe Jewish dietary laws at home, reports Daniel J. Elazar of the Jerusalem Institute for Public Affairs. Synagogue attendance is low, at only 22 percent, but the comparison between synagogue attendance in Israel and church attendance in the U.S. may be misleading. About half of the three-hour Saturday morning service is devoted to reading and study of the Pentateuch and some extracts from the prophets, providing a lesson both in the Bible and the Hebrew language for the Jewish people in exile. Israeli schoolchildren use the language of the Bible on the playground, and take mandatory Bible study throughout primary and secondary school.

Elazar observes,

> Israel's Jews are not divided into two groups but into four: ultra-orthodox, religious Zionists, traditional Jews, and secular. Some 8 percent are ultra-Orthodox. These are the strangely (to Western eyes) garbed, black hatted Jews who are featured in all the pictures, despite the fact that they represent only 8 percent of Israel's Jewish population. Another 17 percent are religious Zionists who normally are lost to view in the studies and the statistics because they are generally lumped with everyone else. The religious Zionists are similar to the modern or centrist Orthodox Jews in the diaspora, partaking of most or all aspects of modern civilization, except that they maintain Orthodox observance of Jewish religious law and tradition. The third group consists of the vast majority of Israeli Jews, some 55 percent, who define themselves as "traditional."... They cover the whole range of belief and observance from people of fundamentalist belief and looser practice to people who have interpreted Judaism in the most modern manner but retain some of its customs and ceremonies.[11]

It might be added that inhabiting the Promised Land is one of Judaism's central commandments. There was a deep religious sensibility among the secular Zionists who set out to rebuild the Land of Israel. David Ben-Gurion, the country's first prime minister, rejected all secular beliefs, yet he personally gave Bible lessons to Israeli students and fought to secure a central role for the Bible in the school curriculum.[12] Devotion to the State of Israel distinguishes nominally secular Israelis from really secular American Jews, whose fertility divides by denomination quite as clearly as it does for American Christians.

U.S. Jewish Fertility by Religious Current

	Average Number of Children per Woman
Ultra-Orthodox	6.72
Modern Orthodox	3.39
Conservative	1.74
Reform	1.36
Secular	1.29

Source: Anthony Gordon and Richard Horowitz, National Jewish Population Survey (2000)

That Israel's exceptional fertility stems from religious commitment rather than ethnicity is suggested by the enormous contrast between orthodox and secular Jewish birth rates in the United States. Nowhere is the fertility gap between religious and non-religious more extreme than among American Jews. As a group, American Jews show the lowest fertility of any ethnic group in the country. That is a matter of great anguish for Jewish community leaders. According to sociologist Steven Cohen, "We are now in the midst of a non-Orthodox Jewish population meltdown.... Among Jews in their 50s, for every 100 Orthodox adults, we have 192 Orthodox children. And for the non-Orthodox, for every 100 adults, we have merely 55 such children." Reform and secular Jews average one child per family; the Modern (university-educated) Orthodox typically raise three to four children, and the ultra-Orthodox seven or eight.

CHAPTER 14

EUROPE'S RUIN AND AMERICA'S FOUNDING

America is different because it was founded to be different. America remains a Christian nation because it overcame the centrifugal forces of ethnic rivalry through a radical and unprecedented device: the creation of a new country founded on a proposition—rather than commonality of language, race, or history. At the moment of Europe's most catastrophic failure, people of faith chose to risk everything to found the country that became the United States of America. Earlier we saw how national idolatry triumphed over Christian universalism during the Thirty Years' War. But that terrible conflict did not extinguish Christian universalism. In the third year of the war, the seed of what became American Christianity left Europe on the *Mayflower*. The Pilgrim Fathers' decision to decamp to the new world was not made casually. The war pushed them out. America's founding came in direct response to Europe's failure. The Pilgrims fled the European continent as it plunged into a tragedy that would undo the civilizing efforts of the preceding thousand years.

Years after the Pilgrims landed on Plymouth Rock, their leader William Bradford recalled the fearful deliberations of the English Separatists in the Dutch port of Leyden in 1620. They had few illusions about the dangers of resettlement in the American wilderness, and in fact half of them would die during their first winter there. The risks of staying, though, were just as frightening; Spain, at war with the Dutch Republic since it overthrew Spanish rule in 1568, was about to invade. And "the Spaniard," Bradford wrote, "might prove as cruel as the savages of America." Bradford wrote:

> It was granted the dangers were great, but not desperate, and the difficulties were many, but not invincible; for although there were many of them likely, yet they were not certain. It might be that some of the things feared might never befall them.... They lived here but as men in exile and in a poor condition; and as great miseries might possibly befall them in this place; for the twelve years of truce were now out, and there was nothing but beating of drums and preparing for war, the events whereof are always uncertain. The Spaniard might prove as cruel as the savages of America, and the famine and pestilence as sore here as there, and liberty less to look out for remedy.[1]

Their fears were well grounded. The history in which they would have been entangled if they had stayed is well worth examining. A year after the *Mayflower* sailed, Spain sent an army into Holland, and in 1625 the Spanish took the great Dutch fortress of Breda, just sixty miles from Amsterdam; Velasquez' canvas depicting the city's surrender hangs in Madrid's Prado Museum. The Dutch defenders kept the Spanish army away from their coastal cities only by opening the dikes and flooding the countryside. Had the Pilgrims stayed and the Spanish won, the Pilgrims likely would have been burned as heretics.

The Pilgrims' Dutch refuge had always been uncertain. Americans today rarely appreciate the raw courage of the Dutch during their Eighty Years' War with Spain. The Revolt of the Netherlands against Spain in 1568 pitted a small people against the unchallenged land power of the sixteenth century—a far riskier rebellion than the American Revolution two centuries later. Not America but the Dutch Republic was the first democratic government in the modern West, a haven for refugees from religious persecution, including Iberian Jews and French Huguenots. America's concept of liberty derived in large measure from Dutch antecedents; the flag of freedom, the red-white-and-blue, was a variant of the Dutch orange-white-and-blue, the colors of the House of Orange and Prince William the Silent, who led the Dutch against their Spanish overlords. Johann von Oldenbarneveldt, William the Silent's political adviser and the intellectual author of the republic, inspired the American founders, along with his colleague, the legal theorist Hugo Grotius.

But the advent of the Thirty Years' War in 1618 ruined the Dutch republicans. Oldenbarneveldt had concluded a peace treaty with Spain in 1605 that recognized Dutch independence for an interval, creating a twelve-year period of stability, during which the Separatists sought refuge in Holland. The outbreak of war in Bohemia in 1618 made a shambles of the peace with Spain; as Austria went to war against its breakaway Protestants, Hapsburg Spain allied with Austria and set out to settle its old account with the Netherlands.

William the Silent's successor, Maurice of Orange, arrested Oldenbarneveldt and Grotius and allied with the Calvinist clergy to crush the republican opposition to his government. (Maurice would die in 1624 leading the unsuccessful defense of Breda.) Holland prepared for war, and the Calvinist clergy now demanded the suppression of any dissenting religious activity. For instance, they demanded that the little community of English Separatists merge into the Dutch Reformed Church. Holland's sole

ally, James I of England, offered military aid to Holland—on the condition
that the Dutch place all English religious groups in their country under his
jurisdiction—which would have forced the Separatists back to the established Church of England. Mobs brawled in the streets over religious differences; in April 1619 one of the Separatists, James Chilton, was beaten
senseless. Even if the Spanish did not come, the Separatists faced absorption
into either the Dutch or English official church. And if the Spanish came,
they would be the first to burn.

The Anabaptists, Sabbatarians, Hutterites, and related sects could not
possibly have prevailed in Europe. A largely illiterate population could not
resort to Scripture for a personal experience of revelation. Seventeenth-
century Europe simply did not produce many individuals prepared to stake
their salvation on a unique conversion informed by personal engagement
with Scripture. The first Anabaptist vision of a new kind of European polity, Thomas Müntzer's vision of a community of property, ended horribly
during the German Peasants' War of 1525. (The Pilgrims also experimented
briefly with community property in Massachusetts before dropping the
idea.) Luther denounced the peasant uprising and its Anabaptist supporters as a danger to social order. Religion from the top, joined to state power
and enforced by civil law, was the only system that could hold Europe
together. The American settlements, by contrast, recruited literate and committed individuals.

The Protestant radicals could flourish only by creating for themselves
a new kind of country, one whose citizens would select themselves out of
the world's nations. The European tribes, whom the Church had nurtured
into nationhood, wanted to become the New Israel in their own tribal skin;
the Protestant radicals sought rather to adopt individuals into a new chosen
people in a new promised land.

Which brings us back to the Massachusetts Bay Colony. The Pilgrim
Fathers had no doubt that God had sent them on their mission in the Wil-
derness just as he had brought Israel out of Egypt. Their governor John
Winthrop warned them, "When God gives a speciall commission he lookes

to have it strictly observed in every article." In his famous 1630 sermon, "A Model of Christian Charity," Winthrop enjoined the Massachusetts colonists to hold themselves to a higher moral standard, for God had chosen them just as he chose ancient Israel, and would punish their transgressions all the more severely:

> Neither must wee thinke that the Lord will beare with such faileings at our hands as he dothe from those among whome wee have lived; and that for these 3 Reasons; 1. In regard of the more neare bond of mariage between him and us, wherein hee hath taken us to be his, after a most strickt and peculiar manner, which will make him the more jealous of our loue and obedience. Soe he tells the people of Israell, you onely have I knowne of all the families of the Earthe, therefore will I punishe you for your Transgressions, because the Lord will be sanctified in them that come neare him.[2]

Identification with ancient Israel was not a Pilgrim quirk. It was the *sine qua non* of the radical Protestantism that rejected the failing regime of Church and Empire. Starting with the Visigoths, the tribes who coveted the Election of Israel sought to eliminate the Jews; the Christians who instead desired to be adopted into Israel tended towards philo-Semitism. America's founding religion was Calvinist in construction—not in every detail of John Calvin's theology, but in the sense of election by grace. The New England settlers saw themselves as an elect saved by grace from the perdition of the Old World. A red thread leads from John Winthrop's "bond of marriage" between God and the Pilgrims and Abraham Lincoln's characterization of Americans as an "almost chosen people."

The individual Christian seeks adoption into Israel through the personal experience of conversion. Where does he then dwell? Among all the nations of the world, only the Jews had learned to live as true exiles in the Babylon of their dispersion, making their national home in a tabernacle of the spirit while awaiting their return to Zion. By contrast, the European nations without exception ultimately chose national idolatry before Christian universality. But the new Americans constructed a nation amenable to their own concept of Christian universality, for which ancient Israel was the exemplar. The peoples of Europe had entered Christendom collectively, under their own tribal banners. After baptism they continued to live their old national life. The dissenting minority who sought adoption into Israel through personal conversion needed a new kind of nation in which to live; Christians may hope for the heavenly city, but they must dwell in an earthly one. In constructing their earthly city, the dissenting Protestants, almost without exception, looked to Israel.

Thus they brought Jewish practices, particularly Sabbath observance, into Christian practice. The leaders of the Lutheran establishment looked with alarm at "Judaizing" among the Anabaptists and related sects. When Martin Luther published his infamous screed *On the Jews and Their Lies* in 1546, calling for the burning of every Jewish home along with every synagogue, he was not addressing the Jews. His pamphlet was written in response to Judaizing by the Moravian Sabbatarians. Like all the Bohemian Protestants, the Moravians lost most of their number during the Thirty Years' War. Many of the survivors would later emigrate to America like the Pilgrims before them.

Perhaps two-thirds of Americans at the time of the Revolution descended from Calvinists and other Protestant dissenters. Some six hundred thousand English Puritans followed the Pilgrim Fathers to America. To these add the Dutch Calvinists who had arrived before the British, as well as German Anabaptists, Mennonites, and others who sought refuge on the American continent. These radical Protestants all shared the belief that the church of Jesus Christ was made up of *individuals* who were reborn into it, and that these individuals corresponded in some way to God's Elect. More than one hundred thousand German Protestants made their way to America during the seventeenth and eighteenth centuries: Anabaptists (Mennonites) to Germantown in 1683; Palatine Protestants to the Hudson

Valley in 1709; the Moravians (followers of John Huss) in 1722; the German Baptist Brethen in 1723; and so forth. The German Anabaptists all but disappeared in their home country but found a foothold on the new continent. Up to a tenth of the American population in 1776 descended from the Anabaptists and similar sects. Another two hundred thousand Ulster Protestants immigrated to America between 1710 and 1775—including Scots Presbyterians, but also the descendants of French Huguenots, English Baptists, and other dissenters dislodged by the Thirty Years' War and its aftermath.

The Gentile nations of Europe could be held within Christendom only through subordination to empire, that is, through a central power that stood over the nations and acted as the ultimate arbiter among them, supported by the authority of a universal Church. American Christianity melds just as closely with its political model: it is a nation composed of individuals who elected to become Americans as individuals, and left their dreams of ethnic election behind next to their furniture on the farther shore.

A religion that requires a personal conversion experience through individual reading of Scripture does not cultivate institutional continuity. Except for pockets of Mennonite and Amish communities, few congregations are left in the United States that trace their heritage to the upheavals of the Wars of Religion. Congregations settle into complacency and security and forget the experience of divine awe that so unsettled their founders. By the turn of the nineteenth century, Puritan Boston had become a religious desert. Harvard College became Unitarian in 1805, and all but one major church in Boston had embraced Unitarianism. Much of the New England elite ceased for all practical purposes to be Christian. Ralph Waldo Emerson, a Unitarian minister, abandoned his pulpit in 1831 for a career as a Transcendentalist philosopher.

Nonetheless the Judaizing Calvinism of the Puritans continued to assert itself until the Civil War. Jonathan Edwards, the salient figure of the First Great Awakening of 1733, had come from Puritan stock in Massachusetts. Edwards stamped a strict Calvinist theology on the Presbyterian Church of pre-revolutionary America so successfully that George III of England dubbed the Revolution "the Presbyterian War."

The Almost-Chosen People and Its Almost-Tragedy

America nearly repeated the tragedy of democratic Athens and republican Rome. Thucydides and Aristophanes blamed the devastating Peloponnesian War on the desire of democratic Athens' lower classes to live on the labor of others. As the Athenians fought to expand their empire, the American South fought to expand slavery. "Manifest destiny," a term coined in 1845 by the pro-slavery polemicist John L. O'Sullivan to justify the Mexican War, perverted the Puritan vision of a City on a Hill into a pretext for American rapacity.

General Ulysses S. Grant, the victorious commander of the American Civil War and America's eighteenth president, saw the Civil War as a continuation of the 1846 Mexican War, a land-grab for the expansion of slavery:

> [Texas] had but a very sparse population, until settled by Americans who had received authority from Mexico to colonize. These colonists paid very little attention to the supreme government, and introduced slavery into the state almost from the start, though the constitution of Mexico did not, nor does it now, sanction that institution.... The occupation, separation, and annexation [of Texas] were, from the inception of the movement to its final consummation, a conspiracy to acquire territory out of which slave states might be formed for the American Union.[3]

Democratic America resolved to make war upon Mexico in 1846 in order to seize territory for the expansion of slavery, Grant observed: "The Southern rebellion was largely the outgrowth of the Mexican war. Nations, like individuals, are punished for their transgressions. We got our punishment in the most sanguinary and expensive war of modern times."

Three hundred thousand Southern men died in the Civil War, or 30 percent of the South's military age population, the equivalent of 15 million casualties for the modern United States. If the South fought the war to preserve chattel slavery, what possessed the 80 to 90 percent of Southerners who owned no slaves to die for a practice from which they drew no present benefit? Southerners had been fighting for the right to bring slaves to new territories for a generation prior to the outbreak of war, in Kansas and elsewhere. Cotton, their principal cash crop, exhausted the soil in a decade's planting, and the planter took his slaves and moved on. Slavery and the Southern economic system would choke to death without expansion. Had the South been successful in its war for independence, it would have embarked on a campaign of conquest and imposed slavery on the whole southern half of the Western Hemisphere.

Professor Robert E. May wrote the classic account of the South's Athenian ambitions in *The Southern Dream of a Caribbean Empire* (1973), citing hundreds of contemporary Southern sources. He writes, for example:

> The *Memphis Daily Appeal*, December 30, 1860, wrote that a slave "empire" would arise "from San Diego, on the Pacific Ocean, thence southward, along the shore line of Mexico and Central America, at low tide, to the Isthmus of Panama; thence South—still South!—along the western shore line of New Granada and Ecuador, to where the southern boundary of the latter strikes the ocean; thence east over the Andes to the head springs of the Amazon; thence down the mightiest of inland seas, through the teeming bosom of the broadest and richest delta in the world, to the Atlantic Ocean."[4]

The difference between the pagan democracy of Athens and the Christian democracy of America is evident in the Northern response. America undertook the costliest of all its wars as a moral crusade to prevent the American project from backsliding into one more of history's imperial monsters. Lincoln easily could have averted the war by agreeing to let the South acquire slave territories outside of the continental United States. His 1860 election victory (by a minority of votes in a four-way race) provoked a crisis. Prior to Lincoln's inauguration, the future Confederate president Jefferson Davis supported a compromise that would have allowed the South to acquire slave territories to the south. Georgia senator Robert Toombs, along with Davis, the South's main spokesman, pleaded for an agreement that would have given the North "the whole continent to the North Pole" and the South "the whole continent to the South Pole," as Professor May reports.

It was Lincoln, not the Southerners, who turned down the compromise. "A year will not pass, till we shall have to take Cuba as a condition upon which they will stay in the Union.... There is in my judgment, but one compromise which would really settle the slavery question, and that would be a prohibition against acquiring any more territory," he wrote. Lincoln preferred to fight. Said congressman Ortis Ferry of Connecticut, "Let but the ties which bind the states to the federal government be broken and the leaders of the rebellion see glittering before them the prizes of a slaveholding empire which, grasping Cuba with one hand, and Mexico with the other, shall distribute titles, fame and fortune to the foremost in the strife. Such, in my opinion, is the real origin of the present revolt, and such are the motives which inspire its leaders."

We know from their songs why the soldiers of America's Civil War fought. "We are a band of brothers / Native to the soil / Fighting for the property / We gained by honest toil," the South sang. Union soldiers intoned a messianic message that has more in common with Malachi than Montesquieu. Julia Ward Howe's "Battle Hymn of the Republic" remains the most characteristic American utterance. Even today the heart pounds and the blood surges to this clumsy imitation of the King James Bible with its inelegant prosody, rough as the tramp of boots.

> I have seen Him in the watch-fires of a hundred circling camps,
> They have builded Him an altar in the evening dews and damps;

I can read His righteous sentence by the dim and flaring lamps....

That this was a holy war there can no doubt. Northern textile manufacturers did not have to conquer the South to buy its cotton. Free labor of the North did not need to fight the Southern slaveholders for land, for on the eve of war in 1861, the South offered to accept restrictions on the expansion of slavery within the United States if only Lincoln would annex Cuba.

In the history of statecraft, the American Constitution is a unique and enduring monument. America's democracy rose "on two wings," Michael Novak argued in a 2003 book: the faith of the Hebrew Bible, and the natural law theory handed down from the Scholastics through Locke and other philosophers.[5] Apt as Novak's characterization is, it describes an unresolved tension as much as an enduring synthesis. The Virginia of Thomas Jefferson and James Madison looked back to Greco-Roman democracy, while New Englanders like John Adams thought first in Hebrew terms. What the Civil War proved is that the American Republic, which was born with two wings, could in extreme circumstances fly on only one. Balance of powers is not what saved America. More than any other president, perhaps, Lincoln ignored constitutional restraints. He suspended the right of habeas corpus, which in the view of his critics trampled over the people's constitutional rights, for the greater good. Lord Acton, the great Catholic philosopher of political liberty, so abhorred Lincoln's concentration of federal power that he supported the Confederacy—wrongly, in my view. What drove the Union in its hour of crisis was a sense of supernatural avenging justice.

There is more information about America's character in "The Battle Hymn of the Republic" than in all the perorations of the political philosophers. To sustain a rational order based on the premise of individual rights, America appealed to a supernatural guarantor of such rights—the God of covenants. Americans believed that God would avenge the violation of such rights.

If America is an almost chosen people, Abraham Lincoln was its almost prophet. As Douglas L. Wilson put it, "Lincoln seems to have resisted the religious beliefs of his parents, [but] he retained throughout his life a fatal-ism that one may believe was fostered by the Calvinist bent of his Baptist upbringing." Observes historian James Takach, "Indeed, more than one Lincoln scholar has connected Lincoln's belief in the Doctrine of Necessity to the Calvinist doctrine of predestination.... He retained the fatalistic premise at its core: that man does not control his own destiny." Similarly, David Herbert Donald observes that Lincoln, from his earliest days, "had a sense that his destiny was controlled by a larger force, some Higher Power."[6] And Alonzo C. Guelzo says the Second Inaugural Address "contains the most radically metaphysical question ever posed by an American president. Lincoln had come, by the circle of a lifetime and the disasters of war, to confront once again the Calvinist God...who possessed a conscious will to intervene, challenge and reshape human destinies."[7]

"Fondly do we hope—fervently do we pray—that this mighty scourge of war may speedily pass away. Yet, if God wills that it continue, until all the wealth piled by the bond-man's two hundred and fifty years of unrequited toil shall be sunk, and until every drop of blood drawn with the lash, shall be paid by another drawn with the sword, as was said three thousand years ago, so still it must be said, the judgments of the Lord are true and righteous altogether," Lincoln said in his Second Inaugural address. In a famous March 15, 1865, letter to Thurlow Weed, Lincoln explained that his just-delivered speech would not be "immediately popular," because "men are not flattered by being shown that there is a difference of purpose between the Almighty and them. To deny it, though, in this case would be to deny that there is a God governing the world." Lincoln's celebrated statement that God held both sides in the Civil War to strict account for their transgres-sions echoes John Winthrop's warning that God would hold America to stricter account "because he would sanctify those who come near him." What applied to ancient Israel applied also to the almost chosen people of America. The Almighty has His own purposes. "Woe unto the world because of offenses; for it must needs be that offenses come, but woe to that man by whom the offense cometh."

Americans chiseled the text of the Second Inaugural address onto Lincoln's Memorial: "If we shall suppose that American slavery is one of those offenses which, in the providence of God, must needs come, but which, having continued through His appointed time, He now wills to remove, and that He gives to both North and South this terrible war as the woe due to those by whom the offense came, shall we discern therein any departure from those divine attributes which the believers in a living God always ascribe to Him?" The biblical faith of Israel refracted through Calvin acknowledges the divine attribute of justice along with the attribute of mercy.

As the evangelical historian Mark Noll observes in *America's God*, that is not always a source of comfort. "Views of providence," Noll writes, "provide the sharpest contrast between Lincoln and the professional theologians of his day." He adds that "the American God may have been working too well for the Protestant theologians who, even as they exploited Scripture and pious experience so successfully, yet found it easy to equate America's moral government of God with Christianity itself. Their tragedy—and the greater the theologian, the greater the tragedy—was to rest content with a God defined by the American conventions God's own loyal servants had exploited so well."[8]

Americans have locked Lincoln up in a marble box on the National Mall—a mock-Greek temple imitating the temple of Zeus at Olympus— and hoped he would stay put in it. Calvinism died with the Civil War: Americans decided that they would rather not have a God who demanded sacrifice from them on this scale. They did not want to be a Chosen People held accountable for their trangressions. Instead they wanted a reticent God who withheld his wrath while they set out to make the world amenable to their own purposes. The New England elite went to war as convinced abolitionists singing of the coming of God who trampled out the vintage of the grapes of wrath and wielded a terrible swift word. They came back convinced that no idea could be so righteous or so certain as to merit the unspeakable sacrifices of their generation. In his book *The Metaphysical Club*,

Louis Menand argues that the horrors of the Civil War desanguinated the idealism of such young New Englanders as the future Supreme Court Justice Oliver Wendell Holmes Jr. and the psychologist William James. The war purged them of their Puritan convictions and left in its place the vapid pragmatism that has reigned since then in American elite culture.

In place of the paternal God of "The Battle Hymn of the Republic," Americans got the avuncular God of Social Gospel, the ebullient Anglo-Saxon pretention of Theodore Roosevelt, and Wilsonian "Idealism." America's reaction to the Civil War, the costliest conflict between the Thirty Years' War in Germany and the Second World War on the Russian front, recalls Sholom Aleichem's Tevye the Carpenter: "God of mercy, choose another people." The terrible sacrifice of the Civil War had soured Americans on their covenant with the God of the Bible. Americans did not want to be the instrument of a Divine Providence that would hold them to account for their transgressions, in the vision of Winthrop and Lincoln. They no longer wanted Puritan election—certainly not at the price level of the Civil War.

Calvinism—specifically the belief that God's purposes transcended our knowledge and might conflict with our wishes—had remained the decisive residual influence on Lincoln and his generation. After the Civil War, it was replaced by the conceit that political tinkering and social engineering could remake the world in America's image—a backhanded way of stating that there is nothing really special about America, and that America's unique character as a country whose citizens selected themselves from out of the other nations does not really distinguish it from nations defined by blood, tradition, and geography. From this muddy well came both the naïve universalism of the Southern Baptist Jimmy Carter and the Wilsonian optimism of George W. Bush.

The Future of American Religion

The God of liberal Protestantism (and his carbon-copy, the God of Reform Judaism) has no purposes of his own; he idles on his throne, while we arrogate to ourselves the destiny of the world. In the absence of the Calvinist God, the denominations that broke from the Roman Catholic Church in pursuit of his service had no real reason to exist. The former radicals became the Protestant mainline; and the only remarkable thing about the Protestant mainstream is that it has maintained its membership until the last generation. The death of mainline Protestantism is not contested. Congregationalism, Presbyterianism, and Methodism began a rapid decline in the 1960s. They are declining not only as congregations but as individual families. American Presbyterians have on average 1.3 children—the same as Episcopalians, and only slightly more than Reform Jews. They have lost not only the desire to worship but the will to live.

But the notion of American election has shown a tenacity that few analysts of American religion might have expected. Evangelicals—a movement rather than a denomination—now comprise 28 percent of Americans, slightly fewer than Catholics but probably more consequential in the public square. To the extent that evangelicals evince a theology, they are less likely to affirm the Calvinism of Winthrop or Lincoln than home-grown doctrines such as the Dispensationalism of John Darby, or Pentecostalism, which began as a street-front church movement a century ago. These groups are boisterous, impassioned, and apocalyptic—moonshine compared to mint tea, next to mainline Protestantism. The Mormons are not evangelicals (most other denominations do not even consider them to be Christians), but their sociology is similar to that of the Dispensationalists, Pentecostals, and so forth. All of them believe that their present leaders are capable of prophecy—that either by reading the Bible or in some other way they receive revelations from God. They share with the liberal denominations the comforting idea that human beings can see into God's plan—either by substituting human action for Providence, as in the case of the Social Gospel, or by prophetic insight. Jonathan Edwards' legacy remains a force to contend with, though, in the "New Calvinist" wing of the evangelical movement. In 2009, *Time* magazine called the "new Calvinism" one of the ten most important ideas shaping America today.[9]

It is still too early to guess how deeply this revival will affect the evangelical movement at large.[10]

Americans cannot help but return to the idea of Election. This is a genetic trait of the American body politic, not a matter of whim. Unlike the Europeans, Americans have never had the option of settling into churches of national self-admiration in which the familiarity of national traditions blend into Christian doctrine. No one described the contrasting European model better than T. S. Eliot, in his 1948 essay "Notes towards the Definition of Culture":

> There is an aspect in which we can see a religion as the *whole way of life* of a people [emphasis original], from birth to grave, from morning to night and even in sleep, and that way of life is also its culture.... It includes all the characteristic activities and interests of a people: Derby Day, Henley Regatta, Cowes, the twelfth of August, a cup final, the dog races, the pin table, the dart board, Wensleydale cheese, boiled cabbage cut into sections, beetroot in vinegar, nineteenth-century Gothic churches and the music of Elgar. The reader can make his own list. And then we have to face the strange idea that what is part of our culture is also a part of our lived religion.[11]

American Christians have no such culture to confuse with religion. They have only the Bible, the American national epic. A very few have a residual attachment to the Latin mass, the English Book of Common Prayer, the hymns of J. S. Bach, the Old Slavonic of the Russian Orthodox service, or other imports from European religious culture. But the ethnic denominations that once dotted the American spiritual landscape—German and Scandinavian Lutheranism, Dutch Reformed Christianity, and Eastern Orthodoxy—stand vacant as North Dakota farm towns. Americans are a deracinated and mobile people. Christianity does not offer them the comfort of continuing tradition but only the stark promise of triumph over death. Unlike the Europeans of past generations, they can take no comfort in the seeming permanence of the cultivated habits of everyday life, the *faux* immortality of national culture—something in which the Europeans themselves have ceased to believe. Americans' hope for immortality is entirely spiritual.

The evangelicals see their lives as pilgrimage, and they cling to the road map that has been given them. This road map is the life of Israel, as told in the Bible. The stations along the redemptive journey of every individual recapitulate the history of Israel: Christ's sacrifice on the Cross relives the Exodus from Egypt, the conversion of the individual repeats the crossing of the Jordan as the tribes of Israel entered the Land of Canaan, and the descent of the Holy Spirit to Christ's disciples on Pentecost recapitulates the giving of the Torah on Mount Sinai.[12] Reliving the history of Israel is central to the religious life of Protestants who reject the Catholic understanding of Communion, that is, the real presence of Christ in the Eucharist. In the absence of communion with the body of Christ, Protestants seek an intense personal identification with Jesus; and because the narrative about Jesus' life on earth recapitulates the history of Israel, to be evangelical is to relive Israel's history. Thus the evangelicals, like the English Puritans and the German Anabaptists and Sabbatarians, identify with the Jews as a living people of which they aspire to be members. The sufferings and trials of Israel are their trials and sufferings, and God's promise of redemption to Israel stands as surety for God's promise to them.

The evangelical movement seeks redemption from sin and death. And Americans who see their lives as a journey toward salvation cannot help but see a salvific dimension in the journey of America, and an echo of the covenant in the inalienable rights of Americans. That is why Americans of faith insist so passionately on the religious character of the Founding. It is also why Americans of faith, including Catholics as well as observant Jews, are closer to one another than to their lapsed coreligionists. As Joseph Bottum notes, "Among conservative churchgoers, the horizontal unity of Mere Religion cuts across denominations. Serious, believing Presbyterians, for example, now typically feel that they have more in common with serious, believing Catholics and evangelicals—with serious, believing Jews, for that matter—than they do, vertically, with the unserious, unorthodox members of their own denomination."[13]

The Civil War destroyed the continuity of American religion, but even in the darkness, Americans instinctively grope their way to the religion of their founding. What might emerge out of America's denominational chaos is uncertain. Bottum speculates, "Perhaps some joining of Catholics and evangelicals, in morals and manners, could achieve the social unity in theological difference that characterized the old Mainline."[14] To date, Catholic intellectuals such as Bottum, George Weigel, Michael Novak, Hadley Arkes, and the late John Richard Neuhaus have articulated a clearer vision of public policy in light of the founding than most of their evangelical counterparts. It seems pointless to argue whether the American political model is better or worse than any other. It is the world's only successful model. It is not easily reproduced, because the American model first of all requires the presence of Americans. European nationalism bled itself to death during the two World Wars of the twentieth century; Europe exists as it does today only because America reconstructed the defeated Axis powers after 1945. And on its present trajectory, Europe will not exist in recognizable form a century from now. Japanese and South Korean democracy were the gifts of American occupation; neither country is a candidate for long-term survival at present fertility rates. America remains the City on the Hill. Those who best understand America in the context of the rest of the world view America through the lens of religion. Sternly as Augustine may have instructed Christians to regard their earthly city as an exile, people made of flesh and blood have never found it possible to draw a bright line between the City of God and the Babylon of their earthly residence. In one of two ways, they always have sought to sanctify their earthly city. In one way or other they have always "Judaized"—that is, sought an earthly city to correspond with the heavenly city.

The Europeans were not content with adoption into Israel; they wanted to replace Israel. And they themselves became the god that failed.

The Americans chose to build a City on the Hill that would select—in parallel to the Christian idea of conversion—individuals who wished to become part of it. Because this act of self-election devolves to the individual, it never can be embodied in an established Church. So America's civic religion always will remain separate from the myriad of contending sects which minister to its citizens. What once seemed an insignificant minority of Christians decided to create a new polity, an earthly City on the Hill that could never replace, but could emulate, the City of God. And the stone that the builders rejected has become the cornerstone of the foundation of world Christianity.

American Christianity in the Global South

If anyone had forecast in 1620 that a yet-unfounded American republic would become the sole Christian nation centuries hence, that vision would seem prophetic in retrospect. Sociologist Philip Jenkins, the chronicler of Christianity in the Global South, reports an even more remarkable forecast made in 1640:

> Though prophecy rarely lends itself to empirical verification, one exception might be an observation of St. Vincent de Paul's, writing about the year 1640. This was one of the grimmest periods of European history, the most desperate days of the Thirty Years' War. In those awful days, Vincent noted that Jesus promised that his Church would last until the end of time, but he never mentioned Europe. The Church of the future, Vincent said, would be the Church of South America, of Africa, of China and Japan. Although we might argue about the inclusion of Japan in that list, St. Vincent's basic point remains sound and

prophetic. Christianity, a religion that was born in Africa and Asia, has in our lifetimes decided to go home.[15]

As Jenkins reports, "According to the statistical tables produced by the respected Center for the Study of Global Christianity, some 2.1 billion Christians were alive in 2005, about one-third of the planetary population. The largest single bloc, some 531 million people, is still to be found in Europe. Latin America, though, is already close behind with 511 million, Africa has 389 million, and 344 million Asians profess Christianity. North America claims about 226 million believers." Both Christian and Muslim sources, it appears, agree that Christianity is winning the battle for souls in Africa. One Muslim cleric asserts that 6 million Muslims convert to Christianity each year. And it is possible that China may become the world's largest Christian nation. Sinologist Francesco Sisci reports,

> Not since late antiquity has the world seen a migration of peoples like the great urbanization of China now in progress. By 2025, migrants will make up two-fifths of China's billion-strong urban population, a fifth of all the Chinese, according to the McKinsey Global Institute. Many analysts have observed that this great confluence of ethnicities and languages has prepared the ground for a great wave of Christian conversion. At the end of World War II, with a nationalist government supportive of Christian missions, barely two percent of Chinese were Christians. The World Christian Database now counts 111 million Chinese Christians, while an internal survey conducted in 2007 by China's government puts the number substantially higher: 130 million, nearly 10 percent of the total population.[16]

The great wave of evangelization in the global South alters the strategic landscape. After September 11, 2001, the late Professor Samuel Huntington of Harvard earned belated celebrity for a 1993 treatise entitled "The Clash of Civilizations." He summarized his thesis, "The fundamental source of conflict in this new world will not be primarily ideological or primarily economic. The great divisions among humankind and the dominating source of conflict will be cultural. Nation-states will remain the most powerful actors in world affairs, but the principal conflicts of global politics will occur between nations and groups of different civilizations. The clash of civilizations will dominate global politics. The fault lines between civilizations will be the battle lines of the future."[17] Huntington sorted the world into great cultural blocs: Western (the U.S., Europe, and a few others), Confucian (China and its periphery), Hindu, Russian Orthodox, and Muslim.

Huntington helped to restore religion and culture to the agenda of political science, but his brushstrokes were too broad. The cultural civil war inside each civilization may be just as important as, and in some cases far more important than, the conflict among civilizations. Americans of faith may find more in common with the 130 million Chinese who identify themselves as Christians, or for that matter with Ugandan Anglicans, or Indian Catholics, than with their secular or loosely affiliated neighbors. Huntington never explained, moreover, why some cultures should clash and others should not. No one questions the great cultural divide between Hindu India and Christian America. Yet not a single observer has suggested that India and the United States have anything about which to quarrel.

More than a hundred thousand Americans serve overseas as Christian missionaries. Protestant denominations of American origin are the fastest-growing religious communities in the world. The spread of Pentecostalism from a store-front church a century ago to a mass of 350 million congregants, a third the size of the Catholic Church, has no precedent in the history of evangelization. Virtually all of the vast increase of China's Christian communities—to the government-estimated 10 percent of the country's population—has occurred in the so-called "house churches" inspired by the American evangelical model. By contrast, China's Catholic population has languished at the 10 million mark. A hundred years of mainline

Protestant missionary work has left little imprint on China, while the Chinese themselves spontaneously identify with American-style evangelical Protestantism. Anglicanism, a dying denomination in the United States and a moribund shell in the United Kingdom, has taken on a new and vibrant life as an evangelical African denomination. Although Catholicism remains the largest Christian denomination in India by official count, new evangelical converts there may well have outstripped the 500-year-old Catholic presence in India.

Jenkins observes that American Christian denominations are at the forefront of an "historical turning point" in Christianity, "one that is as epochal for the Christian world as the original Reformation." In the October 2002 edition of the *Atlantic*, Jenkins wrote, "It is Pentecostals who stand in the vanguard of the Southern Counter-Reformation. Though Pentecostalism emerged as a movement only at the start of the twentieth century, chiefly in North America, Pentecostals today are at least 400 million strong, and heavily concentrated in the global South. By 2040 or so there could be as many as a billion, at which point Pentecostal Christians alone will far outnumber the world's Buddhists and will enjoy rough numerical parity with the world's Hindus."

Whether the line of demarcation that divides people of faith from their secular compatriots will predominate over the great historic divide among cultures remains to be seen. But the ties of faith that cut cross nation, language, and culture have a powerful parallel on the world scene: the emergence of the United States of America as the unchallenged superpower. America's global power may decline, to be sure. But if America declines, it will not be the victim of a more potent challenger, as when Rome displaced Greece in the second century B.C.E., or France displaced Spain in the seventeenth century, or England and Germany displaced France during the nineteenth. America's decline instead would usher in a fracturing of the global political order; the Pax America would have no successor, and world relations would devolve into chaos. America's collapse would more closely resemble the fall of Rome.

The parallel between the first great wave of Christian evangelization in the declining years of the Roman Empire and the present seems obvious. The peoples of the Global South may be uneducated, but they are not stupid. As globalization forces Latin Americans, Africans, and Asians out of rural life and into cities, they watch cable television, surf the Internet, and talk with relatives and friends overseas. They may not think of America quite as the City on the Hill, but they understand what America means in the world, in contrast to sclerotic Europe or moribund Japan. And, remarkably, they understand America first of all in religious terms: their identification with America takes the form of an impassioned commitment to the religious attitudes which embody the American character. The global embrace of American Protestantism is a phenomenon broader and deeper than curiosity about the American political system or American culture. Among the hundred million new Christians of Africa or the more than hundred million "house church" Christians of China, few could quote the Declaration of Independence or the Gettysburg address. But most can quote the Bible.

The new Christians of the Global South understand America better than the political scientists. The vital issue at the time of America's founding was a theopolitical question, not a geopolitical one: How does the individual human being stand with respect to mortality? The same question still grips the peoples of Latin America, Africa, and Asia today.

We can pretend that our life is an accident of natural selection played out in an indifferent universe that affords us nothing more than the chance to entertain ourselves while we wait for death. Or we can seek a purpose beyond our own life. Exercise, hormone replacement therapy, and plastic surgery give the inhabitants of the industrial world the opportunity to banish the specter of mortality until the sixth or seventh decade of their lives. But mortality is a constant presence in the fragile lives of the poor people of the Global South. Belonging to a people who transcend mortality—the People of God—is the alternative to membership in the doomed tribes of the changing world. To an increasing number of the people of the Global

South, Americans are those who select themselves into the People of God. That is the aspect of the American character that the poor in developing Africa and Asia aspire to imitate—as individuals today, and in the future, perhaps, in new political structures that emulate John Winthrop's City on a Hill. American political success may ultimately be transferrable. But not through naïve liberal universalism, nor via a neoconservative reprise of Wilsonian idealism, but through individuals who seek adoption into the People of God and create a polity founded on the common love of God and his people.

CHAPTER 15

♠♠♠

CAN AMERICAN DEMOCRACY BE EXPORTED?

If the rights of man stem from only nature and not from God, they depend not on faith, but only on reason that discovers them—the same way that reason discovers any other principle of nature: the principles of political organization are "deduced," as Leo Strauss put it, "from the desire for self-preservation" in Thomas Hobbes' formulation.[1] But, as we have seen again and again through history and in the great events of our own epoch, when men lose faith, they also lose the desire to live, and with it the desire for self-preservation. Natural right, as understood by secular philosophers from Hobbes to Strauss, nonetheless appealed to a generation of American intellectuals who sought the benefits of religion without its premise of faith. If the principles of a good society are a matter of deduction rather than faith, there is nothing exceptional about America, except that the Americans deduced the correct principles somewhat in advance of other peoples. Thus other peoples can simply be taught to build a good society in the same way that they can be taught to build a bridge or a power plant. An American-style constitution may not work quite as well in Iraq as it does at home—neither will an Iraqi power plant, for that matter—but it should serve as a functioning approximation.

That is the premise of the Bush Freedom Agenda, the grand American strategy to establish stable democracies in the Middle East, starting with Iraq. With this Quixotesque adventure, the Bush administration took the great mandate it received after September 11, 2001, and turned it into the electoral debacle of 2008. It was perhaps the worst application of good intentions ever to plague American foreign policy.

Some months after America's invasion of Iraq, then President George W. Bush envisioned a world of democratic states. "We've witnessed, in little over a generation, the swiftest advance of freedom in the 2,500 year story of democracy," he told the National Endowment for Democracy on November 6, 2003, citing the American victories in World War II and the Cold War.

> We've reached another great turning point—and the resolve we show will shape the next stage of the world democratic movement.... Our commitment to democracy is also tested in the Middle East, which is my focus today, and must be a focus of American policy for decades to come. In many nations of the Middle East—countries of great strategic importance—democracy has not yet taken root. And the questions arise: Are the peoples of the Middle East somehow beyond the reach of liberty? Are millions of men and women and children condemned by history or culture to live in despotism? Are they alone never to know freedom, and never even to have a choice in the matter? I, for one, do not believe it. I believe every person has the ability and the right to be free.

The president answered "skeptics of democracy" who "assert that the traditions of Islam are inhospitable to representative government":

This "cultural condescension," as Ronald Reagan termed it, has a long history. After the Japanese surrender in 1945, a so-called Japan expert asserted that democracy in that former empire would "never work." Another observer declared the prospects for democracy in post-Hitler Germany are, and I quote, "most uncertain at best"—he made that claim in 1957. Seventy-four years ago, the *Sunday London Times* [sic] declared nine-tenths of the population of India to be "illiterates not caring a fig for politics." Yet when Indian democracy was imperiled in the 1970s, the Indian people showed their commitment to liberty in a national referendum that saved their form of government.[2]

Bush's naïve belief in the curative powers of democracy extended to the Lebanese terrorist organization Hezbollah, whose suicide bombers had killed hundreds of U.S. Marines in Beirut in 1983. At a March 16, 2005, press conference, Bush opined that if Hezbollah came to power, its constituency would force it to concentrate on fixing potholes:

> Our policy is this: We want there to be a thriving democracy in Lebanon. We believe that there will be a thriving democracy, but only if—but only if—Syria withdraws...her troops completely out of Lebanon.... I like the idea of people running for office. There's a positive effect when you run for office. Maybe some will run for office and say, vote for me, I look forward to blowing up America. I don't know, I don't know if that will be their platform or not. But it's—I don't think so. I think people who generally run for office say, vote for me, I'm looking forward to fixing your potholes, or making sure you got bread on the table.

There are two problems with the former president's vision. One is the demographic death of every single one the countries that the United States liberated after World War II and the Cold War. After Europe and Japan went to ruin in the World Wars of the twentieth century, America imposed its model on the vanquished. This would appear to be a positive outcome if not for one snag—that is, the fact that all of the vanquished countries are dying.

The second problem is that all the free elections held in the Islamic world, with or without American encouragement, have returned Islamist radicals hostile to America.

The Bush "Freedom Agenda" sounds good—don't we all want to think that everyone in the world is an American under the skin?—but as a practical matter, its batting average is zero. Its proponents are committing the fallacy of composition: all the peoples of the world may be Americans in potential, but America is composed of individuals who fled their own flawed cultures in order to become Americans. In 1620, only a fringe of dissenting Protestants believed in self-governance, based on the profoundly religious premise that every man and woman must engage revelation through Scripture. Improbably, the castaways of Europe founded the future American superpower. The English, to be sure, adopted democracy in parallel to America, but most of America's competitors believed not in democracy, but rather some form of collectivism: either in Throne and Altar, or in Rousseau's popular will, with some nationalist or racial coloring.

The Operation Was Successful, but the Patient Died

Most of the countries that owe their new democracy to American intervention will be much smaller (and much grayer) by mid-century; most of them will have dwindled to the point at which national existence will be unsustainable.

Projected Population Declines
for Countries Liberated by America, 2010–2100
(Constant Fertility Scenario)

Bosnia	-69.5%
Bulgaria	-67.7%

Projected Population Declines
for Countries Liberated by America, 2010–2100
(Constant Fertility Scenario)

Ukraine	62.2%
Romania	-60.4%
Belarus	-59.3%
Croatia	-59.1%
Poland	-57.1%
Republic of Moldova	-56.9%
Japan	-55.1%
Russian Federation	-53.3%
Hungary	-48.0%
Germany	-46.0%
Italy	-39.0%
Serbia	-38.1%
Estonia	-38.1%
Czech Republic	-37.8%

Source: United Nations Population Division

As President Bush said, the United States liberated Germany, Italy, and Japan from murderous and tyrannical governments. By the end of the century, though, the number of living Germans will fall by almost half, and the number of Japanese by more than half, and about three-fifths of them will be over sixty years of age. America destroyed the German and Japanese delusions of racial superiority and their hopes of empire, and offered them instead a modest position in the world under the wing of American power. It appears that Germans and Japanese don't breed in captivity. Having lost their Christianity to nationalism, and lost their nationalism to losing, the Europeans do not appear to want to be much of anything. Although the United States judiciously kept Japan's Emperor on the Chrysanthemum Throne, the Japanese have lost almost all connection to the Buddhist and Shinto religion of their past.

The Dresden firestorm of February 1945 and the nuclear attack on Hiroshima and Nagasaki in August of that year killed more than the few hundred thousand people known to have died in those bombings. In a broader sense, those attacks killed all the Germans and Japanese who ever lived, and all the Germans and Japanese who ever would live. Wounded animals crawl into a hole and die; humiliated cultures turn sterile and pass out of memory. Germany and Japan eschewed democracy for a reason, believing that their hope for survival lay in collective identity. In light of the facts, one might say that this belief was not wrong, only evil and tragic. The advent of democratic governments among the losers of World War II and the Cold War solved a problem for America—it replaced loathsome and hostile regimes—but it has done nothing to solve the basic problem of the countries concerned, namely, their survival into the next century. Democracy, to be sure, is not the problem. But neither is it the solution. For the captive nations freed after the collapse of Communism, the picture is even worse than for Japan and Germany; most of them will suffer population declines of more than half.

"The ideas of economists and political philosophers, both when they are right and when they are wrong, are more powerful than is commonly understood. Indeed the world is ruled by little else. Practical men, who believe themselves to be quite exempt from any intellectual influence, are usually the slaves of some defunct economist. Madmen in authority, who hear voices in the air, are distilling their frenzy from some academic scribbler of a few years back," wrote John Maynard Keynes.[3] The "Freedom Agenda" derives from the Enlightenment philosophy of Hobbes, which assumes an isolated individual preoccupied with physical survival. The problem of *cultural* survival—the possibility that a people (or a majority of a people) might cling to a backward or even barbaric culture, because that culture offers them a bulwark against mortality—does not occur to Enlightenment political philosophy. As Franz Rosenzweig said, the philosophers remind one of a small child who sticks his fingers in his ears and shouts, "I can't hear you," in the face of mortality.

Elective Antipathies in the Muslim World

Almost without exception, "free and fair" elections in the Middle East, held under American supervision or with American approval, have put America's enemies into power. Six years after President Bush suggested that Hezbollah—then and now at the top of America's list of proscribed terrorist organizations—might be tamed by electoral politics, the Iranian- and Syrian-backed militia is in effective control of the Lebanese government, and still more interested in jihad than in potholes. At the end of January 2011, Lebanon's parliament chose Hezbollah's candidate, Najib Mitaki, as the country's new prime minister, replacing the Saudi-backed Saad Hariri. The political crisis that toppled Hariri arose from the findings of an international tribunal investigating the 2005 car-bomb assassination of Hariri's father, former Prime Minister Rafik Hariri. The tribunal identified Hezbollah as the culprit in the assassination, and Hezbollah—which is more powerful than the Lebanese army—threatened a civil war. Without a shot fired, the Lebanese parliament wilted under Hezbollah's threat and brought in their front man.

The elder Hariri's murder in 2005 prompted demonstrations that the press dubbed "the Cedar Revolution." On March 4, the *Washington Post*'s Charles Krauthammer wrote of "the dawn of a glorious, delicate, revolutionary moment in the Middle East."[4] The *National Review*'s John Derbyshire opined prematurely that "this has been a bad few weeks for us pessimists…with 1989-style demonstrations out in the streets of Beirut."[5] A prominent Bush detractor, *Newsweek*'s Fareed Zakaria, conceded that "Bush is right" and "may change the world." That was then.

In January 2006, Hamas swept the first elections held since 1996 for the Palestinian Legislative Council (PLC), the legislature of the Palestinian National Authority (PNA), winning seventy-four seats. The ruling Fatah faction won only forty-five. No elections have been held since.

Tayyip Erdogan's Islamist AK (Justice and Development) party won a clear victory in the July 22, 2007, general election with 47 percent of the votes cast. In September 2010, 58 percent of voters supported Erdogan's position in a constitutional referendum that gave the president and parliament effective control of the judiciary and reduced the role of the army in Turkish politics. Turkey has ceased to be an American ally for all practical purposes.

Since Iraq's 2010 elections, which produced a parliament divided along ethnic and sectarian lines, Prime Minister Nouri al-Maliki—a Shi'ite who owes his position to Iran—has emerged as the country's dominant political figure. For the time being, Iran and America share power in Iraq. The Shi'ite militia leader Moqtada al-Sadr, whose armed forces fought pitched battles with American forces during 2004 and 2005, returned from exile in Iran in January, and al-Maliki invited several of al-Sadr's supporters to join the government. "In persuading Moqtada al-Sadr to back Maliki, Iran provided a major boost to Maliki's efforts to remain prime minister. Once al-Sadr's Sadrist Trend (the strongest Shia party resisting Maliki's leadership) gave in, all of the other Shia groups eventually followed," wrote Marina Ottaway of the Carnegie Foundation for International Peace.[6] In his first speech to his followers on returning to Iraq, al-Sadr threatened armed resistance if America delays plans to remove all American troops by the end of 2011: "We are still resisting the occupation through armed, cultural and all kinds of resistance, so repeat after me: no, no to occupiers."

"Pakistan's 1970 election—the freest and fairest in the nation's history—resulted in civil war, war with India, and the partition of the country into Pakistan and Bangladesh," wrote Stanley Kurtz of *National Review* in 2007. Pakistan's attempt to suppress the Bengali revolt produced casualties reported variously from 200,000 to 3 million; an additional 8 million Bengalis fled to India for safety. "Pakistan is not a democracy," Kurtz added. "Pakistan has never been a democracy. Should Pakistan adopt the electoral trappings of democracy in the near-term, that would not make Pakistan an authentic liberal democracy. Free and fair elections just might dissolve Pakistan into chaos, and/or begin a process of evolution toward Islamist domination. Elections or not, if Pakistan achieves stability any time soon, it will not be due to democracy. Pakistani stability in the near-term can only be the result of a precarious balance between political factions that are largely illiberal and undemocratic."[7]

One might add that when the Ayatollah Khomeini came to power in Iran, more than 98 percent of Iranians voted "yes" in a referendum on whether Iran should become an Islamic republic.

After nearly 4,500 U.S. dead in Iraq and 1,400 in Afghanistan, as well as a trillion dollars in spending, it is hard to have a dispassionate discussion about the success or failure of American policy in Iraq. No matter how badly things turn out in Iraq, there will be protests that all would be well if only we had "stayed the course." After eight years of occupation and vast expenditures of blood and treasure, it seems fair to ask what such a course might be; if the U.S. were to occupy Iraq indefinitely, and spend limitless amounts of money, it could make Iraq look like anything it wants to be. Left to its own devices, though, Iraq will become a satrapy of Iran.

Under American occupation, Iraqis have held national elections, and in that sense America can take credit for sponsoring a new democracy. But the stability that made the elections possible was dearly bought, and bought at the expense of deadlier conflict down the road. A comparison to the Thirty Years' War is instructive. We have seen how the great field marshal Albrecht von Wallenstein taught armies to live off the land, and succeeded so well that nearly half the people of Central Europe starved to death. General David Petraeus, who commanded America's Central Command (CENTCOM) during the "surge" of 2008, taught the land to live off him. Wallenstein put a hundred thousand men into the field, an army of terrifying size for the times, by turning the imperial army into a parasite that consumed the livelihood of the empire's home provinces. Petraeus recruited an identical number of Sunni Arabs by distributing (literally) bags of money. Starting with Iraq, the American military has militarized large parts of the Middle East and Central Asia in the name of pacification. And now America is engaged in a grand strategic withdrawal from responsibility in the region, leaving behind men with weapons and excellent reason to use them.

Petraeus' "surge" drastically reduced the level of violence in Iraq by absorbing most of the available Sunni fighters into an American-financed militia, the "Sons of Iraq," or Sunni Awakening. With American money, weapons, and training, the remnants of Saddam Hussein's regime have turned into a fighting force far more effective than the defunct dictator's state police. Petraeus re-created the military balance of power between Sunnis and Shi'ites by reconstructing the former's fighting capacity while persuading pro-Iranian militants to bide their time. To achieve this balance of power, though, he built up Sunni military power to the point that—for the first time in Iraq's history—Sunnis and Shi'ites are capable of fighting a full-dress civil war with professional armed forces. "Nation-building" in Iraq failed to construct any functional feature of civil society (a concept hitherto unknown to Mesopotamia) except, of course, for the best-functioning organized groups of killers that Iraq has ever had. The Iranians had no interest in disrupting the surge. If they had, the American military would have made short work of their local proxies, who never could outfight the U.S. Marines. Having armed all sides of the conflict and kept them apart by the threat of arms, the United States now expects to depart, leaving in place governments of national reconciliation that will persuade well-armed and well-organized militias to play by the rules. The British played at divide and conquer, whereas the Americans propose to divide and disappear.

A regiment of Iranian regulars crossed the border into southern Iraq on December 16, 2009, and planted the Iranian flag over an inactive Iraqi oilfield at Fakka. At first the Iranian army denied the incursion, but then announced two days later in an Arab-language broadcast, "Our forces are on our own soil and, based on the known international borders, this well belongs to Iran." No oil was flowing from the Fakka installation, but Iran had made its point: the Iraqi government's tepid response to the little invasion showed how beholden the government in Baghdad was to Tehran. "Sunni politicans denounced what they called the feckless response of the Iraqi security forces—the incursion was met with no resistance—whom they accuse of being compromised by Iranian influence," the *Washington Post* reported shortly afterwards. "Since the U.S.-led invasion in 2003, Shiite Iran's influence has steadily grown in Iraq. Many of the Iraqi leaders installed early on by the Americans spent years in exile in Iran, and Iranian money, weapons and intelligence agents have flooded across a border that neither the Iraqis nor the Americans have been able to control."[8]

Diplomatic cables made public by WikiLeaks reveal consternation among America's Arab allies over Iran's creeping influence in Iraq. In a March 22, 2009, meeting with President Obama's counterterrorism adviser John Brennan and other U. S. officials, King Abdullah of Saudi Arabia said he had "no confidence whatsoever in Iraqi PM Maliki, and the U. S. Ambassador to Saudi Arabia is well aware of my views." The King added that he had refused former President Bush's entreaties that he meet with Maliki—because he had met Maliki early in Maliki's term of office, and the Iraqi had given him a written list of commitments for reconciliation in Iraq, but had failed to follow through on any of them. For this reason, the King said, Maliki had no credibility. "I don't trust this man," the King stated. "He's an Iranian agent." The King said he had asked both Bush and former vice president Cheney, "How can I meet with someone I don't trust?" Maliki has "opened the door for Iranian influence in Iraq" since taking power, the King said, and he was "not hopeful at all" for Maliki, "or I would have met with him."[9]

Do Muslims Want American-Style Democracy?

President Bush asked why Arabs should desire freedom any less than Americans. The answer is that political freedom has a price: it requires an extraordinary level of trust. In a democratic republic, individuals assign their voting rights to a representative with whom they have no blood tie, in a distant capital city they may never visit, and entrust this representative to strike bargains with other representatives of people they do not know. When this remote and abstract process results in damaging or unwelcome decisions, the citizen of a democracy must accept them and hope that a future round of voting and negotiations will produce a different outcome. Voters are willing to accept such reverses only when they believe that the rights of every citizen are sacred, and that the decision of the people by democratic process has an authority that no one may profane by violence. The vote is sacred because the rights of every citizen are God-given and therefore sacred. In short, democracy demands trust in an abstract idea of rights, and sufficient faith in the process to accept unfavorable outcomes.

Iraq is an artificial entity cobbled together by British diplomats after the First World War, combining Kurdish, Arab Sunni, and Arab Shi'ite provinces of the defunct Ottoman Empire. A third of Iraqis still marry their cousins, in one of the most clan-centered societies in the world. It is whimsical to assume that Iraqis will behave like Americans, as anthropologist Philip Carl Salzman argues:

> The Arab Middle East has remained largely a pre-modern society, governed by clan relationships and violent coercion. People in both the countryside and the cities tend to trust only their relatives, and then only relative to their degree of closeness. People define their interests in terms of the interests of their own group, and in opposition to those of other groups. A pervasive cult of honor requires that people support their own groups, violently if necessary, when conflict arises.
>
> What is missing in the Arab Middle East are the cultural tools for building an inclusive and united state. The cultural glue of the West and other successful modern societies—consisting of the rule of law and constitutionalism, which serve to regulate competition among unrelated groups—is absent in the Arab world. The frame of reference in a tribalized society is always "my group vs. the other group." This system of

"balanced opposition" is the structural alternative that stands in stubborn opposition to Western constitutionalism.[10]

Bush dismissed as "condescension" the idea that the desires of other peoples might be different from ours. Arab political philosophers, though, have a keen understanding of the difference, and condescension seems too mild a term for an American complacency that ignores their protests.

We have already met Professor Ali Allawi, Iraq's most distinguished political philosopher. In patient and lucid prose, Allawi attempts to explain to his American readers why his country differs so radically from theirs:

> The modern West—particularly its English-speaking part—is defined by a decisive shift away from the collective and the sacred and towards the individual and the secular. In the self-image of the West, the individual is ennobled and given the power to determine the course of his or her personal development, together with that of society, through the idiom of rights and the practice of a democracy based on laws and rules. The main purpose of society becomes to provide the environment for individuals to develop their potential and, in the process, to enrich and advance society as a whole. Other modern societies reject the notion that the individual should be the undivided focus of attention; they reverse the formula. The interests of the group—be it the party, the clan, the military or the nation—becomes paramount.[11]

In his Second Inaugural Address, George W. Bush appealed to theology: "America's vital interests and our deepest beliefs are now one. From the day of our Founding, we have proclaimed that every man and woman on this earth has rights and dignity, and matchless value, because they bear the image of the Maker of Heaven and earth." If American democracy is rooted in a certain theology, though, it seems appropriate to ask whether a different theology would lead to different political conclusions.

Islam rejects the Western notion of individuality; in the Islamic view, Allawi explains, individuality according to the Western concept is not merely undesirable but impossible, an affront against the absolute sovereignty of Allah. "Islam departs from the mainstream of modern constructs of the individual and the group," he observes. The notion of a human individual is not only absent from Islamic thinking, but impossible to describe in the Arabic language. Only God has individuality and uniqueness; the individual is merely an instrument, as it were.[12] "Therefore to claim the right and the possibility of autonomous action without reference to the source of these in God is an affront."

In the American founding, the biblical concept of Covenant undergirds individual rights, for these are granted irrevocably to every member of society by a God who limits his own power as an act of grace. The biblical theology of the West leads to one concept of society; Muslim theology leads to a radically different concept, for an absolutely transcendent God leaves no room at all for the individual. The individual acquires from God whatever appearance of individuality he might have, but has no autonomy, in sharp contrast to the Western notion. Allawi adds:

> Rediscovering or developing the political basis of a new Islamic civilization has to take place in this context. The question becomes whether there is wholesale acceptance of the West's definition of universal values and acknowledgement that Islam must move towards adopting them, or whether Islam should continue to seek the meaning of the universal—including that in political values and institutions—in its own legacy....
>
> In essence, Muslim democracy is a pathway to a secular and ultimately Western definition of the political rather than a re-expression of the political in Islam...democracy is unlikely to resolve the conundrum which Muslims face when they are

dealing with the political: the need to evolve a privileged place
for the sacred in the structuring of the Islamic political order.[13]

The "sacred," as Allawi makes clear, requires the reduction of the individual
to a mere instrument without autonomy.

In Western philosophy, Allawi's vision of a totalizing society that elim-
inates individual autonomy is closest to the "general will" propounded by
the French political theorist Jean-Jacques Rousseau. As Jean Bethke Elshtain
explains, the "general will" presumes a sovereign state that is "closed, indi-
visible, monolithic" in its power. Rousseau "sacralizes" politics, which is
"made into an object of sacred devotion.... The citizen goes through a
sacred rite—enters as a sinner ruled by a bad form of instinct—and emerges
as an avatar of justice, having been cleansed of the old and having put on
the new."[14] Rousseau's philosophy is diametrically opposed to the Pilgrims'
Christian politics, and to their radical respect for God-granted individual
rights. Christianity would have no place in his totalizing state, Rousseau
explained, for the Christian faith gives men "two leaders and two home-
lands, subjects them to contradictory duties, and prevents them from being
simultaneously men and citizens." Rousseau contrasts this "bizarre type of
religion" with what he calls "the wise system of Mohammed," who succeeds
in "completely uniting" religion and the state.[15]

An Islamic political order must be founded upon sharia, albeit (in
Allawi's view) a flexible and adaptable sharia:

> Islamic civilization developed out of the tensions between the
> sacred law and the exigencies of political life. Whenever rulers
> strayed too far from the divine ideal, the Sharia would be brought
> to bear to correct the imbalance. Jurists would fulminate against
> the godlessness of royal courts, the intrusion of alien practices,
> or the irreligiousness of the public.... Whenever the sharia stood
> in the way of the resolution of practical problems—say, in the
> transfer of power from one ruler to the next—new dispensations

would have to be created, simply to allow for continuity in the community's life.[16]

Of course, to adapt sharia to a political order presumes a single source of religious authority; that rules out a multi-confessional state, let alone a secular one.

Is the American Way Better?

Is it entirely unreasonable for Middle Eastern Muslims to reject American-style democracy? Democracy founded on the inalienable rights of the individual has costs as well as benefits. American democracy protects behavior that most in the Muslim world—and most Americans—consider revolting: pornography, extreme forms of sexual deviance, gratuitous violence in television and cinema, and blasphemy. Andre Serrano's 1987 *Piss Christ*, a photograph of a crucifix submerged in the artist's urine, won an award from the Southeastern Center for Contemporary Art with funding from the National Endowment for the Arts and was exhibited in 1999 at the Brooklyn Museum, again with public funding. In a 1990 obscenity trial, a jury decided in favor of the Cincinnati Contemporary Arts Center, which had exhibited photographs by Robert Mapplethorpe depicting sadomasochistic homosexual acts, also with public funding. The vast majority of Americans find the work of Serrano, Mapplethorpe, and innumerable others objectionable, but the American legal system has found no way to limit its exhibition, or even to restrict the use of public funding to support it. Only with extreme effort can parents prevent the septic tide of internet pornography from seeping into their children's computers.

Unlike Iranians or Saudis, Americans do not execute a Mapplethorpe or Serrano for blasphemy. But Western countries used to execute blasphemers, for the same reason that Muslim countries execute blasphemers today. "As for heretics, their sin deserves banishment, not only ... by excommunication, but also from this world by death. To corrupt the faith, whereby the soul lives, is much graver than to counterfeit money, which supports temporal life. Since forgers and other malefactors are summarily condemned to death by the civil authorities, with much more reason may heretics as soon as they are convicted of heresy be not only excommunicated, but also justly be put to death."[17] Those are the words of the thirteenth-century Catholic authority St. Thomas Aquinas, the most influential of all Catholic thinkers. St. Thomas did not merely support the death sentence for individual heretics, but weighed in vigorously on behalf of the Crusade against the Albigensians, which killed perhaps a million people in Provence.

As the Catholic writer Michael Novak explains, tough times required tough measures:

> Thirteenth-century societies were highly fragile. Beyond ties of kinship, many citizens experienced little to bind them to others. Most were subjects of a few, and one ruling aristocrat was often overturned by another...geographical isolation was often intense, and shifting patterns of warfare, baronial allegiance, and foreign occupation awakened acute local insecurity. Under political anarchy, the common people and the poor suffered much. Under all these uncertainties, the chief consensual bond among people was Catholic faith and Catholic ritual. Virtually all unifying conceptions of relationship and social weight, meaning and order, came from that faith.[18]

Novak well might be describing Muslim countries today. If social conditions in Iraq or Afghanistan resemble those of thirteenth-century Europe, where most citizens had no loyalties "beyond ties of kinship," why should Christians (or Jews) object to an Islamic state that kills heretics the way Christians did eight centuries ago? The short answer is that today—in contrast to the thirteenth century—it is impossible to isolate a backward state from the globalized world. National survival requires the kind of talent that democracy fosters. America has produced not only a Robert Mapplethorpe and an Andre Serrano, but also a Steve Jobs, a Bill Gates, not to mention a Thomas Edison. Americans are prepared to tolerate, even to protect some extraordinarily bad individuals in the hope of also fostering some extraordinarily good ones.

America's free market, though, has social costs: Rust Belt communities collapsed in the ruin of American heavy industry during the 1970s and 1980s. The American economy generated ample jobs during the great economic expansion of 1984–2008, but in different parts of the country. People who had grown up within walking distance of several households in an extended family moved to anonymous suburban subdivisions whose social center was the shopping mall. Adolescents' social lives once revolved around a religious community; now they flirt on Facebook. The community house of worship faded, and the peculiarly American institution of the megachurch sprang up with the subdivisions. More than thirteen hundred such megachurches now host several thousand worshippers each Sunday. Extended families that once gathered weekly now send family pictures by email and gather only on major holidays, if at all. Sociologists lament the atomization of American society. Harvard Professor Robert Putnam, author of the celebrated study *Bowling Alone*,[19] warns that "we now see a public that is withdrawing from communal life, choosing to live alone and play alone. We are becoming mere observers of our collective destiny."[20] Family and clan, as we have seen, are the state-in-miniature for Muslim countries, not only as a practical matter but by Koranic decree. To dissolve kinship-communities into a pool of individuals, in which the founding theology of the nation must compete on level ground with the most extravagant perversions—this great American carnival of freedom appears as atrocious to Muslims today as it would have to the thirteenth-century Thomas Aquinas.

The Christian empire of St. Thomas Aquinas's time still had centuries in which to adjust to a modernity that barely flickered on a distant horizon. Modernity is already upon the Muslims, and the required adjustment time is effectively zero. Democracy in the Muslim world has the main effect of providing vents for frustration, and it should be no surprise that every free and fair election held in the Muslim world during the past decade has advanced the cause of Islamist radicalism.

Sometimes, Optimism Really Is Cowardice

There are a few dissenters from the "Freedom Agenda" in the conservative camp, to be sure. Under the title "The Democracy Delusion," the British conservative Peter Hitchens wrote, "How many Islamic republics would you like? How many do you think the world needs? Spreading democracy across the Muslim world—as so many enlightened people say they wish to do—should certainly increase the number. Yet the enthusiasts for planting democracy all over the planet also tend to be the people who dislike Islamic republics and warn endlessly about their likely use as bases for terror."[21] And Stanley Kurtz pointed out in 2003,

> Arab Muslim societies remain un-modern and un-democratic not just in their attitudes toward political authority and law but also in their social organization. For men and women living within a universe where tribal identity, the duties and benefits of extended kinship networks, and conceptions of collective honor organize the relations of everyday life, democratic principles will be incomprehensible. And therefore democracy would be impossible. How could a modern, democratic bureaucracy function, for example, if officials remain loyal primarily to tribe, faction, or family? The power of such ties preempts any ethic of disinterested public service. A government office becomes a means of benefitting your family and harming your enemies, not applying rules fairly.[22]

These voices of caution, though, are drowned out by the din of support for democracy as a global cure-all. Paradoxically, it now seems almost un-American to acknowledge that American democracy was a singular event in world history—even though America's founders believed that they had to put an ocean between themselves and the corrupt Old World in order to found a state according to the biblical notion of individual sanctity. Behind the ideological reflex, which has resisted repeated lessons to the contrary, lurks a reluctance to face a world in which happy outcomes cannot always be expected. The political advisors who urged President Bush to propagate democracy throughout the Muslim world have not changed their views, despite the fact that Islamists have gained from every electoral opening in the Middle East. No amount of experience will change their minds. They do not know how to. Which brings us to Spengler's Universal Law #22, a modification of Oswald Spengler's famous aphorism: *Optimism is cowardice, at least when the subject is Muslim democracy.*

☙☙☙

CHAPTER 16

THE MORALITY OF SELF-INTEREST

Spengler's Universal Law #23: *The best thing you can do for zombie cultures is, don't be one of them.*

Today we take the existence of nations for granted: each flag in the long row fronting the United Nations General Assembly on Manhattan's First Avenue represents a state that has as much right to be there as any other. It seems monstrous even to ask whether some of those flags stand for peoples that will perish within our lifetimes, or that of our children. But this attitude is a prejudice of modern political science. In fact, the founding idea of the West was that states fail because peoples fail.

Since the Enlightenment, political science has reduced political questions to a matter of interests. Interests are by and large material: survival, security, material gain, and so forth. These are the rational concerns of human beings, according to Enlightenment theory. The Enlightenment in fact told us nothing new: this idea of politics was formulated with marvelous clarity by Cicero, the great exponent of the Roman republic. Cicero argued in the first century B.C.E. that a republic is "an assemblage associated by a common acknowledgment of law, and by a community of interests."[1] Cicero's "community of interests" is the ancestor of all the secular concepts of the state offered by modern political scientists, from Hobbes' social contract, to Montesquieu's balance of powers, to Leo Strauss' "low but broad" characterization of the American republic.

But how should we think about the self-interest of the "Bo" people, as in the following 2010 obituary?

> The world has lost an ancient language with the death of the last speaker of "Bo" in India's Andaman Islands at the age of 85, an Indian official said Friday. "Boa Sr, who died on January 28 here, was suffering from old age health ailments for some time. She was the oldest member of the Great Andamanese tribe," Tribal Health Deputy Director R.C. Kar told the media.
>
> According to leading linguist Professor Anvita Abbi, the death of Boa Sr of a unique tribe in the Andamans also led to the tragic demise of the world's oldest languages [sic]—Bo. "After the death of her parents, Boa was the last Bo speaker for 30 to 40 years. She was often very lonely and had to learn an Adamanese version of Hindi in order to communicate with people. But throughout her life she had a very good sense of humor and her smile and full-throated laughter were infectious," said Abbi.[2]

After perhaps 70,000 years (Andaman languages may go back that far, to distant origins in Africa), the 85-year-old woman in question *was* her people—the last repository of their hopes, dreams, songs, and stories—with no hope of transmitting them. What could our political scientists have said to her? The Bo people no longer exist, not, in any event, as a self-conscious identity, although their DNA may live in other bodies. But so does the DNA of Neanderthals, who have yet to obtain their own ethnic studies department at a major university. An extinct people has no self-interest. How close does a people need to come to extinction before the matter of its "interests" becomes moot? What shall we say, as a practical matter, to the Estonians, Latvians, Lithuanians, Ukrainians, and other European peoples whose populations will shrink drastically within the visible horizon? At what point does a nation that refuses to perpetuate itself cease to have a rational self-interest?

Augustinian Realism

At the outset of the previous Great Extinction of peoples, the intellectual founding father of the Christian West asked a similar question. St. Augustine of Hippo (354–430 C.E.) rejected Cicero's notion of "common interest." The definition of a republic, Augustine insisted, must take into account the traits that lead to its preservation or its downfall. States fail, Augustine argued, because peoples fail, and peoples fail because they love the wrong things. A nation defines itself by what it *loves*, and the wrong sort of love condemns it to eventual ruin.

In *The City of God*, Augustine wrote,

> If we discard [Cicero's] definition of a people, and, assuming another, say that a people is an assemblage of reasonable beings bound together by a common agreement as to the objects of their love, then, in order to discover the character of any people, we have only to observe what they love…. According to this definition of ours, the Roman people is a people, and its weal is without doubt a commonwealth or republic. But what its tastes were in its early and subsequent days, and how it declined into sanguinary seditions and then to social and civil wars, and so burst asunder or rotted off the bond of concord in which the health of a people consists, history shows. [3]

Cicero himself was murdered on the order of Marc Antony after the overthrow of the Roman Republic. Augustine saw in the downfall of Rome a repetition of the tragic pattern of the pagan world: "But what I say of this people and of this republic I must be understood to think and say of the Athenians or any Greek state, of the Egyptians, of the early Assyrian Babylon, and of every other nation, great or small, which had a public government."

Christianity arose out of the failure of the fragile nations of late Roman times, and called individuals out of their nations to join the "tribe of Christians." What would Augustine have said about today's Europeans, or Japanese, or Persians? If a time machine had transported the Church Father to the year 2011, he might have marveled at how little was new under the sun. The self-aggrandizing tribes of the world are once again turning from triumphalism to despondency and, as in the fourth century, willing themselves out of existence.

Augustine might have seen America as the sort of non-ethnic policy that he hoped Rome would become. Americans selected themselves out from among the nations of the world to enter into the political covenant that is the American constitutional state. It has succeeded because it is "a country with the soul of a church," as G. K. Chesterton observed. Individualism founded on God-given rights has triumphed over the alternative—the various manifestations of the collectivist state—Rousseau's "will of the people," for example, and Marx's proletarian dictatorship, and the blood-and-soil nationalism that led Europe and Japan into the World Wars of the twentieth century. The only form of collectivism still embraced by a large part of the world's population is Islam.

Any question about the self-interest of a nation that has doomed itself to extinction is a rhetorical question. But with respect to America, the question is: What is the self-interest of the United States of America with respect to other nations? The answer, I believe, calls for an extension of Augustine's definition of a republic: if the American republic is an assembly of people held together by a common law and a common love, then America's self-interest lies in alliances with countries that share our common love.

Other great nations have adopted some parts of the Western principles that define America and therefore something of what America loves. India has become the world's largest democracy by co-opting the parliamentary system of Britain, its former imperial overlord. The daunting subject of Hindu religion lies beyond the scope of this book; the Indians have transformed the fractious subcontinent into a single nation with a deep democratic culture and profound regard for the rights of individuals. Perhaps the Hindu sense of the sanctity of life has combined with Western political forms to produce a polity with strong parallels to the American system. With fourteen languages spoken by more than 10 million of its citizens, India is not an ethnic state, but a multi-ethnic polity united by a common idea. In this respect India resembles the United States more than either Germany or Japan does.

China is trying (though in service of a one-party state) to harness the free market. What the fall of Communism revealed remains true: states that suppress individual rights on behalf of some expression of the collective will fail, and globalization and technological advance simply accelerate the pace of state failure. Those states that support individual rights have some chance of succeeding. There is no reconciling the conflicts in Chinese society. It remains a dictatorship ruled by the Communist Party, which brutally suppresses attempts to revive such traditional Chinese religious movements as Falun Gong. But the Communist party has tolerated—and on some occasions even appeared to encourage—the spread of Christianity in China, which now claims the faith of a tenth of the country's population.

As the Italian sinologist Francesco Sisci writes, "The leadership views Christianity in a fundamentally different way from how it sees the religions rooted in traditional China. Christianity is inherently open to the modern world and a scientific outlook. Just as China imported science and Western methods of industrial organization, so it could import what Beijing understood to be the spiritual counterpart of Western science. In the view of the party, the naturalization of Christianity in China is not

essentially different from the importation of socialist ideology two generations earlier. Christianity, like socialism, can be translated into Chinese
characters."[4]

To the extent that other nations share the American love for the sanctity
of the individual, they are likely to succeed. To the extent they reject it, they
are likely to fail. Thus actions in the world can promote American interests
because taking the side of nations who share what we love will mean allying
with success. We might call this foreign policy "Augustinian realism." American interest consists of allying with success and containing failure.

Secular political science views nations as mechanical constructs, like
watches. In this view what matters is whether the gears mesh properly and
the mainspring holds its tension, for watches have no spiritual concerns.
But what appears objective and scientific turns out in the broad context
of the life and death of nations to be fantastical and unreal in the extreme,
for nations that fail to reproduce their people will cease to exist. True
political realism begins with Augustine's concern: What is the character
that fosters a people's continuity rather than catastrophe? Augustinian
realism begins with the observation that civil society precedes the character of a nation. The American state can ally with, cajole, or even crush other
states, but it cannot change the character of their civil society, except in a
very slow, gradual, and indirect fashion—for example, through the more
than one hundred thousand American Christian missionaries now working overseas. Authentic realism insists that the state should not try to do
what it cannot do.

It is not necessary to agree with Augustine's evangelical purpose to grasp
the instrumental value of his political insight. To take America as the great
exemplar of an Augustinian Realist state, moreover, is not triumphalism,
for America cannot take for granted that it will remain the only—or even
the most important—instantiation of its own founding idea.

But beyond its instrumental value, Augustinian realism has a moral
dimension as well. America has a moral obligation toward citizens of other
nations who share our civic love—for the same political friendship that

binds together our civil society must include prospective friends in other countries. America has a moral obligation to allies and a moral interest in the welfare of people who are linked to our civil society—our mother country England, for example, as well as the Christians in the global South.

Israel is the example par excellence of a state with a moral claim on American friendship. America's founding began with the Pilgrims' vision of a new Exodus and a new mission in the wilderness, and the new nation learned from the Jews to regard every human being as a living image of God. Israel, moreover, is an example to the world of how moral greatness corresponds to practical success. Israel is a crucial American ally not only because it is the leading military power in the Middle East and a technological powerhouse with more venture capital investment than the whole of Europe (the instrumental dimension of Augustinian realism), but also because of the deep ties between the American founding and the Jewish religion and the strong bonds between Israelis and America's 6.4 million Jews (the moral dimension).

America has no obligation toward states and peoples who have no part in our civic love. We wish everyone well and prefer that all succeed and none fail. But realism demands that we ration our friendship. Consider the winning policy of the Reagan administration during the Cold War, which overcame the most prominent collectivist alternative to American democracy. America did not set out to persuade the Soviet Union to emulate us. We set out to ruin it, and ruin it we did. After Russia repudiated Communism, we proposed to assist in the country's reconstruction. In other words, American interest consists of allying with success and containing failure.

In the course of just two administrations, our foreign policy has passed from adolescence—the Wilsonian fancy that America could remake the world in its own image—to senile renunciation of world leadership, without ever having passed through maturity. Instead of the uncertain, meticulous work of containing failed states, nurturing prospective allies, and deterring prospective enemies, Washington has swung from a utopian effort to fix the world to the baffling pretense that the world somehow will fix itself if only

America leaves it alone. The result is a self-inflicted wound to America's world standing—to the anguish of our allies and the undisguised contempt of our adversaries.

Instead of a president determined to use American hegemony to rid the world of evil, in Barack Obama America has a president determined to rid the world of hegemony. As Barack Obama told the United Nations in September 2009, "No one nation can or should try to dominate another nation. No world order that elevates one nation or group of people over another will succeed. No balance of power among nations will hold." Since America is the only nation capable of exercising hegemony on a world scale or maintaining the balance of power among other powers, President Obama's doctrine is the self-liquidation of American influence—an unprecedented and, on reflection, astonishing position for an American leader.

American foreign policy baffles the rest of the world. Look, for example, at the damage to America's world position during March and April of last year. First came the Obama administration's staged quarrel with Israel over a routine zoning decision for homes in northeast Jerusalem, which is a neighborhood where Arabs had never lived and an area which every proposal for the division of Jerusalem has assigned to the Israeli side. For over thirty years American administrations have avoided making an issue of Israel's claim to an undivided Jerusalem; Obama broke with that precedent in a staged crisis. The White House threatened Israel with an imposed solution and afterwards threatened to demand that Israel abandon nuclear weapons. The White House in effect demanded that Israel concede key matters subject to negotiations in advance. Most alarming to Israel, the Obama administration repudiated the 2004 agreement that President George W. Bush had struck with then Prime Minister Ariel Sharon, in which Israel unilaterally evacuated Gaza in return for American flexibility on West Bank settlement growth. Sharon's chief of staff Dov Weisglass had put this agreement in writing in letters that have since been made public.[5] In May 2011, President Obama demanded an Israeli withdrawal from the West Bank to the 1949 armistice lines (sometimes referred to as the "1967 borders") prior to any Palestinian agreement on the right of return of Arab refugees to Israel and the final status of Jerusalem—the deal-breakers in previous peace negotiations. Israel and its supporters interpreted the president's speech as a unilateral concession to Israel's adversaries and a repudiation of American policy since the 1967 United Nations Resolution 242, which envisioned less-than-complete withdrawal by Israel from territories seized during the Six-Day War.

Obama's pressure on America's Israeli ally has been defended in the name of realism. For, in common parlance, realism in foreign policy denotes the amoral acceptance of the way things are. But the way things are is not necessarily the way they will remain, and it can be unrealistic in the extreme to expect them to do so. During the Cold War, the "realist" position accepted the Soviet Union as a permanent feature of the world scene and sought a long-term accommodation with its interests—while Ronald Reagan was regarded as a reckless visionary for his dangerously "unrealistic" belief that the Soviets could be defeated. Yet the Soviet economy, as we have seen, turned out to be a Potemkin village worth less than its scrap value after the fall of Communism. The Soviets were unable to support Russian military power when forced to compete with an American build-up. The Soviets loved the wrong things, and that false love made them weaker than anyone, except Reagan and his allies, could see. Reagan, Margaret Thatcher, and John Paul II were the authentic realists.

The Emperor Has No Clothes, and the Empire Has No Tailors

What passes for "realism" today comes down to placating the Muslim world as it is, in opposition to the Bush administration's "idealist" project of exporting democracy. In January 2011 this policy exploded when revolts against longstanding Arab autocracies exploded in Tunisia and Egypt and quickly spread to Libya, Bahrain, Yemen, and other Arab countries. The Arab revolt demonstrates that this form of "realism" has no more to do with reality than the "realism" of the early 1980s. Again, as we have seen, the most likely outcome of the Arab revolts will be a series of failed states from North Africa to the Persian Gulf. There are nearly a billion and a half Muslims, but their footprint in world events is small. Globalization and technological advance have given us a world which multiplies the power of innovative individuals. Mass armies have no more military relevance today than horse cavalry in World War I—as Saddam Hussein learned during the First Gulf War. Computation and communication technology, meanwhile, have turned formerly backward parts of Asia into economic giants within a single generation.

This great transformation has left Muslim countries almost untouched. "According to a World Bank estimate, the total exports of the Arab world other than fossil fuels amount to less than those of Finland, a country of five million inhabitants," observed Bernard Lewis. Not one scientific discovery of note, innovative firm of international importance, or contribution to universal culture has come from the Muslim world in the past century. In 2008, only 133 patents were filed in Muslim-majority lands, about a tenth of the number in Israel, while the Israeli total exceeded that of India, Russia, and Singapore combined.

It is not only that the emperor has no clothes, but that the empire has no tailors: except for hydrocarbons, the Muslim world is of small interest to America. Only the multicultural conceit that all cultures deserve equal esteem and should enjoy equal success contravenes the obvious facts. It is America's misfortune to have elected at this juncture a president who bears a deep sentimental attachment to the Muslim world. The Bush administration's idealism stands in deserved disrepute. But the impulse behind its approach to the world—the belief that America's exceptional character is the standard by which all political systems should be judged—is a baby that should not be thrown out with the bathwater.

Why have the past two administrations put the Muslim world at the top of their foreign-policy agenda? Part of the answer, of course, is oil, although we have yet to encounter a regime that, however ill-disposed to America, declines to sell oil on the world market at the market price. But there is a more significant reason. The paradoxical answer is that the claim of Muslim states on American attention rests on their propensity to fail. Many were contrived from Ottoman, British, or Dutch imperial detritus and comprise a welter of contending tongues and tribes. None of these nations foster the kind of entrepreneurial and scientific innovation that success in the global economy demands; most support a religious establishment hostile not only to individual initiative but to religious freedom, the education of women, and other indispensable aspects of modern society.

Egypt, Tunisia, Algeria, Libya, Iraq, Afghanistan, Lebanon, and Pakistan are at near-term risk of state failure. To repeat a point, their loves produce frail and fragile states. And their weaknesses make them dangerous. Iran, whose theocratic ruling stratum crushed the political aspirations of the country's educated youth with violence, is trying to avert a breakdown at home by breaking out into regional hegemony. Intelligence services in Pakistan—where half the people live on $1 a day, half cannot read, and ethnic rivalry remains a perpetual threat to the artificially constructed state—help the Taliban. Syria supports Hezbollah and Hamas. And the Saudis pay protection to al-Qaeda. To obtain visas, weapons, intelligence, and so forth, terrorists require the assistance of someone in government, if not the complicity of the highest state authorities. Such assistance may be a matter of state policy, or a matter of sympathetic officials aiding terrorists for ideological reasons, or a case of corrupt officials selling weapons or even fissile material. The vulnerability of the failed Muslim states makes all these scenarios more likely.

To use force against governments that support terrorists surely lies within the proper scope of American policy, as well as the definition of just war. But there has been no greater folly in American diplomacy—no better example of the cost of ignoring Augustine—than the conceit that American intervention could make modern democracies out of states with a pre-modern civil society. The Bush administration acted properly to overthrow the Taliban in Afghanistan and the regime of Saddam Hussein in Iraq, but overreached when it occupied both countries in order to foster democracy.

We cannot effectively do that, and American troops must leave some day. Then Iran or Pakistan will step in to assert their influence—Iran through its Shi'ite auxiliaries and Pakistan through its longtime Taliban client.

America has neither the means nor the moral obligation to transform failing Muslim states into entities compatible with our civil loves. The very attempt can be disastrous.

And now the Obama administration hopes for what it calls a "reset" of America's relations with the Muslim world. But it appears to be encouraging some of America's worst enemies. The immediate result of the regime collapses in Arab countries will be a shift from secular to Islamic governance, with the paradoxical approval of the United States. America's president really is prepared to gamble core American interests on the sketchy proposition that Egypt and other failed states can turn into Muslim democracies. The *Washington Post* reported March 4,

> The administration is already taking steps to distinguish between various movements in the region that promote Islamic law in government. An internal assessment, ordered by the White House last month, identified large ideological differences between such movements as the Muslim Brotherhood in Egypt and al-Qaeda that will guide the U.S. approach to the region.
>
> "We shouldn't be afraid of Islam in the politics of these countries," said a senior administration official, speaking on the condition of anonymity to describe internal policy deliberations. "It's the behavior of political parties and governments that we will judge them on, not their relationship with Islam."[6]

Islamist governments span a range of ideologies and ambitions, from the primitive brutality of the Taliban in Afghanistan to Turkey's Justice and Development Party, a movement with Islamist roots that heads a largely secular political system. None of the revolutions in the "Arab Spring" has been overtly Islamist, but there are signs that the uprisings could give way to more religious movements. An influential Yemeni cleric has called for the U.S.-backed administration of President Ali Abdullah Saleh to be replaced with Islamist rule, and in Egypt an Islamist theoretician has played a leading role in drafting constitutional changes after President Hosni Mubarak's fall from power.[7]

President Obama may well be the anti-Truman. In 1948, Harry Truman made America the first country to recognize the State of Israel after the United Nations vote on the partition of Palestine—against the advice of his entire cabinet, and despite the threat of his Secretary of State, General George Marshall, to resign and campaign for Truman's opponent in the next presidential election. Truman insisted on recognizing Israel because his reading of the Bible led him to believe that the Jewish people had a sacred purpose in returning to their ancient homeland. President Obama, by contrast, identifies deeply with Islam, the religion of his Kenyan father and Indonesian stepfather, and the culture that his anthropologist mother sought to defend against the incursions of globalization. Truman gambled American policy on a religious impulse, with the result that America ultimately allied with the strongest and most stable state in the Middle East. Obama appears prepared to gamble American policy on support for inherently unstable and potentially hostile regimes. It may be the most detrimental foreign policy decision taken by an American president in living memory.

The fact is that we have urgent security concerns that arise from state failure, and we are justified in employing force to protect ourselves. Iran's attempt to acquire nuclear weapons is and should be the central concern of Western diplomacy; a rogue state can be contained, but not so easily if it can deliver a fission bomb. The vulgar "realism" of the Beltway argues that deterrence proved effective in averting nuclear exchanges during the Cold War. It is true that deterrence did not fail utterly—if it had, no one would be here to debate the matter—but it came very close to failing, for example during the Cuban Missile Crisis and again during Able Archer in the early 1980s. It is utterly unrealistic to assume that deterrence will allow us to avoid actual nuclear war in perpetuity, all the more unrealistic when powers considerably less rational than the Russians are involved.

Realism demands that we prevent Iran and other rogue states from acquiring nuclear weapons. Excising the Iranian nuclear program through targeted air attacks and subversion directed at regime change are the fail-safe means of defanging the Iranian threat.

Turkey's open hostility to American interests, and its diplomatic dalliance with Iran, Syria, and the Hamas terror statelet in Gaza, should remind Washington not to meddle in "moderate Islam." As we have seen, economic reality constrains Turkey's drift towards Islamic authoritarianism: much as its Islamist leaders might prefer a sharia state like Iran, they cannot get there from here. What keeps Islamism at bay in Ankara, in short, is fear rather than moderation. Given Turkey's delicate dependence on world financial markets, the United States has a wide range of options to calibrate Turkish policy through rewards and penalties. Turkish Islamists will never like the United States, but they can be made to respect us sufficiently to keep their behavior within acceptable parameters. If they don't, the United States has alternatives—including support for the creation of an independent Kurdish state.

The Bush administration set out to drain the swamps of terrorism by invading Afghanistan and then Iraq and constructing democratic regimes in those countries. As a result, hundreds of thousands of American military personnel serve within reach of the Iranian terrorist regime that openly threatens to kill them. And then to prevent our soldiers from being killed, America's military leaders argue against using force that would prevent the potential murderers of American soldiers from acquiring nuclear weapons. A punitive expedition against a prospective threat to American security turned into an exercise in nation-building, the nation-builders turned into hostages to Iranian threats, and the hostages became the excuse to concede nuclear capability to a terrorist state. Meanwhile the old foreign-policy "realists"—for example Zbigniew Brzezinski, the architect of the Carter administration's foreign-policy debacle—conclude from this perverse result that America requires "constructive engagement" with Iran. And the president concedes on television that his policy may fail to prevent Iran from acquiring nuclear weapons. The world looks on in confusion and contempt.

A disaster of this magnitude should inspire a reconsideration of first principles. First among these principles, as I have suggested, is that the prospects for a state's failure or success flow from the character of its people and its civil society. A sound congregation can correct a deficient state, but the best-designed state will founder upon a deficient civil society. Thus America should seek alliances with states that in some way approximate its own exceptional character—in other words, that love what we love—employing our good offices to help them succeed after our fashion. And we should isolate and contain the maleficent influences of states that, repudiating our principles, love other things.

America should look to the founding principles of the West, which are to be found in the character of the society rather than the political structures we have adopted—to Augustine's realism. It did not seem strange to Augustine to consign his own polity to the dustheap of history along with the pagan empires of the past. Augustine's verdict on Rome seems harsh to us today. Yet it is likely that many more nations will disappear during the next two hundred years than during the decline and fall of Rome. At present fertility rates, the Ukraine will lose half of its population by the middle of the present century; in two hundred years the population of Germany will decline by 98 percent. For the first time in recorded history, most of the world's peoples are failing of their desire to live. The European nations were founded upon the wrong kind of love, that is, that of their own ethnicity. Post-nationalist and post-Christian Europe no longer worships at the altar of its own blood and soil, but without its old self-love it sees no reason to persist into the next century.

People are failing of their desire to live, fastest of all in the Muslim world. As a practical matter, a generation hence, some of the world's poorer societies will be saddled with an elderly-dependency ratio like Europe's as today's shriveled generation succeeds the very large generation of Muslims now in their working years. America's most important allies of the second half of the twentieth century, the Western European nations, will lose importance in foreign policy as they wither away. Not much later the Muslim nations will suffer the consequences of their present demographic implosion, as the bulge generation now in its working years turns old, and the drastically shrunken generation that follows proves too feeble to support the burden of elderly dependents.

Engaging Success and Ring-Fencing Failure

What, then, is America's fundamental foreign policy interest? It is not to remake the world but to manage America's leading global position in a world made unstable by the sharp juxtaposition of winners and losers. Where the common love of other polities coincides with ours, America has a strategic opportunity to foster friendships that will make the world a stabler and safer place, and also a moral obligation to help other countries who to some extent emulate our founding principles. We cannot implant this Augustinian love—for the God who grants men inalienable rights by irrevocable covenant—on barren soil. We only can respond where other peoples embrace it of their own volition.

First, in the Middle East, America should cut its losses in "nation-building" and remove the bulk of its forces from Iraq and Afghanistan—with limited exceptions, including sufficient troops to deter Iranian efforts to encroach on Iraqi oil fields near the common border and special forces assisting cooperating local elements. American soldiers, sent out as nation-builders, have become hostages rather than peacekeepers. Their continued presence is detrimental to American interests.

Second, America should not allow rogue states to threaten our security—much less acquire nuclear weapons—and must employ force where required to prevent them from doing so. North Korea has been contained with Chinese help, but Iran presents an unacceptable risk to America and its allies, including Israel and the Arab oil-producing states in the Persian Gulf. America should make clear its willingness to use force to eliminate the Iranian nuclear program and, if Iran does not yield, neutralize the risk through air attacks and aggressive efforts to change the regime.

Third, America should deploy ground personnel to neutralize threats to its interests, through limited intervention by special forces when possible, avoiding large-scale deployment of occupation forces. The mission of the American armed forces should be to destroy our enemies, not to build the civil society of other countries. It is cheaper to seal off the failed states from the rest of the world than to attempt to occupy them and control the travel of their citizens. America should seek the agreement of other powers for such operations but not fear unilateral action under exceptional circumstances—as in the case of Iran's nuclear program.

Fourth, America should abandon balance-of-power politics in southern Asia in favor of alliance with our natural ally India, a democratic nation whose interests diverge little from American goals. To what end does American policy seek to maintain a balance of power between India and Pakistan? India ranks fourth in scientists and engineers in the World Economic Forum Survey for 2010, whereas Pakistan ranks eighty-third, after Cameroon and Benin. India also ranks fourth in terms of Gross Domestic Product on a purchasing power parity basis, while Pakistan ranks twenty-sixth. India is one of the most stable states in the world; Pakistan is at risk of state failure. India fights terrorism; Pakistan's intelligence services gestated the Taliban from the outset and continue to sustain it, along with terrorist organizations that threaten India.

Fifth, America should engage China constructively, aiming at a rivalry without hostility. China attempts to combine elements of economic freedom with political dictatorship; its paradoxes are too complex for America to attempt to resolve. Elements of repression—worst of all the one-child policy—vie with aspects of freedom—including partial religious freedom under which a tenth of Chinese self-identify as Christians. China's chief political concern is territorial integrity. China has always been a multi-ethnic, multi-lingual empire rather than a nation-state; its regimes historically have been undone by provincial rebellions. Beijing understandably displays extreme sensitivity to the prospect of a "breakaway province," which is how it views Taiwan, and what it fears for Tibet and its largely Muslim far west. The Bush administration accomplished a great deal in winning Chinese trust by agreeing to the principle that Taiwan is part of China, while making clear that Taiwan's prospective incorporation into the mainland will remain a matter for the indefinite future. America has no interest in Tibetan or Uyghur independence movements and should reassure China of its support for Chinese territorial integrity.

China's concerns for energy security can be allayed in part through cooperation in nuclear power, where America still has a technological lead. Economic relations between China and the United States should be a positive-sum game: both sides stand to gain from an economic alliance that leads to currency convertibility, a reduced Chinese savings rate, and an opening of China's domestic market to increased imports from the West. In return for this support for China's legitimate economic objectives, America must require Chinese support for its own objectives, for example, the suppression of Iran's nuclear ambitions. In practice, China can be persuaded to respect American exercise of power so long as it does not impinge on core Chinese interests.

Despite its prosperity, Asia remains unstable. America has squandered its resources in the pursuit of a balance of power in the small. But America is the only power capable of maintaining a balance of power in the large— between India, China, and Japan. If America makes clear its intent to lead, other powers in the region will grudgingly acknowledge its role. If America renounces leadership, the potential for mishaps will become unacceptably high.

Finally, what of Russia? It is a more difficult case: a spoiler, but a rational spoiler, which suffered a catastrophic blow to its world position with the fall of Communism and is in rapid demographic decline but remains a world power. Relations with Russia offer a crucial test case for Augustinian realism. America has limited interests in the so-called Russian "near abroad," but it has deep civil ties and consequent moral obligations to countries formerly in the Soviet sphere. Under the Bush administration, the United States treated the former Soviet sphere as a geopolitical Monopoly board on which to acquire real estate, without, however, distinguishing between vital American interests and the opportunistic exercise of power. The expansion of American influence has proven ephemeral. The 2004 Orange Revolution in Ukraine, half of whose inhabitants are native Russian speakers, persuaded Moscow that America would ignore interests to which Russia gave first priority. Russian-American relations reached a nadir as a result. Ukrainian voters elected a pro-Russian government this year, effectively burying the Orange Revolution. Russia reversed the 2005 "Tulip Revolution" in Kyrgyzstan by supporting a coup against the American-sponsored government. And America's attempt to build up Georgia as a toehold in the Caucasus came to grief after Russia's military intervention in 2008.

Whereas America has limited interests in Ukraine, it has a profound interest in Poland, despite Poland's sad and unstoppable demographic decline. Ties of culture and kinship bind the United States to Poland. Poland freed itself from Soviet rule through the resurgence of Christian civil society, and the heroism of its people was a crucial factor in the West's winning the Cold War. The strength of Poland's civil society manifests itself equally in economic success: Poland was the only country in Europe to sustain economic growth through the present world recession. The Obama administration humiliated Poland in October 2009 when it abandoned the Bush administration's pledge to station antimissile systems there and in the Czech Republic. By failing to draw a clear line between the fundamental American commitment to Poland and targets of opportunity on the Russian periphery, Washington in effect invited Russia to deal with Poland as another wayward element in its sphere of influence, on par with Ukraine. We share with Poland bonds of blood, history, religion, and alliance during the critical moments of the Cold War. America must make clear to Russia that while it understands the Russian interest in neighboring countries with a large proportion of native Russian speakers, Poland is a Western nation that must remain secure under the wing of American friendship, and that no form of intimidation will be tolerated.

Augustinian realism draws a bright line between friendship based on shared foundations in civil society on the one hand and the opportunistic exercise of state power on the other. It attempts for practical reasons to distinguish successful states from failing states and as a moral matter to distinguish those who share our loves from those who do not—whose love of other things is often the source of their incipient failure. America can and must compromise on many issues, but we cannot abandon alliances with nations founded on the principles that define our unique character as a people. Countries with whom we share a common love, in Augustine's understanding, we draw near to us. Others should respect us, and if need be, fear us. A nation that knows it has nothing to lose is a dangerous entity—for example, Iran. We cannot engage it. We shall have to ruin it.

America needs to rediscover its own exceptionalism. Our unique nation was built of brands plucked out of the fire of their own ethnic cultures—individuals who chose to become Americans as the Pilgrims did, to flee the failure of their native countries. America is not the only good or successful country in the world, but it is the exemplar and model for what a good country should be. Its founding proposition, the inalienable rights of human beings granted by covenant with the creator of the universe, offers hope to all the peoples of the world. But it cannot impose this proposition on peoples who are determined to destroy themselves. America is universal in its promise but separate in its national life. Our exceptional nation can do its best for the peoples of the world by reserving its alliance for those countries who in some way share its national premise.

As for the living dead among the nations, "We will not speak of them, but look, and move on."[8]

ACKNOWLEDGMENTS

This book is an apology for conventional thinking, in fact, for the most conventional thinking of all, that is, the orthodox currents of Judaism and Christianity. It proceeds from the belief that the traditional understanding of revealed religion in the West addresses something fundamental in the human condition, such that political philosophy cannot ignore it without losing its compass.

Uwe von Parpart, the founding editor of *Asia Times*, first suggested to me in 1995 that I write a pseudonymous column for the Hong Kong-based daily, and the pen-name "Spengler" was intended as a joke: a writer for an Asian newspaper behind the mask of the author of *The Decline of the West*. To Uwe and his successor at *Asia Times Online*, Allen Quicke (1953–2010), I owe the opportunity to develop the "Spengler" essays over the past decade. Joseph Bottum, then editor at *First Things* magazine, commissioned and edited several essays that prepared the way for this volume, and the present manuscript would not exist without his encouragement and counsel. Conversations and correspondence with friends too numerous to cite contributed to this book; it would be unfair not to mention Dr. Norman A. Bailey, Professor Reuven Brenner, Professor Gabrielle Brenner, Professor Anna Geifman, Professor Russell Hittinger, Professor David Layman, Michael Ledeen, Herbert E. Meyer, Daniel Pipes, Rabbi Meir Soloveichik, George Weigel, and Professor Michael Wyschogrod. Most of all I should thank a group of readers who have prodded and provoked me over the years through the readers' forum at *Asia Times Online*.

Loretta Barrett, my literary agent, made invaluable suggestions for the plan of the book; and Elizabeth Kantor and Harry Crocker, my editors at Regnery Publishing, provided thoughtful, helpful, and pointed suggestions throughout. Their enthusiasm for the project, deep knowledge, and professionalism made this book possible, for which I am deeply grateful.

♠♠♠

NOTES

Introduction

1. These ratios are based on the Elderly Dependency Ratio calculated by the model of the United Nations World Population Prospects 2010 revision, assuming constant fertility. The model is available at http://esa.un.org/unpd/wpp/unpp/ panel_indicators.htm.

2. Jared Diamond's 2005 book, *Collapse: How Societies Choose to Fail or Succeed*, blames exhaustion of resources and environmental damage. The extinct people of Easter Island and the pre-Columbian Mayans chopped down too many trees, Diamond observes, and thus he argues that environmental damage is the greatest threat to our civilization. (Never mind that America has expanded its forests by 20 million acres during the past quarter century: disaster stories of this sort resonate with a public fed on media reports of global warming and apocalyptic disaster movies.) Easter Island, though, is something of a rarity in world history. The cultures about which we know the most—and from which our own civilization descends—failed from a different cause. Classical Greece and Rome died for the same reason that Western Europe, Japan, and other parts of the modern

world are dying today: they lost their motivation to bring children into the world. The infertile Greeks were conquered by Rome's army and the inexhaustible manpower of the farms of the Italian peninsula; as the Romans later grew childless, they were overrun by a small force of barbarian invaders.

3.   Rob Banks, "Suicide Contagion," Indigenous Health Research, CDU, http://www.cdu.edu.au/newsroom/origins/edition1-2007/origins1-2007-suicide-contagion.pdf.

4.   Laurence J. Kirmayer et al., "Suicide Among Aboriginal People in Canada," The Aboriginal Healing Foundation Research Series, 2007, http://www.ahf.ca/downloads/suicide.pdf, p. xv.

5.   Christina Lamb, "Rising suicides cut a swath through Amazon's children," *Telegraph*, November 19, 2000, http://www.telegraph.co.uk/news/worldnews/asia/1374881/Rising-suicides-cut-a-swath-through-Amazons-children.html.

6.   John Noble Wilford, "Languages Die, but Not Their Last Words," *New York Times*, September 19, 2007, http://www.nytimes.com/2007/09/19/science/19language.html.

7.   "90 percent of world's languages will disappear in 100 years: UN," newKerala.com, http://www.newkerala.com/news/fullnews-30561.html.

8.   Eric Kaufmann, *Shall the Religious Inherit the Earth? Demography and Politics in the Twenty-First Century* (London: Profile Books, 2010), 19.

9.   Franz Rosenzweig, *Der Stern der Erlösung* (Freiburg im Breisgau; Universitätsbibliothek, 2002), 350. Translation by the author.

Chapter 1

1.   Neil MacFarquar, "U.N. Sees Falling Middle East Fertility Rates," *New York Times*, April 3, 2009, http://dotearth.blogs.nytimes.com/2009/04/03/un-sees-big-drop-in-middle-east-fertility-rates/.

2.   Eric Kaufmann, *Shall the Religious Inherit the Earth?* (New York: Cambridge University Press, 2010), 125.

3.   http://www.mardomsalari.com/Template1/News.aspx?NID=95289.

4.   "Iran: Mahmoud Ahmadinejad urges girls to marry at 16," *Guardian*, November 21, 2010, http://www.guardian.co.uk/world/2010/nov/21/iran-ahmadinejad-girls-marry-16.

5.   Mohammad Jalal Abbasi-Shavazi et al., "Education and the World's Most Rapid Fertility Decline in Iran," International Institute for Applied Systems Analysis, Interim Report, approved May 13, 2008, http://www.iiasa.ac.at/Admin/PUB/Documents/IR-08-010.pdf.

6.   See Seyed Farian Sabahi, "The Literacy Corps in Pahlavi Iran," *Cahiers d'etudes sur la Mediterranie orientale et le monde turco-iranien*, No. 31 (January–June 2001).

7.   Zohreh Soleimani, "Children of the Revolution," BBC Radio World Service, first broadcast October 1, 2008, http://www.bbc.co.uk/worldservice/documentaries/2008/09/080925_children_of_revolution_one.shtml.

8.   Adolf Hitler, *Mein Kampf,* Vol. 1, Chapter 11, Section A.

9.   Ali A. Allawi, *The Crisis of Islamic Civilization* (New Haven, CT: Yale University Press 2009), 272.

Chapter 2

1.   Kaufmann, op. cit.

2.   Phillip Longman, *The Empty Cradle* (New York: Basic Books, 2004), 35.

3.   Daniel Bell, *The Cultural Contradictions of Capitalism* (New York: Basic Books, 1976), 170.

4.   Viviana Zelizer, *Pricing the Priceless Child* (New York: Basic Books, 1985), 145–46.

5.   "Why Do Americans Want Children?" *ScienceDaily,* June 20, 1997, http://www.sciencedaily.com/releases/1997/06/970630000458.htm.

6.   Projections under constant fertility from the United Nations World Population Prospect model 2010 revision, United Nations Department of Economic and Social Affairs, http://esa.un.org/unpd/wpp/unpp/panel_indicators.htm.

Chapter 3

1.   "Europa Wird Islamisch," *Die Welt,* April 19, 2006, http://www.welt.de/print-welt/article211310/Europa_wird_islamisch.html. Translation by the author.

2.   Bat Ye'or, *Eurabia: The Euro-Arab Axis* (Madison, NJ: Fairleigh Dickinson University Press, 2005); Tony Blankley, *The West's Last Chance: Will We Win the Clash of Civilizations?* (Washington, D.C.: Regnery Publishing, Inc., 2005); Mark Steyn, *America Alone: The End of the World as We Know It* (Washington, D.C.: Regnery, 2006).

3.   "Muslim Demographics," http://www.youtube.com/watch?v=6-3X5hIFXYU.

4.   Quoted by MEMRI from al-Jazeera Television, http://www.youtube.com/watch?v=i7ympF_grrA.

5.   Leo Cendrowicz, "Sorry, We're Closed," *Time,* May 4, 2011, http://www.time.com/time/world/article/0,8599,2069634,00.html.

6.   "IMF Backs G-8 Plan for Supporting Middle East, North Africa," IMF Survey Magazine Online, May 27, 2011, http://www.imf.org/external/pubs/ft/survey/so/2011/new052711a.htm.

7.   "Libya War Paves Way for Deadly Migrant Boat Trips," *Expatica,* May 16, 2011, http://www.expatica.com/es/news/news_focus/Libya-war-paves-way-for-deadly-migrant-boat-trips_148062.html.

8.   "Tunisia Grows Economy, Creates Jobs," World Bank Results Profile, last updated May 27, 2010, http://web.worldbank.org/WBSITE/EXTERNAL/COUNTRIES/MENAEXT/0,,contentMDK:22502249~pagePK:146736~piPK:226340~theSitePK:256299,00.html.

9.   "The Second ALO Report on Employment and Unemployment in Arab Countries," p. 85.

10. Mohamed ElBaradei, "The Next Step for Egypt's Opposition," *New York Times*, February 10, 2011, http://www.nytimes.com/2011/02/11/opinion/11elbaradei.html.

11. Thomas Friedman, "Up with Egypt," *New York Times*, February 10, 2011, http://www.nytimes.com/2011/02/09/opinion/09friedman.html.

12. Mohammed A Tag-Eldin, Mohsen A Gadallah, Mahmoud N. Al-Tayeb, Mostafa Abdel-Aty, Esmat Mansour, and Mona Sallem, "Prevalence of female genital cutting among Egyptian girls," *Bulletin of the World Health Organization* 2008; 86:269–74.

13. The World Bank, "Improving Food Security in Arab Countries," 2009, http://siteresources.worldbank.org/INTMENA/Resources/FoodSecfinal.pdf.

14. Paul Rivlin, "Behind the Tensions in Syria: The Socio-Economic Dimension," Moshe Dayan Center of Tel Aviv University, 2011.

15. "In Brief: Syria unrest a risk for food security," IRIN, May 23, 2011, http://ww.irinnews.org/Report.aspx?ReportID=92789.

16. "Yemeni Opposition Says Saleh Cut Water," myFOXla.com, June 2, 2011, http://www.myfoxla.com/dpps/news/yemeni-opposition-says-saleh-cut-water-dpgonc-km-20110602_13503971.

17. Egyptian political dissident Cynthia Farahat contested the idea that Mubarak was an American ally in a July 11, 2011, interview with *FrontPage*, warning against "a dangerous sham alliance between freedom and its enemies. You will often find freedom-loving people unknowingly working on advancing the agendas of their enemies." See "Egypt Unveiled," *FrontPage Magazine*, July 11, 2011, http://frontpagemag.com/2011/07/11/egypt-unveiled/print/.

18. "List of countries by number of broadband internet users," Wikipedia, http://en.wikipedia.org/wiki/List_of_countries_by_number_of_broadband_Internet_users#cite_note-PointTopicQ42007-7.

19. Roula Khalaf, "Hopes for renewal risk colliding with reality," *Financial Times*, February 13, 2011, http://www.ft.com/cms/s/0/9f2c3862-3794-11e0-b91a-00144feabdc0.html#axzz1Flf3UD62.

20. Margie Fishman, "Panel dissects scenarios for Egypt's future," Emory Report, http://www.emory.edu/EMORY_REPORT/stories/2011/02/event_panel_discusses_scenarios_egypt_future.html.

21. Andrew England, "What next for Egyptian business?" *Financial Times*, February 16, 2011, http://blogs.ft.com/beyond-brics/2011/02/16/what-next-for-egyptian-business.

22. "Arab World Experts at Davos Call for Multi-Sector Reform," Associated Press, January 26, 2011.

23. Charles F. Westoff and Thomas Frejka, "Religiousness and Fertility Among European Muslims," in *Population and Development Review*, 2007, vol. 33, pages 785–809.

24. Anne Genereux, "The End of High Fertility: Senegalese Immigrant Reproduction in France," paper presented at the annual meeting of the American Sociological Association, Montreal Convention Center, Montreal, Quebec, Canada, August 10, 2006.

25. Laurent Toulemon, "Fertility Among Immigrant Women in France: New Data, a New Approach," prepared for Population Association of American 2006 Annual Meeting, Los Angeles, California, March 30-April 1, 2006.

26. Harry Wallop, "Britain to be biggest country in Europe by 2050," *Telegraph*, July 29, 2010, http://www.telegraph.co.uk/news/uknews/7916924/Britain-to-be-biggest-country-in-Europe-by-2050.html.

Chapter 4

1. "Die Wahrheit hinter der islamischen Fassade," *Der Standard*, February 3, 2009, http://derstandard.at/1233586592607/Die-Wahrheit-hinter-der-islamischen-Fassade. Translation by the author.

2. Zand-Bon, "Planet Iran Exclusive: Iranian regime's sanctioned brothels at Imam Reza's shrine in Mash'had," Planet Iran, July 23, 2010, http://planet-iran.com/index.php/news/19414.

3. Faraj Balafkan, "Iran's festive drink and drugs binge," BBC, March 27, 2009, http://news.bbc.co.uk/2/hi/middle_east/7963647.stm.

4. "Iran inflation reaches 10.8 per cent," *Trade Arabia*, February 1, 2011, http://www.tradearabia.com/news/ECO_192783.html.

5. Stanley Reed, "Surprise: Oil Woes In Iran," *BusinessWeek*, December 11, 2006, http://www.businessweek.com/print/magazine/content/06_50/b4013058.htm?chan=gl.

6. Energy Information Administration, Country Analysis Briefs, Iran, http://www.eia.gov/emeu/cabs/Iran/pdf.pdf, p. 8.

7. Spencer Schwartz and Benoit Faucon, "Iran's Falling Oil Output Means Less Revenue, Clout," *Wall Street Journal*, June 26, 2010, http://online.wsj.com/article/SB10001424052748704569204575328851816763476.html.

Chapter 5

1. "New Analysis: 'Turkish model' emerges as Muslim nations face transformation," Xinhua, March 3, 2011, http://news.xinhuanet.com/english2010/indepth/2011-03/03/c_13759959.htm.

2. "From the Bosphorus: Straight—The wisdom of Tunisia's Chebbi," *Hurriyet Daily News*, March 15, 2011, http://www.hurriyetdailynews.com/mob_n.php?n=from-the-bosphorus-straight---the-wisdom-of-tunisia8217s-chebbi-2011-03-15.

3. The Brookings Institution, "September 11, One Year Later: What's Ahead for an Altered Homeland?" September 5, 2002, http://www.brookings.edu/~/media/Files/events/2002/0905homeland%20security/20020905.pdf.

4. Rachel Sharon-Krespin, "Fethullah Gülen's Grand Ambition: Turkey's Islamist Danger," *Middle East Quarterly* Winter 2009, 55–66.

5. Sutay Yavuz, "Fertility transition and the progression to third birth in Turkey," Max Planck Institute for Demographic Research Working Paper 2005-028, September 2005, http://www.demogr.mpg.de/papers/working/wp-2005-028.pdf.

6. Ibid.

7. Ismet Koc, Attila Hancioglu, and Alanur Cavlin, "Demographic Differentials and Demographic Integration of Turkish and Kurdish Populations in Turkey," *Population Research and Policy Review* Vol. 27, No. 4, 447–57.

8. Alan Hall, "Multiculturalism in Germany has 'utterly failed,' claims Chancellor Angela Merkel," *The Daily Mail*, October 18, 2010, http://www.dailymail.co.uk/news/article-1321277/Angela-Merkel-Multiculturalism-Germany-utterly-failed.html.

9. "Chinese imams to study in Turkey with new agreement," *Today's Zaman*, February 19, 2011, http://www.todayszaman.com/news-236014-chinese-imams-to-study-theology-in-turkey-with-new-agreement.html.

10. Dan Bilefsky, "In Turkey, Trial Casts Wide Net of Mistrust," *New York Times*, November 21, 2009, http://www.nytimes.com/2009/11/22/world/europe/22turkey.html.

11. Ivan Watson and Yesim Comert, "Turkey arrests 3 opposition journalists," CNN, February 18, 2011, http://articles.cnn.com/2011-02-18/world/turkey.media.arrests_1_akp-recep-tayyip-erdogan-ergenekon?_s=PM:WORLD.

12. Donald Quaetert, *The Ottoman Empire 1700-1922* (Cambridge University Press, 2005), 117.

13. See Michael Rubin, "Turkey's Turning Point: Could There Be an Islamic Revolution in Turkey?" National Review Online, April 14, 2008, http://www.nationalreview.com/articles/224182/turkeys-turning-point/michael-rubin.

14. Sharon-Krespin, op. cit.

15. Fethullah Gülen, *The Essentials of Islamic Faith* (New Jersey: Tughra Books, 2005), 69.

16. Ibid., 81.

17. Robert Pigott, "Turkey in radical revision of Islamic texts," The BBC *World Service*, February 28, 2008, http://news.bbc.co.uk/2/hi/7264903.stm.

18. Felix Koerner, S.J., *Revisionist Koran Hermeneutics in Contemporary Turkish University Theology: Rethinking Islam* (Ergon Verlag: Wurzburg, 2005), 204.

19. Kemal Kirisci, "Migration Information Source," Migration Policy Institute, November 2003, http://www.migrationinformation.org/Feature/print.cfm?ID=176.

20. European Stability Initiative, "Islamic Calvinists: Change and Conservatism in Central Anatolia," Berlin 2005.

21. See World Bank Report 48508-TR, "Female Labor Participation in Turkey," 2009.

22. "SGK head Zararsız: We have exceptional and advanced practices," *Today's Zaman*, May 25, 2010.

23. Abdullah Takim, "Effectiveness of the Informal Economy in Turkey," *European Journal of Social Sciences*, Vol. 19, No. 2 (2011).

24. Masha Charnay, "Central Asia Grapples With Migrant Labor Dilemma," in Eurasia.net, March 10, 2010, http://www.eurasianet.org/departments/civilsociety/articles/eav030510.shtml.

25. See Altay Atli, "A fraternal welcome for Erdogan in Kyrgyzstan," *Asia Times Online*, February 17, 2011, http://www.atimes.com/atimes/Central_Asia/MB17Ag01.html.

Chapter 6

1. Ali A. Allawi, *The Crisis of Islamic Civilization* (New Haven, CT: Yale University Press, 2009), 273.

2. Ibid., 272.

3. See for example Mike Ghouse, "Mission of World Muslim Congress," World Muslim Congress, July 9, 2011 http://worldmuslimcongress.blogspot.com/2008/01/wife-beating-434.html, where the full text of Bassam A. Abed and Syed A. Ahmad, "Discipline as a Means to Marital Reconciliation: The Husband's Graduated Response to His Wife's Disobedience under Islamic Law" can be seen.

4. Asma T. Uddin, "Domestic violence in the Muslim community," altmuslimah.com, December 12, 2009, http://www.altmuslimah.com/a/b/a/3276/.

5. Rowan Williams, "Civil and Religious Law in England: a religious perspective," The Archbishop of Canterbury website, February 7, 2008, http://www.

archbishopofcanterbury.org/articles.php/1137/archbishops-lecture-civil-and-religious-law-in-england-a-religious-perspective.

6. For a summary of rabbinic writings on the subject see Rabbi Jon-Jay Tilsen, "May a Husband Beat His Wife? Classical Halakhic Sources on Domestic Violence," Congregation Beth El-Keser Israel, http://www.beki.org/domestic.html.

7. Eric Nelson, *The Hebrew Republic: Jewish Sources and the Transformation of European Political Thought* (Harvard University Press, 2010).

8. Michael Novak, *On Two Wings: Humble Faith and Common Sense at the American Founding* (New York: Encounter Books, 2003).

9. Robert Fisk, "The crimewave that shames the world," *Independent,* September 7, 2010, http://www.independent.co.uk/opinion/commentators/fisk/the-crime-wave-that-shames-the-world-2072201.html.

10. See Phyllis Chesler, "Worldwide Trends in Honor Killings," *Middle East Quarterly,* Spring 2010, pp. 3–11.

11. Madhur Singh, "Why Are Hindu Honor Killings Rising in India?" *Time,* May 25, 2010, http://www.time.com/time/world/article/0,8599,1991195,00.html#ixzz1Bn56Jr6l.

12. "Female genital mutilation and other harmful practices," World Health Organization, Sexual and reproductive health, http://www.who.int/reproductivehealth/topics/fgm/prevalence/en/index.html.

13. "What is the Islamic legal ruling concerning female genital mutilation?" Islamopedia Online, April 22, 2010, http://www.islamopediaonline.org/fatwa/what-islamic-legal-ruling-concerning-female-genital-mutilation.

14. "Birth defects warning sparks row," BBC, February 10, 2008, http://news.bbc.co.uk/2/hi/uk_news/7237663.stm.

15. Seyed Mohammad Akrami and Zahra Osati, "Is Consanguineous Marriage Religiously Encouraged?" *Journal of Biosocial Science* (2007) 39, pp. 313–16.

16. "Besserer Schutz vor Bedrohungen," Tageszeitung, October 21, 2008, http://www.taz.de/1/politik/deutschland/artikel/1/islam-professor-muss-umziehen/. Translation by the author.

17. Quoted in Toby Lester, "What is the Koran?" *The Atlantic Magazine,* January 1999.

18. Samir Khalid Samir, S.J., *111 Questions on Islam* (San Francisco: Ignatius Press, 2009).

19. Karl-Heinz Ohlig, Gerd-R. Puin, ed., *The Hidden Origins of Islam: New Research into Its Early History* (New York: Prometheus Books, 2010).

Chapter 7

1. Suha Taji-Farouki and Basheer M. Nafi, *Islamic Thought in the Twentieth Century* (London: Tauris, 2004), 9.

2.   Ibid., 2.

3.   Ibid., 14.

4.   Sayyid Qutb, *Social Justice in Islam*, trans. John B Hardie and Hamid Algar (Oneonta, NY: Islamic Publications International, 2004).

5.   Nicholas Le Quesne, "Trying to Bridge A Great Divide," Time.com, Innovators: Tariq Ramadan, http://www.time.com/time/innovators/spirituality/profile_ramadan.html.

6.   Paul Berman, *The Flight of the Intellectuals* (Brooklyn, NY: Melville House, 2010).

7.   Ibid., 4.

8.   Tariq Ramadan, "In the Middle of the Night: Remaining with the One, one night, one's life," Tariq Ramadan official website, February 2, 2005, http://www.tariqramadan.com/In-the-Middle-of-the-Night.html.

9.   Philip Jenkins, "Infertile Crescent: Iran, Denmark of Tomorrow?" *The New Republic*, November 9, 2007, http://www.tnr.com/article/infertile-crescent.

10. Greg Bruno, "Iran's Revolutionary Guards," Council on Foreign Relations, June 22, 2009.

11. Michael Rubin, "Turkey, from Ally to Enemy," *Commentary Magazine*, July/August 2010.

12. Ramzy Baroud, "Middle East is changing, and Ankara knows it," *The Tehran Times*, June 20, 2010, http://www.tehrantimes.com/index_View.asp?code=221654.

Chapter 8

1.   Anna Geifman, *Death Orders* (Praeger, 2010), 14–15.

2.   Robin Wright, "Since 2001, a Dramatic Increase in Suicide Bombings," *The Washington Post*, April 18, 2008, http://www.washingtonpost.com/wp-dyn/content/article/2008/04/17/AR2008041703595.html.

3.   Author interview with Herbert Meyer.

4.   John Lewis Gaddis, *The Cold War: A New History* (New York: Penguin, 2005).

5.   Robert Gates, *From the Shadows* (New York: Simon and Schuster, 2007), 272–73.

6.   Christopher Andrew and Oleg Gordievsky, *KGB* (HarperCollins, 1992), 605.

7.   Author interview with Herbert Meyer.

8.   "Iran plant Bau einer Raketenstellung in Venezuela," Die Welt Online, November 25, 2010, http://www.welt.de/politik/ausland/article11219574/Iran-plant-Bau-einer-Raketenstellung-in-Venezuela.html. Translation by the author.

9.   Dore Gold, Speech before the Henry Jackson Society, October 12, 2009, http://www.henryjacksonsociety.org/stories.asp?id=1278.

10. See Ariel Cohen, "Iran's Claim Over Caspian Sea Resources Threatens Energy Security," The Heritage Foundation, September 5, 2002, http://www.heritage.

org/research/reports/2002/09/irans-claim-over-caspian-sea-resources-threaten-energy-security.

11.   Quoted in "Does Iran Have Something in Store?" *Wall Street Journal*, August 8, 2006.

Chapter 9

1.   Gilbert Murray, *Five Stages of Greek Religion* (Mineola, NY: Courier Dover 2003), 116 et. seq.

2.   David Crystal, *Language Death* (Cambridge University Press, 2000).

3.   Robert Drews, *The End of the Bronze Age* (Princeton University Press, 1993), 3–4.

4.   Aristotle, *Politics*, trans. Benjamin Jowett, Book 2, Part 9, http://classics.mit.edu/Search/index.html.

5.   Thomas F. Scanlon, "The Dispersion of Pederasty and the Athletic Revolution in Sixth-Century BC Greece," in Beert C. Verstraete and Vernon Provencal, eds., *Same-Sex Desire and Love in Greco-Roman Antiquity and in the Classical Tradition of the West* (Florence, KY: Psychology Press, 2006), 64–70.

6.   Plato, *Laws* 636ab, in ibid., 66.

7.   J. D. Beazley, "Some Attic Vases in the Cyprus Museum," in *Proceedings of the British Academy* 33 (1947), 199.

8.   Martha Nussbaum, *The Fragility of Goodness* (Cambridge University Press, 2001), 188.

9.   Victor Davis Hanson, *Carnage and Culture* (New York: Random House, 2002), 29.

10.   *The Geography of Strabo*, Book VIII, Chapter 4, published in Vol. IV of the Loeb Classical Library edition, 1927, available at http://penelope.uchicago.edu/Thayer/E/Roman/Texts/Strabo/8D*.html.

11.   Charles M. Reed, *Maritime Trades in the Ancient Greek World* (Cambridge University Press 2003), 16.

12.   Jamie Glazov, "The Iraqi War and All with VDH: An Interview with Frontpage Magazine," November 13, 2005, on Private Papers: Victor Davis Hanson on the Web, http://victorhanson.com/articles/hanson111305.html.

13.   Aristophanes, et al., *The Eleven Comedies* (The Echo Library, 2006), 18–19.

14.   Thucydides, *The Peloponnesian War*, trans. Rex Warner (New York: Penguin), 372, 382.

15.   Sophocles, *Oedipus at Colonus*, trans. C. John Holcombe (Ocasa Press, 2008).

16.   Thucydides, *History of the Peloponnesian War*, trans. Richard Crawley (Ebooks@adelaide), 2007.

17.   Søren Kierkegaard, "The Position of Socrates Viewed as Irony," in *The Essential Kierkegaard*, eds. Edna Hong and Howard Hong (Princeton University Press, 2000), 20 et. seq.

18. Aristotle, op. cit., Book 7, Part 16.

19. Michael H. Jameson et. al., *A Greek Countryside: The Southern Argolid from Prehistory to the Present Day* (Stanford University Press, 1994), 396.

20. Polybius, *The Histories* Vol. II, trans. Evelyn S. Shuckburg (London: MacMillan, 1889), 511.

21. Gustave Glotz, *Ancient Greece at Work* (Routledge & Kegan, 1965), 298.

22. *Encyclopedia of Ancient Greece* (Psychology Press, 2006), entry on "Demography."

23. Polybius, *op. cit.*, Vol. I, 39.

24. Frank W. Walbank, ed., *Polybius, Rome, and the Hellenistic World: Essays and Reflections* (Cambridge University Press, 2002), 199.

25. See Richard I. Frank, "Augustus' Legislation on Marriage and Children," in *California Studies in Classical Antiquity*, Vol. 8 (1975), 41–52.

26. John C. Caldwell, "Fertility Control in the Classical World: Was There an Ancient Fertility Transition?" in *Journal of Population Research* Vol. 21 Issue 1 (May 2004).

27. Bryan Ward-Perkins, *The Fall of Rome and the End of Civilization* (Oxford University Press 2005), 4–7.

28. Theodore Mommsen, *The History of Rome* Vol. 4, Part II, trans. William Dickson (London: Richard Bentley, 1866), 519.

29. Naphtali Lewis and Meyer Reinhold, eds., *Roman Civilization: Selected Readings* (Columbia University Press 1990), 626.

30. Unsigned review of *Economie Politique des Romains* by Dureau de la Malle, *Edinburgh Review*, Vol. 83, p. 371.

31. Bureau de la Malle, *Economie Politique des Romains* (Paris 1840), vol. I, p. 419.

32. George Finlay, *Greece under the Romans* (London: Blackwell 1857), 68.

33. Sauvy, *General Theory of Population* (London: Weidenfeld and Nicholson, 1969), 362.

34. E. A. Wrigley, "The fall of marital fertility in nintheenth-century France: exemplar or exception?" (Part I), http://www.ncbi.nlm.nih.gov/pubmed/12159012.

35. In the "Don Juan in Hell" Interlude in *Man and Superman*.

36. Oswald Spengler, *The Decline of the West*, Vol. III, trans. Charles Frances Atkinson (A. A. Knopf 1928), 105.

Chapter 10

1. Sven Muhammed Kalisch, "Islamische Theologie ohne historischen Muhammad—Anmerkungen zu den Herausforderungen der historisch-kritischen Methode für das islamiche Denken," http://www.uni-muenster.de/imperia/md/content/religioesestudien/islam/_v/kalisch_islamische_theologie_ohne_historischen_muhammad.pdf. Translation by the author.

2. Patricia Crone and Martin Hinds, *God's Caliph* (Cambridge University Press, 1986), 24–25.

3. Yehuda Nevo and Judith Koren, *Crossroads to Islam: The Origin of the Arab Religion and the Arab State* (New York: Prometheus Books, 2003).

4. Kalisch, op. cit., 14–15.

5. Rosenzweig, op. cit., 60.

6. William Montgomery Watt, *The Faith and Practice of Al-Ghazali* (London: George Allen and Unwin Ltd, 1953), 14–16.

7. See Robert R. Reilly, *The Closing of the Muslim Mind* (Intercollegiate Studies Institute, 2010), 105.

8. Ibid., 62–63.

9. Rosenzweig, op. cit., 199.

10. "Renowned Syrian Poet 'Adonis': The Arabs are Extinct, Like the Sumerians, Greeks, and Pharaohs; If the Arabs are So Inept They Cannot Be Democratic, External Intervention Will Not Make Them So," MEMRI, March 16, 2006, http://www.memritv.org/report/en/1643.htm.

11. Netan'el Helfgot, ed., *Community, Covenant and Commitment: Selected Letters and Communications of Rabbi Joseph B. Soloveitchik* (K'tav Publishing House, 2005), 301.

12. Jon D. Levinson, *The Death and Resurrection of the Beloved Son: The Transformation of Child Sacrifice in Judaism and Christianity* (Harvard; Cambridge, 1993).

13. Fatwa from Islam Online, http://www.islamonline.net/servlet/Satellite?pagename=IslamOnline-English-Ask_Scholar/FatwaE/FatwaE&cid=1119503544988.

14. Some forms of Shi'ite Islam encourage forms of self-sacrifice in addition to jihad. On the Feast of Ashura, the anniversary of the death of Husayn ibn Ali in 680 C.E., thousands of Shi'ites come to the site of his final battle at the Iraqi town of Karbala and cut themselves until they bleed profusely. Blood symbolism is common in Shi'ite Islam. Spurting blood is the preferred symbol of Iran's Islamic revolution. Fountains shooting red dye at Tehran's Behesht-e-Zahra cemetery recall the blood of the young Iranians interred there, who fell in the Ayatollah Ruhollah Khomeini's suicide battalions during the Iran-Iraq war of the 1980s.

15. Rosenzweig, op. cit., 254.

16. See Heinrich Stuhrmann, ed., *Deutscher Soldatenspiegel für den heiligen Krieg. Ernst Moritz Arndts Katechismus für den deutschen Kriegs- und Wehrmann* (Godesberg: Deutschen Evangelischen Volksbund, 1914). Translation by the author.

17. Quoted in Jeffrey Verhey, "War Enthusiasm," in *The World War I Reader*, Michael Neiberg, ed. (NYU Press, 2007), 154.

18.   Quoted in Brock Millman, *Managing Domestic Dissent in First World War Britain* (Taylor and Francis, 2000), 32.

Chapter 11

1.   Rodney Stark, *The Rise of Christianity: A Sociologist Reconsiders History* (Princeton University Press, 1996), 95–97.

2.   Aldous Huxley, *The Grey Eminence* (London: Chatto and Windus, 1942), 213.

3.   Ibid., 203.

4.   Russell Hittinger, "The Churches of Earthly Power," *First Things*, June-July 2006.

5.   Rosenzweig, op. cit., 377.

6.   M. A. Roberts, ed., *Beowulf,* (Literary Touchstone Edition, Prestwick House, 2005), 99.

7.   Nicholas Wade, *Before the Dawn* (Penguin: New York 2006), 150–53.

8.   Phillip Wynn, "Wars and Warriors of Gregory of Tours' Histories," in *Francia Forschungen zur westeuropäischen Geschichte* Vol. 28, 2001 (Ostfildern, 2001).

9.   René Rémond, *Religion and Society in Modern Europe* (Blackwell Publishers, 1999), 110–11.

10.   Jack Weiner, *El Poema de mio Cid* (Edition Reichenberger 2001), 6.

11.   Catholic Encyclopedia of 1913, entry on *Gesta Dei per Francos.*

12.   John Hellman, *Simon Weil: An Introduction to Her Thought* (Wilfrid Laurier University Press, 1982), 37–38.

13.   Henri De Lubac, *Catholicism: Christ and the Common Destiny of Man* (Ignatius Press, 1988), 58.

14.   I discuss this issue in an essay entitled "Zionism for Christians," in *First Things*, June/July 2008.

15.   Adrian Hastings, *The Construction of Nationhood: Ethnicity, Religion, and Nationalism* (Cambridge University Press, 1997), 59.

16.   Linda Colley, *Forging the Nation 1707-1837* (Yale University Press, 2009), 30.

17.   Anthony Levi, *Richelieu and the Making of France* (Constable, 2000), 199–200.

18.   Aldous Huxley, op. cit., 184–85.

19.   Ibid., 133.

20.   Ibid., 185.

21.   Quoted in Luis Suárez Fernández and José Andrés Gallego, *La crisis de la hegemonía española, siglo XVII* (Ediciones Rialp, 1986), 12.

22.   Stanley G. Payne, *Spain: A Unique History* (University of Wisconsin Press, 2011), 106.

23.   Quoted in Fritz Stern, *The Politics of Culture Despair* (University of California Press, 1965), 88.

24. Michael Geyer and Hartmut Lehmann, Religion und Nation, Nation und Religion (Quoted in Wallstein Verlag, 2004), 26. Translation by the author.

25. Quoted in Peter Watson, *The German Genius* (New York: HarperCollins, 2010), 533.

26. Christian Dube, *Religoese Sprache in Reden Adolf Hitlers* (Books on Demand, 2005), 169. Translation by the author.

Chapter 12

1. Georges Grente, *Le beau voyage des cardinaux français aux États-Unis et au Canada* (Plon, 1927), 308. Translation by the author.

2. Gilles Gougeon, *A History of Quebec Nationalism* (Essex, England: Miles Kelly Publishing, 1994), 59.

3. Denyse Delcourt, "Parler mal » au Québec," http://mondesfrancophones.com/espaces/langues/parler-quebec/.

4. Damien-Claude Belanger, "L'abbe Lionel Groulx et les consequences de l'emigration canadienne-francaise aux Etats-Unis," in *Quebec Studies* (Spring-Summer 2002). Translation by the author.

5. Catherine Krull and Frank Trovato, "Where Have All the Children Gone? Quebec's Fertility Decline: 1941-1991," *Canadian Studies in Population*, Vol. 30(I), 2003, http://www.canpopsoc.org/journal/CSPv30n1p193.pdf, p. 197.

6. Ibid., 193–220.

7. Ibid., 199.

8. Address of His Holiness John Paul II, Welcoming Ceremony in Warsaw, June 2, 1979, http://www.vatican.va/holy_father/john_paul_ii/speeches/1979/june/documents/hf_jp-ii_spe_19790602_polonia-varsavia-okecie-arrival_en.html.

9. Stephen Engelberg, "A Look at Nazi Era Is Urged in Poland," *New York Times*, November 7, 1990, http://www.nytimes.com/1990/11/07/world/a-look-at-nazi-era-is-urged-in-poland.html.

10. Waldemar Chrostowski (Academy of Catholic Theology in Warsaw), "The Suffering, Chosenness and Mission of the Polish Nation," Religion in Eastern Europe, http://www.georgefox.edu/academics/undergrad/departments/soc-swk/ree/Chrostowski_Suffering.html.

11. George Weigel, *Witness to Hope: The Biography of Pope John Paul II* (New York: HarperCollins, 2005), 90.

12. Chrostowski, op. cit.

13. Neal Pease, *Rome's Most Faithful Daughter:Tthe Catholic Church and Independent Poland* (Ohio University Press, 2009), 6–7.

14. Author's interviews with Hungarian government economists.

15. Brian P. Clare, *Piety and Nationalism* (McGill-Queens Press, MQUP 1993), 155.

16.   Hugh F. Kearney, *Ireland: Contested Ideas of Nationalism and History* (NYU Press, 2007), 43.

17.   Mary Eberstadt, "How the West Really Lost God," in *Policy Review* no. 143 (June 1, 2007).

18.   Rafael Gómez Pérez, *El franquismo y la Iglesia* (Madrid: Ediciones Rialp, 1986), 268. Translation by the author.

Chapter 13

1.   "U.S. Stands Alone In Its Embrace of Religion Among Wealthy Nations," Pew Global Attitudes Project, December 19, 2002, http://pewglobal.org/2002/12/19/among-wealthy-nations/.

2.   Tomas Frejka and Charles F. Westoff, "Religion, religiousness and fertility in the U.S. and in Europe," Max Planck Institute for Demographic Research, Rostock, Germany in its series MPIDR Working Papers with number WP-2006-013; available for download at http://ideas.repec.org/p/dem/wpaper/wp-2006-013.html.

3.   The regression coefficient of religion on fertility across the universe of 40 European countries is 38 percent. More important is that the statistical significance (t-statistic) is extremely high.

4.   Author's calculations.

5.   Leslie Leyland Fields, "A Counter Trend—Sort Of," *Christianity Today*, August 1, 2006, http://www.christianitytoday.com/ct/2006/august/16.30.html.

6.   Richard Rorty, *Contingency, Irony and Solidarity* (Cambridge University Press, 1989), 5.

7.   Lee Smith, *The Strong Horse: Power, Politics and the Clash of Arab Civilizations* (New York: Random House, 2009), 153.

8.   Daniel Schorr, "Israel's demographic time bomb," *Christian Science Monitor*, August 31, 2001, http://www.csmonitor.com/2001/0831/p11s1-coop.html.

9.   "Address by PM Ehud Olmert to the opening of the Knesset winter session," Israel Ministry of Foreign Affairs, October 8, 2007, http://www.mfa.gov.il/MFA/Government/Speeches+by+Israeli+leaders/2007/Address+by+PM+Ehud+Olmert+to+the+opening+of+the+Knesset+winter+session+8-Oct-2007.htm.

10.   "Olmert warns of 'end of Israel,'" BBC, November 29, 2007, http://news.bbc.co.uk/2/hi/middle_east/7118937.stm.

11.   Daniel J. Elazar, "How Religious are Israeli Jews?" The Jerusalem Center for Public Affairs, http://www.jcpa.org/dje/articles2/howrelisr.htm.

12.   See David Ben-Gurion, *Ben-Gurion Looks at the Bible*, trans. Jonathan Kolatch (New York: Jonathan David Co., Inc., 2008).

Chapter 14

1.   Nathaniel Morton, William Bradford, Thomas Prince, and Edward Winslow, *New England's Memorial* (Congregational Board of Publication, 1669), 262.

2.   Cited in Alan Heimert and Andrew Delbanco, *The Puritans in America* (Harvard University Press, 1985), 90.

3.   Ulysses S. Grant, *Memoirs*, Chapter 3, "Army Life—Causes of the Mexican War—Camp Salubrity," http://www.bartleby.com/1011/3.html.

4.   Robert E. May, *The Southern Dream of a Caribbean Empire, 1854-1861* (Louisiana State University Press, 1973), 164.

5.   Michael Novak, *On Two Wings: Humble Faith and Common Sense at the American Founding* (Encounter Books, 2001).

6.   James Takach, *Lincoln's Moral Vision: The Second Inaugural Address* (University of Mississippi Press, 2002), 62.

7.   Ibid., 92.

8.   Mark Noll , *America's God* (Oxford University Press, 2002), 438.

9.   David Van Biema, "The New Calvinism," *Time*, March 12, 2009, http://www.time.com/time/specials/packages/article/0,28804,1884779_1884782_1884760,00.html.

10.   See the Barna Group report, "Is There a 'Reformed' Movement in American Churches?" Barna Group, November 15, 2010, http://www.barna.org/faith-spirituality/447-reformed-movement-in-american-churches.

11.   Quoted in Chris Jenks, *Culture* (London: Psychology Press, 2005), 203.

12.   In this respect evangelical Protestantism stands very close to Judaism. As Rabbi Joseph Dov Soloveitchik explained, the Jewish practice of redemption of the first-born requires every male Jew to relive Abraham's binding of Isaac on Mount Moriah, the definitive event preparing the Covenant. All Jews relive the Exodus at Passover—they are enjoined to consider themselves as having actually taken part in the departure from Egypt—and relive the giving of the Torah at Mount Sinai through the public reading of the Torah in synagogue. See Helfgott, op. cit., 301.

13.   See Joseph Bottum, "The Death of Protestant America," *First Things*, September/October 2008.

14.   Ibid.

15.   Philip Jenkins, "Believing in the Global South," *First Things*, December 2006.

16.   Francesco Sisci, "China's Catholic Moment," *First Things*, June/July 2009.

17.   Samuel P. Huntington, "The Clash of Civilizations," *Foreign Affairs*, Summer 1993.

Chapter 15

1.   Leo Strauss, *Natural Right and History* (University of Chicago Press, 1950), 181.

2. "Remarks by President George W. Bush at the 20[NaN] Anniversary of the National Endowment for Democracy," National Endowment for Democracy, November 6, 2003, http://www.ned.org/george-w-bush/remarks-by-president-george-w-bush-at-the-20th-anniversary.

3. J. M. Keynes, *The General Theory of Employment, Interest and Money* (Boston: Harcourt 1936), 383.

4. Charles Krauthammer, "The Road to Damascus," *Washington Post*, March 4, 2005, http://www.washingtonpost.com/wp-dyn/articles/A5695-2005Mar3.html.

5. "Irrational Exuberance?" JohnDerbyshire.com, March 10, 2005, http://johnderbyshire.com/Opinions/Britain/irrationalexuberance.html.

6. Marina Ottaway, "Iraq: An Uneasy American-Iranian Condominium," Carnegie Endowment, January 10, 2011, http://www.carnegieendowment.org/publications/index.cfm?fa=view&id=42259.

7. Stanley Kurtz, "Democracy Myth," *National Review*, November 26, 2007, http://www.nationalreview.com/articles/222934/democracy-myth/stanley-kurtz.

8. Michael Hastings, "Border oil dispute worsens fears about Iran's influence over Iraqi government," *Washington Post*, January 9, 2010.

9. American Embassy Riyadh (2009-03-22). "Viewing cable 09RIYADH447, COUNTERTERRORISM ADVISER BRENNAN'S MEETING WITH," http://cablegate.wikileaks.org/cable/2009/03/09RIYADH447.html.

10. Marni Soupcoff, "Philip Carl Salzman: Why Arabs suffer," *National Post*, January 11, 2008, http://network.nationalpost.com/np/blogs/fullcomment/archive/2008/01/11/philip-carl-salzman-why-arabs-suffer.aspx#ixzz1D3aNXhRY. See also Salzman's *Culture and Conflict in the Middle East* (New York: Humanity Books, 2008).

11. Ali A. Allawi, *The Crisis of Islamic Civilization* (Yale University Press, 2009), 2.

12. "In classic Islamic doctrine, the problem of the nature of the individual as an autonomous entity endowed with free will simply does not arise outside of the context of the individual's ultimate dependence on God. The Arabic word for 'individual'—al-fard—does not have the commonly understood implication of a purposeful being, imbued with the power of rational choice. Rather, the term carries the connotation of singularity, aloofness, or solitariness. The power of choice and will granted to the individual is more to do with the fact of acquiring these from God, at the point of a specific action or decision—the so-called ikti-sab—rather than the powers themselves which are not innate to natural freedoms or rights. Al-fard is usually applied as one of the attributes of the supreme being, in the sense of an inimitable uniqueness. It is usually grouped with others of God's attributes (such as in the formula al-Wahid, al-Ahad, al-Fard, al-Samad: The One

in essence, state and being, and the everlasting), to establish the absolute transcendence of the divine essence. Man is simply unable to acquire any of these essential attributes." Ibid., 11.

13. Ibid., 184–85.
14. Jean Bethke Elsthain, *Sovereignty* (New York: Basic Books, 2008), 131.
15. Ibid., 134.
16. Allawi, *The Crisis of Islamic Civilization*, 161.
17. Quoted in Michael Novak, "Aquinas and the Heretics," *First Things*, December 1995.
18. Ibid.
19. Robert D. Putnam, *Bowling Alone* (New York: Simon and Shuster, 2000).
20. "Bettertogether," The Saguaro Seminar, 2000, http://www.bettertogether.org/aboutthereport.htm.
21. Peter Hitchens, "Democracy Delusion," *The American Conservative*, May 1, 2010 issue, http://www.amconmag.com/article/2010/may/01/00038/.
22. Stanley Kurtz, "After the War," *City Journal*, Winter 2003, http://www.city-journal.org/html/13_1_after_the_war.html.

Chapter 16

1. Quoted in Augustine, *The City of God*, in Marcus Dods, ed., *The Works of Aurelius Augustus, Bishop of Hippo: A New Translation* (T. & T. Clark, 1871), 49.
2. Alastair Lawson, "Last Speaker of ancient language of Bo dies in India," BBC News, February 4, 2010, http://news.bbc.co.uk/2/hi/8498534.stm.
3. Augustine, op. cit., 527.
4. Francesco Sisci, "China's Catholic Moment," *First Things*, June/July 2009.
5. See Jerusalem Media and Communication Centre, "Letter from Dov Weisglass to US National Security Advisor Condoleeza Rice," April 19, 2004, http://www.jmcc.org/Documentsandmaps.aspx?id=697.
6. Scott Wilson, "Obama administration prepares for possibility of new post-revolt Islamist regimes," *Washington Post*, March 4, 2011, http://www.washingtonpost.com/wp-dyn/content/article/2011/03/03/AR2011030305531.html.
7. Ibid.
8. Dante, *Inferno*, Canto III, Verse 51.

INDEX